FEMALE SMUGGLERS
OF THE 19TH CENTURY

FEMALE SMUGGLERS OF THE 19TH CENTURY

DEE GORDON

First published in Great Britain in 2025 by
PEN AND SWORD HISTORY
An imprint of
Pen & Sword Books Ltd
Yorkshire – Philadelphia

Copyright © Dee Gordon, 2025

ISBN 978 1 03611 519 7

The right of Dee Gordon to be identified as Author of this work has been asserted by her in accordance with the Copyright, Designs and Patents Act 1988.

A CIP catalogue record for this book is available from the British Library.

All rights reserved. No part of this book may be reproduced, transmitted, downloaded, decompiled or reverse engineered in any form or by any means, electronic or mechanical including photocopying, recording or by any information storage and retrieval system, without permission from the Publisher in writing. NO AI TRAINING: Without in any way limiting the Author's and Publisher's exclusive rights under copyright, any use of this publication to "train" generative artificial intelligence (AI) technologies to generate text is expressly prohibited. The Author and Publisher reserve all rights to license uses of this work for generative AI training and development of machine learning language models.

Typeset in Times New Roman 12/16 by
SJmagic DESIGN SERVICES, India.
Printed and bound in the UK by CPI Group (UK) Ltd.

The Publisher's authorised representative in the EU for product safety is
Authorised Rep Compliance Ltd., Ground Floor, 71 Lower Baggot Street,
Dublin D02 P593, Ireland.
www.arccompliance.com

For a complete list of Pen & Sword titles please contact
PEN & SWORD BOOKS LIMITED
George House, Units 12 & 13, Beevor Street, Off Pontefract Road,
Barnsley, South Yorkshire, S71 1HN, England
E-mail: enquiries@pen-and-sword.co.uk
Website: www.pen-and-sword.co.uk

or

PEN AND SWORD BOOKS
1950 Lawrence Rd, Havertown, PA 19083, USA
E-mail: uspen-and-sword@casematepublishers.com
Website: www.penandswordbooks.com

Contents

Acknowledgements

I WOULD LIKE to thank Brian Phillips at the CET Archive in Brighton, who went above and beyond to help in my research. There was also invaluable information and assistance given by authors Richard Platt and Douglas Huke, and welcome cooperation from George Pritchard at cornwallsmugglers.com. Other interested individuals who were forthcoming with valuable input were Tim Davies from the Reference Library in Scunthorpe and L. Garratt at the Dorset History Centre. Others did their best to help with what has been a tricky subject to research, including Margaret Coward at Combe Martin Museum, Cathy Shelbourne at the Ipswich Maritime Trust, and James Franklin at Culture Vannin (The Manx Heritage Foundation). J. Morton at northeastlore.com and Ellen Carr at the Norfolk Family History Society provided some valuable tips, and Joanne Penn (Joanne Penn Genealogy) took a different approach with her own helpful research. My visits to Hastings Fishermen's Museum, Hastings Wreckers Museum and Bexhill Museum also proved fruitful, although not as fruitful as the wonderful British Newspaper Archive (online), which has been one of my main sources given the paucity of primary sources on the subject.

Introduction

FEMALE SMUGGLERS IN the eighteenth century veered towards the piratical, with some famous names to the fore (Anne Bonny and Mary Read), but the nineteenth was a very different century for men and women. Duties were coming down, making smuggling slowly less viable, especially from the mid-nineteenth century onwards, and tourism was increasing, changing smugglers from those in small boats to those as passengers on much larger vessels, better suited to women. As Jo Stanley pointed out in *Bold in Her Breeches*, it would take 'several lifetimes' to fully research all the primary sources of this subject, but oral history has often been as reliable as written documents.[1] This book uses legends and folktales alongside facts, and also places an emphasis on the smugglers rather than the preventive forces because the former are much more entertaining.

As an introduction, there is an interesting argument against smuggling by John Wesley at the end of the eighteenth century, when he exhorted, 'If you could not live without it, you ought to die, rather than steal. For death is a less evil than sin.'[2] In spite of this, many men and women in England chose to live with their brandy, gin, tea, and tobacco, rather than to die, or live, without them. A surprising number of women participated in what they called the 'free trade' by procuring and running goods, financing smuggling voyages, purchasing significant quantities of goods for resale, or simply buying an anker (nineteenth-century measure of wine or spirits) or two at harvest time, in spite of the risks.

However, the identities of female smugglers and their stories were often concealed from public scrutiny, sadly for modern historians. We therefore do not have images of these formidable women, other than some cartoons and some classic portraits e.g. William Heath's 'Why, Polly! You an't on the smuggling tack I hope!' Other portraits illustrate how whole communities, including women, were involved in smuggling – for instance Julius Caesar Ibbetson's oil painting of *Smugglers on the Irish Coast* in 1808 showing young women on a beach as contraband is being landed.

Since the 1671 Customs Act placed duties on goods from alcohol to lace, fruit to tea, British subjects found many items too expensive to enjoy unless they were obtained illegally. Not only were the prices less on smuggled goods, but smuggling paid well with a few hours' hard work comparable to that of a farmhand's average weekly wage so that smuggling had become an attractive sideline, especially for poor fishermen. So while smuggling is usually viewed as the work of violent criminals, it was common for entire villages to assist the smuggling operations, aiding the smugglers while hampering the customs men. Britain was at war almost constantly throughout the nineteenth century and taxes, especially on luxury goods, helped to fund the cost. Benjamin Franklin said nothing in this world is certain except death and taxes, and he could have added smuggling. Charles Lamb, nineteenth-century essayist, regarded smugglers as the only honest thieves who rob 'nothing but the Revenue' because the latter imposed restrictions on the few luxuries of the common people.

Salt carried a tax until at least 1825, becoming a popular item for smugglers, with small amounts easily carried by women, and was as important as spirits and tobacco for large profits. The Hon. Henry Shore wrote that 'smuggling in salt was extensively carried on by old women, who obtained their supplies from the fish-curing establishments, and secreting it in ways familiar to the feminine mind [!], carried it about the country for sale. Many were committed to gaol for this offence.'[3]

In 1806, Napoleon had started an embargo against English trade, the so-called Continental System, to weaken the English economy. Taxes on imports from the continent made many goods too expensive to buy – result: smuggling. Interestingly, the heyday of smuggling was during the wars against France and Napoleon from 1803 to 1815 when large areas of coastline were left unguarded. By 1851, only forty-eight articles were dutiable. The emphasis shifted to tobacco, especially after further reductions in import duties after 1861, less bulky and more profitable than spirits. Smuggling flourished in the nineteenth century judging by some of the seizures recorded in the 1830s with a steady rise of petty smuggling by passengers as opposed to fishermen. Foreign travel was no longer the sole privilege of the upper classes and passengers from 1850 were allowed to bring into the UK a half pound of tobacco or cigars for personal use without duty, and in 1875 one pint of spirits was added, i.e. the first duty-free allowances.

On the advice of Richard Twining, of Twinings Tea, William Pitt the Younger had introduced the Commutation Act (1784) reducing taxation on tea from 119 per cent to 12.5 per cent. Twining estimated that at least half the tea drunk in England was smuggled, and it was still one of the two most smuggled commodities in 1820, alongside liquor. Smuggled tea often came from Holland where it might be purchased for seven pence per pound and sold at two shillings a pound, a third of what legally procured teas sold for.

Mary Waugh has written of the fight against smuggling which 'gained ground slowly after 1800 as measures intended to thwart Napoleon destroyed the privacy of many favourite landing places' e.g. the Martello Towers along the coast. After the defeat of Napoleon at Waterloo in 1815, '250,000 soldiers and sailors returned home and many turned to smuggling in the absence of employment.'[4] The Coast Blockade Service was formed to counter the smugglers but the smuggling of spirits and tobacco continued into the 1870s and beyond. Smugglers felt they were 'providing a public service by supplying goods at affordable prices and maintaining an Englishman's right to free trade.'[5] But as the country began to adopt a Victorian conscience, smuggling became perceived as a crime. Jan Toms illustrates how much more profitable smuggling was than being employed by customs in her account of James Snudden, father of eight, living on slow payments from the local board (the so-called Seizure Awards) and poor financial management. He died in 1822 aged 39, leaving his widow 'faced with destitution' and appearing in the 1834 List of Paupers in Newport.[6] The combined introduction of the Preventive Waterguard and the Coastguard Service meant that by the end of the 1820s smuggling had begun its decline.

Author Trevor May also pointed out how the increase in tourism in the nineteenth century meant that more effort had to be made to control smuggling, which in the individual case might be small in scale, but in total could add up to a considerable sum. He also refers to smuggling from the mid-nineteenth century most often committed by 'inconsiderate and unprincipled passengers' with new smugglers, many of them women, 'trying to slip something past customs or crew members bringing something back for the family or to sell on the blackmarket', with steamships providing opportunities for concealing contraband in coal bunkers or among machinery.[7]

In *Smuggling*, a Board of Customs report dated 1858 refers to 'ladies and ladies' maids' being 'silly and perverse enough to risk pounds that they save pence and both incur and inflict endless trouble and annoyance for the tremulous and vulgar joy of cheating the revenue and evading the vigilance of the Officers.'[8] While the eighteenth century saw more bold runs on open beaches, the nineteenth century saw more ingenious forms of smuggling as detailed in the following chapters.

Generally, females were based on the land side of the operation as opposed to being on a vessel. If they didn't sell, transport, or hide the smuggled goods, they provided protection, alibis, or assistance to those who did. Smugglers, on vessels or on shore, often had an 'investor', someone who remained in the shadows, a wealthy silent partner (male or female) with a reputation beyond reproach – the least likely person in a community to be in league with smugglers.

Ultimately, a lot of 'history' – especially female history – is guesswork. Afraid of knowing too much, the communities looked the other way and were happy to buy cheap brandy, tea, snuff, or lace without asking too many questions. As Kipling said in his poem, 'A Smuggler's

Song': 'Watch the wall, my darling, while the Gentlemen go by!'[9] Researching smuggling is a tortuous and fascinating conundrum. The very nature of the smuggling trade required it to be cloaked in secrecy: nothing written down, no traces left behind. Loyal customers often included the vicar, the magistrate, and the squire. Deliveries to local people were made quietly and discreetly under cover of darkness; payment by 'cash or favours' only.[10]

Even more outrageous was an early nineteenth-century practice whereby women tied bladders filled with brandy and gin under their skirts and walked brazenly through the town with them swinging under their skirts, safe in the knowledge that the revenue men were forbidden from putting their hands up the good wives' petticoats. Any risks were not from the revenue men, but from local youths who thought the greatest joke ever was to pierce the bladder with a knife or other sharp implement and watch the booze flood out over the carrier's shoes, stockings, and onto the ground. Many women confined themselves to benefiting from the system rather than participating in it.

Interestingly, Richard Platt writes that women 'who did not co-operate with their smuggling menfolk'[11] were in for a difficult life – bearing in mind that this was long before domestic abuse was recognised. The stories of women which follow show that many wives were happy to be involved, while others felt obligated by their dire financial circumstances. Some enjoyed the excitement, some kept a low profile and enjoyed the profits, some turned a blind eye, some were afraid and tried to dissuade their menfolk. There were women like the silk 'throwsters' of Somerset in 1822 (who spun silk ready for weaving) who were directly affected by the duty on silk which allowed the smuggling of foreign silk, putting many of their 2,000 colleagues out of work. Then there were women, particularly in inland areas, whose lives were barely touched by the smuggling 'industry'. In other words, all (female) human experience is here! Deliberately absent, however, are the nineteenth-century Chinese opium smugglers, often female, who are better described as pirates than smugglers.

Chapter One

Cornwall

CORNWALL WAS ONE of those areas where it was virtually impossible to police and enforce the prevention of smuggling. Small tree-lined creeks, like those along the rivers of the south coast of Cornwall, were used extensively for smuggling, thanks to its 'long, sparsely-inhabited coastline and its many coves'. The area had 'a justifiably fearsome reputation at high tide in a gale, since there were innumerable rocks that even now will rip steel hulls to shreds, at calm low water many of them have broad, gently shelving stretches of sand that were ideal for bringing small boats ashore to meet the waiting strings of ponies'.[1] This meant that owners of small, swift boats wishing to evade exorbitant tariffs on imported goods stood a good chance of evading customs officials. With punitive duties imposed on luxury items such as brandy, lace, and tobacco, which were available a few hours away in France and Holland, there is little wonder that smuggling became a major industry in the eighteenth and nineteenth centuries. It was Cornwall's close geographical and cultural ties with Breton ports that gave Cornish smugglers their unique advantage – even the Cornish and Breton languages are similar. By the nineteenth century, a large proportion of the population of Cornwall – an estimated 10,000 people, including women and children – were thought to take part in the smuggling business.

Coverack, on the Lizard Peninsula, was once home to Sarah Bosanko who, in 1802, remarried two years after her notorious smuggler husband John Corlyons was drowned. His smuggling activities prospered to such an extent that he had been able to afford a much larger merchant ship with a crew of six for his frequent trips across the Channel to Roscoff in France when, upon returning, Sarah would hang out his red shirt on the battery above the house as a sign that the coast was clear. Her son, also John, born in 1794, was only 6 years old when his father drowned but may have become involved as a young man with his uncle Edward, his father's brother, who had been deeply involved in smuggling with his brother. However, it seems young John was caught and pressed into the Navy (Revenue Service). It was a practice well exercised by the Navy to actively press fishermen with smuggling experience into the service as they were not only good, experienced, and hardy sailors, but they also knew the coasts in great detail. Many so pressed rose quickly to become officers in the service, as did John Junior.[2] So in the nineteenth century Sarah had moved from being a smuggler's wife to the mother of a revenue officer.

Moving away from the more obvious role of smugglers' wives, there is one particular account, in 1807, which demonstrates one of the ways that local women could be involved in aiding and abetting local smugglers. Well known, and notorious, among locals was the Carter gang in the eighteenth century, headed up by John Carter, a notorious smuggler in the Penzance area, known as the King of Prussia, given his links with Prussia Cove. Bessie Bussow ran the kiddleywink (or 'kiddlywink', the old Cornish name for a small beer house) above the cove and had always been amply provided with rum, like many landladies. The cove was by 'a perfect natural harbour that seems to have been designed for smugglers' with 'old cart tracks [that] can still be seen carved into the surface of the rocks between the two coves' and was later re-named Bessie's Cove.[3] Local legend has it that tunnels led from the inn to the beach below, and Bessie was well known and trusted by Carter and his crew. When Carter was 70 years old (1807), his lugger was making for home with the revenue men giving chase (one version says it was a Navy ship called the HMS *Fairy* in pursuit). Whatever the case, the King of Prussia felt that they were coming 'too close to his kingdom and opened fire! The enemy was driven back and held off for the night. The next morning however the smugglers found themselves fired upon from the hedge at the top of the hill by a number of men on horses. They quickly took refuge in Bessie Bussow's kiddleywink, perhaps escaping into the tunnels.'[4]

Before this 'battle' Carter had built 'a range of defences' in the area 'armed with a number of guns'. However, the landing party now destroyed Carter's guns and this seems to have terminated his smuggling career: he died sometime before 1822.[5]

According to a written account by a John Cornish in 1899, Carter's role was taken on by Will Richards, who had taken part in the 1807 battle. 'Cappen' Richards lived in Prussia Cove, using smaller open boats rather than the larger luggers and cutters. Some years later he was waiting on the removal of a cargo 'of kegs' from storage in a shaft behind his home, with horses ready to move it on, when four custom house men arrived. 'Chatting with the enemy, Cappen Will learnt that they had been sent off in such a hurry that they had neither food nor drink, and it was coming in a cold and stormy night.' As evening closed in, another way for women to help their menfolk is illustrated by the intervention of Mrs Richards, who made 'some broth for the poor fellows out there in the cold, and her good man invited them in'. Long before those four men left that kitchen, 'the kegs were up from the old shaft, and the horses loaded and gone'. Mrs Richards is a classic example of how women assisted in keeping the customs men at bay, and their own men safe.[6]

In 1805, a smuggler called Christopher Pollard was tried for assault, incitement, and smuggling, and a principal witness was Anne George who, according to the counsel's brief, was a woman of notorious character, described in *Smugglers' Britain* as a 'malicious gossip'.[7] The Cornwall Live website goes further, describing her as running 'smuggling and wrecking operations with the local parson'.[8] The brief described her as being the wife of Joseph George who had been the 'keeper of the First and Last Inn in Sennen Cove, a place which had the reputation of being the resort of all the idle blackguards in the county' and which has convenient tunnels running down to Sennen Cliffs. Sennen certainly seems to have been the centre of free trading in this part of Cornwall. Joseph had acted as 'smuggling agent' for his landlord, and, using their knowledge of his illicit transactions, the Georges had for some time refused to pay any rent for the inn. 'At length the owner, very unwisely, decided to eject them. Infuriated by this, the innkeeper's wife had thereupon turned king's evidence against the landlord, and reaped her revenge in seeing the latter served with a long term of imprisonment.' It was also claimed that some years previously following an argument with her brother-in-law, John George, over a few pounds of tobacco, she had again 'turned kings evidence, accused the victim of her malice of firing on a revenue officer, and so incriminated him that the poor wretch was actually convicted and hanged in June 1802.'[9]

In a district in which almost every inhabitant – including, no doubt, Anne George – had probably had some hand in smuggling, the presence of such a malicious and unscrupulous informer no doubt accounted for the difficulty in obtaining witnesses for the defence. The brief continued: 'The terror and dismay, indeed, which this woman has been the means of spreading throughout the county are not to be described. Independent of the present prosecution no less than five persons have been capitally indicted by her means, one of whom, John George, had already been executed, and so callous is her conscience, and deadly her revenge, that persons who may have given her slight cause for offence are now trembling for fear of the consequences, expecting to be made the next victim of the detestable passion with which she is actuated.' On this occasion the jury chose not to believe her evidence and Pollard was found not guilty and allowed to go free.[10]

Not only were women useful to the smugglers as signallers and carriers of messages between gang members and obstructing revenue officers, but they also brought goods in from the shore. The voluminous skirt was particularly useful, for the women wound yards of silk and lace round their bodies and reached home as a rule quite peacefully with their contraband.[11] In 1806, one particular individual came to the aid of notorious Devon smuggler Jack Rattenbury as per his memoirs. He had escaped from constables en route to prison when the constables had stopped at the Indian Queen pub at Bodmin for refreshment – a pub now demolished, but which gave its name to a village (now Indian Queens) on the site. Rattenbury and another prisoner ran to a cottage nearby and the woman living there took him through her house into the garden and pointed out what road he should take, resulting in him successfully making it back to his home in Devon.[12]

It seems that the place most likely to win the award for having had the most smuggled goods pass through was a small village near Plymouth called Cawsand. It provided a safe anchorage and even Lord Nelson stayed at the local Ship Inn, 'not in the course of any smuggling activities though!' Cawsand also had a thriving pilchard industry when the boats weren't being used for illicit purposes. Transporting goods over land was very expensive, meaning that to make a profit contraband had to be sold locally, and Plymouth was one of the largest towns in the region, a ready market for the smuggled goods. Brought in by small, fast boats, the liquor would be carried by women, in bladders under their petticoats, and they were often so heavily laden that their bodies seemed deformed, waddling rather than walking.[13] *Smugglers' Britain* points out the only real snag, from the women's point of view, was not the excise officers but that a 'knowing sailor might pierce the bladder with a deftly placed jack-knife just for a lark'.[14] Thousands of casks of spirits were landed here every year and in 1804, the revenue services estimated that about 17,000 kegs of spirits were landed in Cawsand and Kingsand in the previous year. In the early 1800s these twin coastal villages were the main centres of smuggling contraband in the West Country.[15] It wasn't just alcohol that was popular in the area: for example, at Looe in 1816, 'a French vessel came in with a cargo of fruit and children's toys in the form of carved wooden horses [which] proved to be filled with fifty-one pairs of silk stockings and nine lace shawls'.[16]

Continuing with Cawsand, Susanna Eddey, whose uncle Henry was a renowned smuggler, married a toll collector (Richard Chapell) in

1833. Henry's grandson wrote an account about Henry's smuggling, referring specifically to brandy (and salt) being smuggled from France, anchored off the coast until it was clear to retrieve them, and then poured into large sheep and goat bladders 'for transportation by the Cawsand women under their crinoline dresses'. The contraband would be transported by cart or donkey to buyers across the country. Henry was eventually caught, and served two years in Exeter jail but promptly resumed his trade on his release. When his laden boat was boarded by Customs officers soon after at Penlee Point (at the entrance to Plymouth Sound), he jumped overboard and made his way to Cawsand where his wife gave him dry clothing and hid him 'under furniture'. But the officers

> found him there, and he was sent to Exeter assizes, where he was sentenced to a choice between five years transportation to Botany Bay, Australia, or five years in the Navy. He chose the latter and completed his time there and retired as a purser's steward with a pension of £13 a year, dying in 1885 aged 79, and was buried at Maker [between Cawsand and Rame Head].[17]

The grandson, also Henry, apparently married the coastguard's daughter, Harriet, illustrating how the two opposing forces often came together.[18] While the women of Cawsand used bladders hidden under their skirts, the neighbouring village of Devoran also has smuggling stories to tell, including one about local women using cloam pitchers (jugs with handles, as favoured by Mistress Poldark!) with double bottoms to conceal the contents, i.e. brandy.

Early in the nineteenth century, the small rocky island of Great Mewstone at the entrance to Wembury Bay (in Devon) was inhabited by the children of a local outlaw, who had been sentenced to banishment on the island, regarded as a mini-Alcatraz.[19] Young Silas Finn – or Fyn or Finny – and someone named Black Joan, who may have been his sister, relayed signals to the smugglers, eventually moving to

Looe Island, both islands remote and difficult to reach other than by boat. Looe Island, a mile from the town of Looe, is now a nature reserve. According to cornishbirdblog.com, 'Black Joan' may have been Finn's wife or even just a savvy business acquaintance, and got her name from being a person of colour which could indicate that she was not, indeed, his sister! (The mystery continues.) One fateful night the worst happened to an adult Silas when by chance the excise men caught him red-handed with a large amount of smuggled goods. Silas panicked and did something said to have been completely out of character. He struck a deal with the authorities. To secure his own freedom, Finn agreed to turn in some local smugglers. The plan was hatched for the Finns to light a lantern and signal from the cliffs at Portwrinkle. The open beaches of nearby Whitsand Bay made a fine landing when the coast was sufficiently clear for covert runs, but smugglers seeking a more discreet approach headed for Looe, and brought the goods ashore on Looe Island. The Finns stored contraband in a cave which was hidden even from the smugglers, who paid a fee for each tub concealed. The cave's custodians liaised with a farmer on the mainland. When he was able to divert the customs authorities, or when he knew they posed no threat to a landing, he would ride his white horse along the coast. If there was danger, the farmer would walk the horse home.[20]

At sea, Finn's friends in their boat loaded with contraband landed on the beach when they thought it was safe, but no sooner had they hit the sand than the customs men swooped and they were arrested with a cargo of brandy, lace, tea, and tobacco. The captured smugglers were Finn's friends Amram Hooper and his sister Jochabed. Finn had betrayed a man that he had probably known all his life. Nevertheless, Silas and Joan were both widely considered as honourable characters by the community and Joan said to be a successful smuggler in her own right. Further stories are of Silas and Joan (and indeed Jochabed) living on the rabbits and rats that inhabited these islands and Richard Platt, author of *Smugglers' Britain*, claimed they, as a result, exterminated all these animals on the islands.

The Hoopers were amongst the last smugglers to live on Looe Island. Apparently, Jochabed behaved in a manner expected of a man of her time – 'she could row a boat, smoked and swore, and would even use her fists to great advantage when the occasion required. She wore a man's hat, a blue knit frock and sea boots; her skirt was always rolled up and fastened above her knees' and even the revenue officers did not care to get too close to her![21] There is a painting in Looe's Guildhall, *Arrest of the Smuggler in East Looe, 1820*, painted by John Robertson Reid which is said to show the Hoopers, with a mysterious figure in the background who could be Joan Finn. Amram was said to be the chief smuggler of the time, although several sources maintain that he and his family didn't smuggle the goods themselves but would 'hide contraband goods for a fee and then get them across to Looe when the coast was clear.' He and his sister and (perhaps) daughter Matilda are involved in many smuggling stories. Parish registers do confirm the baptisms of Amram and Jochabed, and there appears to have been a Hooper family bible which also lists Elizabeth Hooper (the wife?) and three children by her first marriage! The National Trust website ends the Black Joan story with the news that she married and raised three children, and was widowed when her husband 'fell off a rock'! How much of the Finn/Hooper stories are legend is difficult to assess, but there are few legends that are not based on truth.

There is more to this smuggling family… Matilda Finn was nicknamed Black Till but this could have been confused with Black Joan's name. One story is of Black Joan as a murderess – killing one unknown man on the island (whose skeleton was discovered) and another account of her shooting a Jamaican seaman in the head following an argument in the Jolly Sailor Inn in Looe, the seaman now said to haunt the pub. Although jailed for this crime, she was acquitted despite the evidence, probably due to the magistrate being one of her best customers. As for Black Till, if there was such an individual, it is rumoured that she would pretend to be in distress in her rowing boat to distract the attention of any officers so that her father, Silas, could move contraband goods. This latter story only appears online[22] but there is another more widely reported regarding the Jolly Sailor Inn, a smugglers' haunt, regarding 'the quick-thinking landlady' who famously 'concealed an illicit keg beneath her petticoats during an unexpected search. While the preventives searched, she calmly knitted.'[23]

In November 1811, the *Manks* (sic) *Advertiser* carried a story about brandy being stuffed inside the bodies of butchered geese and then snuck onto a Royal Navy ship off the coast of Cornwall with 'the smugglers, being women' not detained. In *Cornish Wrecking* there is a claim that 'on the Cornish coast and elsewhere the moment a wrecked vessel touched the shore she was considered fair plunder and men, women and children worked to break her up, night and day.' Author Cathryn Pearce was quoting from a book by the Reverend Smith (*The Wreckers or a Tour of Benevolence from St Michael's Mount to the Lizard Point*) who wrote that

> the neighbourhood is sadly infested with the wreckers. When the news of a wreck flies round the coast, thousands of people are instantly collected near the fatal spot; pick-axes, hatchets, crow-bars and ropes are their usual implements for breaking up and carrying off whatever they can … the hardships they endure (especially the women) in winter to save all they can, are almost incredible.

Tales of Cornish Wreckers refers to both smuggling and wrecking as community, rather than male, activities. One incident in Mullion in 1817 features 'thousands of men, women and children' working on a local wreck to 'break her up by night and day. The precipices they descend, the rocks they climb' and the suffering involved in seizing the remaining fragments are both 'frightful and alarming'. A similar incident is described in 1826 in Hele Bay when women are foregrounded as plundering the wrecked *The Ocean*. Among the 'number of persons from the adjacent villages' crowding down to the beach, women 'were the greater part of these miscreants carrying away whatever they could lay their hands on', being 'dextrous in concealing bottles of wine and other things so as to elude a search … As the day advanced, the plunderers, male and female, became intoxicated' with respectable inhabitants unable to control the pillaging. The book *Bold in Her Breeches* comments that women 'could not afford the luxury of conforming to ideas about respectable womanly behaviour' and were drawn to piracy and wrecking to fend off starvation.

According to author Mary Waugh, the women of Flushing, opposite Falmouth, became known for buying up contraband from the crews of the packet boats (whose captains lived mainly at Flushing) and carried these to Truro 'or the mining settlements further inland'. She then points out that they were 'no doubt aided by an Excise clerk convicted of fraud in 1822' (but not named). Waugh also mentions an incident in 1822 at the village of Point, a secluded coastal village, when officers seized fifty-nine casks in a barn. One officer was left in charge but when the other officers returned four casks were missing, prompting a search which resulted in their being attacked by a 'woman with a shovel and an innkeeper and his daughter'.

There is a slightly different version of this last incident, by John Vivian. This refers to a customs officer named John Real who found a jar of brandy and a barrel of gin in a garden owned by Mr Nicholls, the keeper of a public house at Point. As he was about to remove the contraband, a woman (not identified) came out of the house 'with a shovel in her hand' and made several unsuccessful attempts to break the jar. Some twenty locals got involved, protesting at the digging up of the garden, and throwing stones, but the officers managed to get the liquor into their boat. The result was that several of the protesters were charged with assault. At the Assizes, Elizabeth Nicholls, the innkeeper's daughter, described how the officer arrived to search for the spirits while she was sowing seeds, but was held back by an officer's pistol preventing her from leaving. Having denied any knowledge of the existence of contraband, she was not charged.

Vivian also writes of a search by officers which took place in a house in The Warren, St Ives, one of a row of fishermen's cottages (now Grade II listed) – they were delayed by the woman of the house insisting on tidying the bedroom before they entered, meaning she could throw smuggled tobacco out of the bedroom window 'on to the rocks below'. This meant the officers found nothing and the tobacco could be moved somewhere more secure.

Maria Branwell, mother of the Brontë sisters, the nineteenth-century authors, was born in Penzance in 1783 into a wealthy merchant family with an affluent lifestyle. Maria's father was 'a town bigwig and very well-connected' in what was then a bustling cosmopolitan port, but smuggling was so rife that the family could hardly avoid it. Opposite their home was the seventeenth-century Admiral Benbow tavern, the base for a group of cut-throat smugglers known as the Benbow Brandy Men, with whom Thomas Branwell had a 'business partnership'. He also had a 'conviction for obstructing local revenue men' and was in business with two of Penzance's 'busiest tax dodgers, James and John Dunkin, who ran a shop four doors away from Branwell's Corner'. They described themselves as merchants of Penzance, while the *Reading Mercury* described them as 'the most notorious smugglers in that part of the kingdom'. In reality it seems they were both, with illicit links no doubt helping to fund some of the Brontës' books. It is impossible to exclude Maria from some peripheral involvement at least.

The excellent cornwallsmugglers.com website features a couple of local women who did not manage to evade the Customs officers. One report in their listings (May 1845) is with regard to two women and a man who were 'apprehended and brought before W.Clements, the Wadebridge magistrate, charged with having sold to two shop-keepers of that place several parcels, stated to be smuggled tea and tobacco, amounting in purchase to the value of £5 and upwards'. The parcels are described as

> covered with coarse wrapping paper, on the inside of which was a layer of about half an inch of the tea and

> tobacco, the bulk of the parcels being nothing but bags of sawdust. It is supposed the parties have carried on a long and profitable trade, and that the persons who have been duped by them have suffered the matter to pass in silence to prevent their names being made public as no little disgrace attaches to those who would thus deal in supposed contraband goods.

However, someone did indeed contact the 'constables of Bodmin' and a 'search was made for the parties'. After what is referred to as 'a most careful watch', a Mr Harris succeeded in 'capturing the females, who were committed to take their trial at the next sessions' – though the results of the trial have proved untraceable or may be in missing copies of the *West Briton* newspaper.

A similar account is listed in May 1850 when 'two young women named Roskilly were charged with smuggling' before Lieutenant Hill, magistrate at the Town Hall, Falmouth. The first case was against the eldest sister, but the evidence failed, and the complaint was dismissed. As for the youngest sister, witnesses had been

> deposed to searching the house and shop of the defendants, and on following Miss Roskilly upstairs, one of the witnesses picked up a bag containing five pounds of Cavendish tobacco. [Cavendish tobacco is black, usually used in pipes.] There appeared some doubt as to the identity of the bag, but it was quite clear that tobacco was not such as was duty paid, and the bench convicted the defendant.

As it was the first offence they mitigated the fine 'from £100 to £25' but when the money was about to be paid 'the young woman said it should not be done, as the informer would have half the amount; rather than that she would stay six months in prison'! Again, the final result has proved untraceable and is perhaps only accessible in local trial records not held digitally.

A year later, another woman featured. This was Jane Toms, charged in January 1851 with 'having smuggled a quantity of cigars, coffee, and spirits'. Mr Downing defended the prisoner, who pleaded not guilty. Mr China, the chief officer, stated that

> he went to the house of the prisoner in Mulberry Square, and on his going into the first room, he found twelve or eighteen empty cigar boxes, and the two produced, which had two pounds in them. In the second room he entered, he found nothing, but in the third room he found the bag of coffee now produced, which weighed 41lbs. In the passage opposite the kitchen door he saw a small keg, and told one of his men to start the bung, which being done, he found it contained spirits.

It seems the prisoner made no remarks about the cigars, but said 'she had bought the coffee in small lots' and 'totally disowned knowing anything about the spirit, until the officer ordered it to be taken away, when she said it was some she had bought at Mr Carne's; it was one gallon and thirty-two parts of a gallon of brandy'. The other officers corroborated this. Mr Downing cross-examined the officers as to the amount of duty payable on the quantity taken, which would only be about £3. He 'endeavoured also to show that the brandy was some which had been taken by the officer in September, and given back; and that prisoner's husband being now in prison for a lot of goods taken in September, she ought not be convicted'. The bench considered the prisoner guilty, but the quantity being small, they mitigated the penalty to £25, or six months' imprisonment. The prisoner chose the fine, which was duly paid.[24]

The *West Briton* newspaper (5 October 1855) is also given as a source for a brief story about the second stewardess of the *Drake* steamer, who was brought before the bench, charged with 'having brought on shore about seven gills of gin. She was found guilty, and sentenced to pay the amount of treble the duty, and the costs.'

This shows how smuggling was changing from macho men in open boats to more sophisticated women.

The *Royal Cornwall Gazette* (1801–1851) was another local newspaper that carried a brief story of a female smuggler. In January 1851, Hannah Maria Greenstreet was charged at the Guildhall in St Ives by the Collector of Customs, John Shelley, 'with carrying, concealing and conveying 6lb of manufactured tobacco on which the proper duties had not been paid. The Mayor's sentence was 40s with 10s costs and in default of payment.'

This same newspaper in September 1891 went into far more detail about an old lady of 80 who was interviewed in 'a stuffy back room in London' about her life in Camborne. She was born there and became a servant, her husband being a petty officer on board 'a man-of-war packet' who 'pricked his finger, took ill, and died'. She said that 'All the things as he'd brought from overseas was seized by the Customs. We made a bit of money sometimes that way.' When asked if she meant she and her husband were smugglers, she said, apologetically: 'Well, you see, sir, there is no harm in it down in Cornwall; of course, up here it's different.' However, she was asked about the smuggling, and was happy to provide more detail:

> It was this way, sir. The man-o'-war packets were lighter and didn't draw so much water, and they didn't stay so long on the stations – they was often backward and forward. The men … used to buy cheeses and things as was cheap here, then when they got to Lisbon, Halifax, or the Islands, they'd change 'em for things as was cheap there, mostly tobacco and rum. Many a pound of good Cavendish have I sold for 1s 4d. They used to bring the rum ashore in great demi-johns, then we'd pour it out into pans and sell it to the trochers.

She explained that 'trochers' were women who used to come into Falmouth to take the rum away into the country to sell to the farmers, using three or four pigs' bladders blown out with wind and tied round their waists under their clothes, and returning with them full of rum. 'They were very respectable people, but the Customs' used to treat them terrible'. The newspaper described this as 'altogether charming topographic morality' with a petty officer on a naval packet ship not the usual idea of a smuggler.

Landladies and landlords were regularly under suspicion of colluding with smugglers for obvious reasons. Mrs Elizabeth Baragwanath, landlady of the Sloop Inn on the Wharf at St Ives (which is still there) pleaded guilty in court to handling tobacco which had been found and seized by officers (*c.* 1898). She was apparently able to pay 'treble the duty and value on the tobacco involved'. Her family had occupied the house for nearly fifty years and in January 1899, the *West Briton* spoke to her because 'She has its history at her fingers ends; back to the time of an old smuggler known only as Old Tub … one of the best remembered characters in St. Ives' and she had many a well authenticated tale of savage conflict between King's Officers and St Ives smugglers 'on the foresands'.

The following simplified version of an article in the *Paisley, Herald and Renfrewshire Advertiser* of 28 March 1868 is included because (a) it is obviously about Cornwall, (b) it is too interesting to ignore, and (c) it suggests we are talking nineteenth century.

> The coastguards' men have occasionally to put off in their boats to overhaul any craft of suspicious appearance. They often had to cope with men armed to the teeth, half smugglers and half pirates … women sometimes even took a part in these fraudulent, though bold enterprises, and many a Cornish heroine has distinguished herself among her companions … one coastguard allowed his heart to become entangled … by the pretty face of a fisherman's daughter; she was beautiful, and … had promised to marry him. Their marriage was delayed for a few days because the coastguard lover was directed,

> with some of his comrades, to give chase to a suspected brigantine. At the moment when they were about to board her, a shot, fired by a cabin boy, announced that the crew had made up their minds to defend themselves. The brigantine was taken after a smart resistance but the young man who had fired the pistol was sought for in vain. Some days later the sea threw up on the beach of a Cornish cove the corpse of a female dressed as a sailor, in whose face the coastguard 'recognised the features of his intended'.

Had she fallen into the water by accident or had she dived into the waves because of the 'shame that awaited her, if she had been found by her lover in such evil company?'

One of many local mysteries.

The prolific Victorian novelist, Devon-born Sabine Baring-Gould, also wrote books on history and folklore such as *A Book of the West* (1902). One story refers to a woman called Granny Grylls, whose job in her younger years was to recover tubs that had been concealed in the sands of Cawsand Bay.

> At Maker there lived a handsome woman – she is now dead – who used to go up and down the street, carrying a baby in long clothes. Somehow the baby never got out of long clothes. One day a preventive man in passing greeted her 'A quiet baby yours, never cries.' 'No. I reckon her don't cry terrible, but her's got a lot o' spirit for all that.' And so the baby had. It was a keg of contraband brandy.

This was how she removed 'run' liquor from its cache in the sand. While Baring-Gould writes about Granny Grylls as factual, to close this chapter is a more obvious legend, in that it features in *Roar of the Sea* – a tale of the Cornish Coast – one of his most enduring novels, with its simple, strongly characterised plot. It was first published in

1892 and remained in print as mainstream paperback until the late 1960s. The covers were, by then, decorated with a bosomy maiden, the heroine of the book, Judith Trevisa. Set on the North Cornwall coast, the story tells of Judith's relationship with the arch-wrecker and smuggler, Cruel Coppinger, also associated with Devon, and her steely determination to stand up to him. Although the book is fiction, Coppinger and his life are very much based on fact.

Chapter Two

Devon

DEVON'S LONG INDENTED coastline was well suited to smugglers looking to land illicit cargo, unobserved. It was not necessarily regarded by the population as a crime, more of a necessity to defeat nineteenth-century poverty, and supported – as elsewhere – by local clergy, judges, and even the aristocracy. Interestingly, the Collector of His Majesty's Customs at the Port of Dartmouth reported that smuggling in the area actually increased early in the nineteenth century.[1]

Shipwreck was a bigger danger for the smugglers than being convicted of smuggling, with the death penalty or transportation a rarity. While it has been difficult to trace women directly involved in smuggling, research does reveal some interesting stories. In fact, one story tells of a whole 'houseful' of 'wailing women' who opened the door to officers wanting to search the house of a renowned smuggler, Jackman, in Brixham, although the dating of this event is unclear. They told the officers Jackman was dead and would be buried in Totnes, but of course the coffin was full of brandy.[2]

A far more famous, and notorious, smuggler than Jackman was John (known as Jack) Rattenbury, 'The Rob Roy of the West'. He was aided by many women during his career throughout the eighteenth and nineteenth centuries and even features in a novel (Sabine Baring-Gould's *Winefred*, set on the East Devon coast) where the eponymous heroine becomes caught up in the activities of the Rattenbury family. In his own memoirs, Rattenbury refers to an 1807 incident, which concerned an attempt by a sergeant and several men to arrest him at Beer as a deserter from the Navy. At bay in an inn cellar, armed with knife and reaping hook, Rattenbury held off the attacking party for four hours, then escaped thanks to a diversion caused by women raising a 'false alarm of shipwreck'.[3]

Another incident in his memoirs is dated 1812 when returning with a 'cargo of spirits from Alderney' and was pursued, fired upon, and captured. However, when the captain of the *Catherine*, the brig that had chased him down, searched the ship they only found a solitary pint of gin in a single bottle – the rest of the cargo having been put over the side. Nevertheless, the crew were imprisoned on board the *Catherine* for a week and taken to Brixham where the prisoners' wives were anxiously waiting. Next morning, when the captain and chief officer were ashore, the women came off the beach in a boat, and were helped aboard the brig. Rattenbury and three of his men took the opportunity to jump into the boat used by the women, and pushed off. The second mate, in charge of the vessel, caught hold of the oar Rattenbury was using, breaking the blade, and the smuggler then threw the remaining part at him but the mate was prevented from using his firearm by Rattenbury's wife, Anna, who knocked it out of his hand. Picking it up, he fired again, but the boat's sail was up, and the fugitives were well on the way to shore, 'amid a shower of bullets'. They then dispersed, two of them being re-taken and sent aboard a man-of-war bound for the West Indies, but Rattenbury made his way safely home and was joined there by his wife. She may have been the recipient of one of Rattenbury's hauls around this time, i.e. 'lace concealed inside a turkey!'[4]

His Lyme Regis-born wife was certainly a prominent figure in Rattenbury's world following their marriage in 1801. At the end of that year, she 'collared' a lieutenant who was trying to manoeuvre Rattenbury onto a boat at Bridport as part of a pressgang, having arrived on the scene at just the right moment, oblivious to the lieutenant's nine colleagues! With the support of male and female bystanders, Rattenbury escaped (again). In 1819 she was sent to speak to the revenue officer of a cutter that Jack had managed to avoid near Seaton by jumping from his lugger into his dinghy, 'leaving behind 300 kegs of spirit and several bales of tea' being smuggled from France. She asked the officer if she could have Jack's clothes which he had abandoned on the captured lugger. Rather surprisingly, he agreed!

On 23 August 1865, Rattenbury featured in the *Belfast Morning News*. He had died in 1844, and it seems that the story was at the beginning of the century. Following a haul of kegs of brandy, his boat landed on 'the soft sand at Smuggler's Cove, near the Parson and Clerk rock' (between Dawlish and Teignmouth). However, the coastguard were informed of their arrival and 'hastened back to their district, and were on the coast between Teignmouth and Starcross, under a cheery certainty of capture'. A scout had been sent to the Parson and Clerk, discovering that the cargo had been moved to 'some private grounds that reached to the shore. Up the smugglers went through the shrubberies, and the kegs were carried hastily into the barn of a farm house belonging to a female relative of Rattenbury.' As this could afford only temporary refuge, a safer place of concealment was necessary 'for the morrow'. The farmer had died, and the ordinary preparations had been made for his funeral. The female relation 'in the midst of her grief' was 'true to her blood' and consented that the contraband kegs could be hidden in the chamber of the deceased. 'There he lay in his coffin, with the lid unclosed and a candle each side. Rattenbury, a daring fellow, without compunction or delicacy, intent only on gain' and to avoid 'the preventive force', brought the contraband in batches from the barn, with assistance from a crew member. He locked the door, and 'commenced operations. Noiselessly and quickly they cut off the head of the defunct farmer, and taking out the body filled the coffin with kegs of brandy, shrouded decently, and replaced the head on the pillow. Done in a trice, and the body, doubled up in a cloak, was brought in the dark to the barn.' Did his female 'relative' know what he had done? Perhaps not.

Another wife features in the story of another famous West Country smuggler, Cruel Coppinger, operating from the eighteenth to the nineteenth century, who married a rich older woman after being shipwrecked off the North Devon coast in 1792. He divided his activities between Devon and Cornwall (there is a Coppinger's Cave at Steeple Brink in Cornwall). A few years later, Mrs Coppinger reportedly

> hid a quantity of very valuable silks in the kitchen oven, while her husband engaged the officer's attention by permitting them to find a number of spirit-kegs. The officers discovered, much to their disgust, not only that they were empty but that they had been empty so long that not even the ghost of a smell of the departed spirit could be traced.[5]

But the harried Ann Coppinger had, in her haste, made a grave mistake in hiding the precious contraband in the oven, as it was hot and ready for baking: the valuable silks were cooked to a cinder. The marriage was predictably violent and Coppinger ended up in the King's Bench prison in Southwark in 1802 after being married for around a decade, separating the couple in all senses of the word. He was later reputed to be living in Barnstaple, funded by his wife, who died there in 1833, but her husband is buried at Hartland church.[6]

There are plenty of legends with regard to Cruel Coppinger, who may have been born 'a Viking' (i.e. from Scandinavia) who moved to Ireland before enjoying a comfortable life in Brittany which was destroyed during the French Revolution, meaning that he ended up in the West Country having been supplying contraband from Brittany to Cornwall. It seems likely that Ann, who some sources call Dinah, was a victim of domestic abuse, as suggested by Trevor May in *Smugglers and Smuggling*, as there are also stories of Coppinger tying her to the bed and threatening her with a whipping unless she persuaded her mother (who died in 1800) to hand over cash when he needed it.

In November 1823, eighteen fishermen's wives from the village of Hope were imprisoned in Exeter Gaol for 'insulting' the coastguard. The women had been caught red-handed, in Bolt Barn above The Square in Inner Hope, getting donkeys ready to carry smuggled goods inland to Churchstow, Devon. It is said that on their release the women returned to Hope Cove with the prison's copper kettles!

The woman on smuggler Richard Pepperell's boat on 4 September 1848 remains a bit of a mystery. The boat was being chased by the lieutenant of the coastguard of Salcombe after entering the harbour at nightfall. The two male occupants, one named as Pepperell, landed and headed for the shore, closely pursued by the coastguards; but the woman on board remained, and was taken into custody. One report gives the name of this woman as Jarvis, another says it was Pepperell's wife Ann. The coastguards later succeeded in taking Pepperell but the other man escaped. The boat contained thirty bales of tobacco-stalks, weighing 2,598lb. The following week Kingsbridge magistrates sentenced 42-year-old Pepperell to imprisonment at Exeter Gaol, this being his fourth smuggling offence. He escaped before getting as far as the gaol and a reward of £20 was offered for his capture. Just a month later, he was re-captured during another smuggling attempt at Stoke's Bay and the reward was paid to the coastguards responsible for his re-capture. This time the authorities took no chances in getting him incarcerated and he was still in gaol in 1851 when, on 5 July, Ann arrived with a man named Jenkins, off Bolt Head (South Hams) in a small open boat laden with twelve bales of tobacco-stalks from Guernsey. As they waited to enter Salcombe harbour after nightfall, they spoke to a passing Fowey pilot boat, the *Rebecca* and, giving the crew several handfuls of tobacco, 'asked them to take a note on shore to the party waiting to collect the contraband. The *Rebecca*'s crew agreed to this but instead placed the note into the hands of the coastguard, who immediately manned a boat, and Mrs Pepperell and her accomplice were soon safe in custody.' In addition to the notorious Richard and his wife Ann, there seem to have been other black sheep in the Pepperell family, but no more named ewes.[7]

Wrecking was common on the North Devon coast, which was known as the Sailors' Grave, bearing in mind that if there was even one survivor there was no chance of salvage. Wrecking is the practice of taking valuables from a shipwreck which has foundered or run aground close to the shore. It is even more unusual for a woman to be involved in wrecking than in smuggling, but one such was Mrs Elizabeth Berry from Mortehoe, who became infamous for holding drowning men under with a pitchfork to make sure they did not survive! She was arrested while removing goods from the wreck of the *William and Jane* on 15 February 1850 which had become lost in thick fog, and she was imprisoned for twenty-one days' hard labour because she could not pay the £1 fine.[8] It appears that she was arrested on her way home from the stranded vessel and, on being questioned by 'the Ilfracombe Receiver about a sack (containing a tub and a bedsack) she was humping along' her aggressive and evasive replies set her on course for the magistrates court, as a warning that it would 'warn her and others against such dastardly conduct in taking away from the unfortunate mariners, especially those lying dead on the shore'. It was said that sailors would rather drown at sea than come into the shores of Mortehoe. There are many unknown drowned sailors buried in Mortehoe's parish church, St Mary's (now Grade I listed) but many more were left at sea, drowned at the hands of the wreckers for their possessions.[9]

As for Elizabeth, known as Betsey or Betsy, she was born in 1798 in West Down, near Ilfracombe, and married John Berry in 1819. They lived in Mortehoe where their life 'would have been hard', and money scarce for their growing family. There are many rumours about Elizabeth, but with local families worried about swift retribution as well as being actively involved, few would ever testify about her actions, certainly not on oath before the magistrates and assizes. She became notorious for luring ships onto the shore by tying a lantern to the tail of a horse to create the impression of land and safety, although once the boats became stranded or damaged, she would drown the sailors and then take their possessions for her own. But she was also an opportunistic looter according to Ruby Bidgood in *Two Villages*. The family – they had nine children – would eventually leave Mortehoe, with many moving for work to Swansea.[10] However, it seems she died in 1877 in Georgeham, close to her Devon roots, so they obviously returned to the area at some point.

There were other tough Devon women during the Elizabeth Berry era. In the *Morning Herald* (London) of 20 May 1823, it was reported that four men from Hope, a small village near Kingsbridge, were sent to gaol a week earlier charged with smuggling. 'The Preventive men stationed on the coast went a few days later to apprehend another man on a similar charge, but the women, some of them the wives of the men taken, turned to, and absolutely drove them from the place.' It seems that the men were 'maltreated … so roughly, that the boatmen have applied to a magistrate for redress. What his decision is we have not yet heard, but these Amazonians have given them the defiance and promise to serve them again in the same manner, should they ever come back upon a similar errand' – which did not seem very likely.

Acting on information that a run had been made at Heddon's Mouth on 30 November 1827, but not yet sent inland, Lieutenant Mackenzie, Commanding Officer of Coastguards, with his Chief Boatman, the Lynton Riding Officer, and others, descended in force on the evening of 3 December on the farm buildings of John Hoyle (some sources name Hayle) at Trentishoe. Questioning Hoyle, they noticed his wife was very agitated and, taking this as a hopeful sign, they searched a barn and found a hole had recently been excavated in the floor to hold thirty-eight tubs of spirits. Continuing their search the next day, they found even bigger holes, described as caves, under another building concealing 174 tubs. The search went on for two more days when they found fifty more tubs of spirits, besides some wine, cordials and preserved fruits. Hoyle got away and roused a mob of men and women at Ilfracombe so that when the captured cargo was brought there in carts, the carters and escorts were attacked. To keep the peace, it was decided to take the evidence to Barnstaple where eventually Hoyle's wife and farm hands as well as some of the rioters were tried. 'Hoyle himself escaped to the continent and his wife was cleared of complicity.' According to Graham Smith in *Smuggling in the Bristol Channel*, the customs 'tried to implicate Hoyle's wife for assisting smuggling and harbouring smuggled goods. But after numerous reports to London and much legal debate the case against her was dropped. Perhaps it was felt that no local jury would convict her.' Obtaining a smuggling conviction from prejudiced juries or magistrates was a constant problem. Plus women outnumbered men in some coastal areas of Devon, giving them a strong voice – for example, in Combe Martin in 1871 there were 726 females compared to 692 males, no doubt many of the menfolk lost to smuggling.[11]

Chapter Three

Dorset and the Channel Islands

DORSET HAD MANY advantages for traditional smugglers. The Purbeck coastline has a plethora of coves and bays with high cliffs, Poole has the second largest natural harbour in the world, with the Dorset moors and the New Forest offering ideal hiding places. On the one hand, there were miles of sandy softly sloping beaches, ideal for landing small vessels, and, on the other, there were the shingle beaches around Burton Bradstock which meant that smugglers, even in the pitch black, could assess how far they were from a safe landing by the size of the pebbles, which varied in size depending on their location. Around 1830, smuggling reached a climax in the Weymouth area, where tunnels were said to be constructed 'from the harbour to merchant's houses and even to the residence [holiday home] of King George III' i.e. Gloucester Lodge, on the seafront.[1]

Women are mentioned in a report from the customs house at Weymouth in 1804.

> The articles generally smuggled from this part of the coast are chiefly brandy, rum and geneva [gin], to which may be added a small quantity of wine, tobacco and salt, the whole from the islands of Guernsey and Alderney, which are imported in casks containing from four to six gallons each in vessels from ten to thirty tons burthen in the winter, and in the summer season in boats … carrying three hundred and fifty casks, which are generally sunk on rafts till a convenient opportunity offers for taking them up, which they put into boats and distribute them along the coast at Portland and on … Chiswell Beach as

> far as Burton Hive [south of Burton Bradstock], which is about sixteen miles in extent. It then gets into the hands of women and others, who disperse it in small quantities in the country for five or six miles round, and what is not got rid of in this manner is conveyed on horses forty or fifty miles up the country.

According to this report, it seems that most of the contraband landed in Dorset was finding its way to 'Hampshire, Wiltshire and Somerset'.[2]

Usually thought of as a male preserve, it can come as a surprise that so many women were actually involved. Some of these would have been smugglers' wives, but not all. Dorset, in the heyday of smuggling, was a very rural and sparsely populated county, with much agrarian poverty. The business of importing goods, usually liquor, from cross-Channel boats under the cover of darkness in order to flout excise regulations was a lucrative sideline that impoverished families living within a few miles of the coast would find too great a temptation to overlook.[3]

In the *Dorset County Chronicle* of 2 July 1829 are details of some court cases when women were 'committed to Dorchester Gaol' for smuggling. These were Susannah Attwool Stone and Ann Shaddock, 'imprisoned until they pay the sum £4 19s; [and] Ann Stone to be imprisoned until she pay the penalty of 10s'. In the issue of 19 November 1829 more names crop up in an account of 'two female smugglers of the names Rebecca Carter and Maria Bagwell (from Chickerell near Weymouth)' who had been 'taken up by the Excise Officers and committed to the county gaol' for having 'in their possession and offering for sale in this town a quantity of prohibited spirituous liquors'. Maria is also listed in a roll call of Dorset land smugglers[4] whose cases came up at Lyme Regis Court where she is described as a dressmaker. (Land smugglers were those who distributed contraband inland.) She was not the only woman in that list – others were Martha Vivian, a labourer, Ann Gummer, needlewoman, and Martha Lumb, chairwoman (or chainwoman –

see below). In *Smuggling in the British Isles*, Platt says that women commonly 'played a peripheral role in smuggling ventures'. They hid, sold and distributed contraband, 'provided protection, alibis and assistance' to smugglers more heavily involved and 'sometimes fought off Revenue men'.

Records at dorsetcouncil.gov.uk for the 11–18 April 1816 reveal the conviction and warrant for the arrest of Martha Hurdle for smuggling 'one silk shawl, five silk half handkerchiefs, thirteen silk handkerchiefs, twenty-four pairs of leather gloves, two lace silk half shawls and twenty-one yards of lace', quite a classy haul. She was fined £20 including costs. The archives at Dorset History Centre also confirmed that Martha Hurdle, 52, a 'widow from Poole' was 'received' on 12 December 1821 for the crime of stealing money and plate. Her trade was given as Chainwoman (which could mean someone making chains in a nearby forge, or could be a misprint for charwoman!), and it is recorded she had four children. Her case was held at the Lent Assizes and her unusually severe death sentence was reprieved to eighteen months' hard labour. Martha died in 1852 so she survived the hard labour, and probably worse. Conditions in Dorset jail were pretty grim for the women as well as the men. The two sexes were segregated, but they had to tolerate iron bedsteads and straw-stuffed 'bed mats' with a diet of bread, some meat, broth, and extra bread if working; if they worked outside the jail confines they had to wear a smock bearing the words DORCHESTER GAOL. They also had to hand over more than two-thirds of earned income for running costs at the prison and to keep the 'gaoler' happy!

The remarkable research in *Dorset Smugglers* details the professions and ages of prisoners arriving at Dorchester gaol for smuggling offences between 1782 and 1853 in a very detailed Roll of Honour, based on the gaol records. Seventy-one of the 833 prisoners listed were women, several accompanied by their babies, one of whom died there in 1829. The baby's mother was 22-year-old Susannah Stone, a needlewoman from Portland serving two months, having failed to pay the fine of £4 19s. One was a 60-year-old blind widow serving three months in 1820 for failing to pay a fine of £23 10s 5d: Levia Rutledge, a 'twine spinner' from Bridport. Others were sentenced to hard labour, such as 19-year-old Eliza Harfal, a servant from Beaminster, serving three months in 1822. The youngest was Mary Ellis, only 15, described as a labourer from Buckland Ripers near Weymouth, and fined £100 in 1826. £100 was quite a common fine for smuggling offences, but one woman was fined just £1 16s in 1834 – this was 18-year-old Mary Stone, a fish carrier of Chesil – presumably for a minor, one-off offence. Other professions included the keeper of a 'hacksters shop' in Morcombelake near Bridport: Mary Miller, aged 30, imprisoned for two months in 1824 for failing to pay the £26 fine. (Hackster is an obsolete term for prostitute which could be the meaning here, although 'ruffian' is a later translation which seems closer to her potential smuggling activity.) There is also the fascinating reference to Sarah Humber who gave birth to her child four months into a five-month sentence in 1830, having failed to pay the reduced £10 fine, not just for smuggling in her case but for 'refusing to swear to the fatherhood of her bastard child'. Not just spirits but tea was being smuggled, resulting in 63-year-old Edith Mead from Wool, near Lulworth, serving six months for smuggling in 1803, one of the last to be imprisoned for smuggling tea as duties had been slashed, and would be completely abolished in 1860.

Further specific examples of prisoners are Charlotte Drake of Bridport and Ann Maidment, a Bridport 'buttoner' who both assaulted and obstructed excise officers. (A buttoner could produce up to seventy-two buttons a day, often from home, and there were thousands of them in the Dorset area.) Then there was Mary Applin of Langton, who committed an undefined 'excise offence'. Martha Lumb (again!) of Weymouth was sentenced to three months' hard labour in 1822 for smuggling, while Catherine Winter, a Weymouth seamstress, served an eighteen-day sentence in 1844 for smuggling at the age of 70! Approximately one-third of the women in this Roll of Honour were from Portland alone, while just six resided in Weymouth, five in Bridport, three in the inland village of Bere Regis and two in Lyme

Regis. The rest were from villages, hamlets, and towns from all around the county. Regardless of the sex of the offender, smuggling was generally considered an honourable trade for the populace as a whole.

In the early part of the nineteenth century, with smuggling at its peak, the hamlet of Fiddleford was a major smuggling depot in North Dorset, in an ideal geographic location, despite its modest size and inland situation. The leader of the local smuggling gang was Roger Ridout, who was jailed at one point although often escaping capture – when in jail he was visited by his wife, Mary, who smuggled in ale for him to drink through the prison bars, strictly against the rules, but cunningly concealed in a pig's bladder. She died not long after, in 1809, two years before Roger. Other female family members could be involved – a smuggling family in nineteenth-century Langton Herring (five miles from Weymouth on the ridge above the River Fleet) were the Vivians – even 14-year-old Martha went to prison for smuggling in 1826.

There is an oft-repeated story about Hannah Seller (or Sillar or Sellars, spellings vary) who was apparently in charge of an inn called The Ship in Distress at the very beginning of the nineteenth century, having been the landlady at Haven House, both at Mudeford in the quay area. She was apparently deeply involved in the 'free trade', allowing both pubs to be used for storage, and would induce customers to assist smuggling vessels in difficulties. Known as the Angel of Smugglers, she died in 1802. The creek named after her – Mother Sillar's (sic) Channel – gave secretive access to The Ship in Distress at Stanpit (on the shore of Christchurch harbour, historically in Hampshire until its 1974 boundary change to Dorset). Christchurch is named by Geoffrey Morley as the epicentre of smuggling – because of its location close to France, the Channel Islands and Holland, its gently shelving sandy beaches, the nearby New Forest, and its proximity to the 'Great Heath' whose difficult ground made it difficult for revenue men to pursue the smugglers.

An enlightening article by Andrew Norman in the February 2010 issue of *Dorset Life* magazine features a Charles Hayward, born

1796, sexton and churchwarden of St George's Church, Langton Matravers. Outwardly respectable, it seems Hayward was a smuggler, but his oldest daughter, Mary, was married to an exciseman which gave Hayward some advantages. This son-in-law, Thomas Trupp, is described as 'a drunkard and a bigamist' but it was certainly useful having a spy in the enemy camp. Norman suggests, logically, that Hayward's 'access to unlimited supplies of wines and spirits, may have made sure that … Trupp was too drunk to fulfil his duties'. His youngest daughter also made a useful marriage – to the butler of Mrs Frances Serrell, a wealthy landowner living at Durnford Hall, who rented Dancing Ledge quarry (on the coast, one mile south of Langton Matravers) to Hayward: the perfect, remote, place to land smuggled goods. It seems unlikely that Mrs Serrell was entirely ignorant of Hayward's smuggling activities. 'Further evidence to suggest that Frances Serrell was not all that she might have been comes with the discovery of a concealed passageway linking the attics of two cottages which she owned, and of a muzzle-loading shotgun in the chimney of a third, next door.' (Langton Matravers has other links to local smuggling, with contraband apparently often stored in the church roof.)

In 1814, a Mrs Moore and Thomas Creed were arrested in Weymouth for the smuggling of silks and lace, 'some of which were found concealed about the person of Mrs Moore' who was about to leave the house to approach the summer visitors. This couple were apparently part of a smuggling trade of luxury fabrics, 'for the purpose of disposing them off to several families that may visit this place during the summer'. Their illegal stock was catering to a booming population of middle-class visitors coming to the Dorset coast, with locals and customers of all classes

> largely turning a blind eye and allowing these businesses to continue. Smuggling itself involved people from all professions, genders and ages. From farm labourers who helped transport goods inland to local clergy who

> bought discounted tea and wine, and wealthy merchants who obtained cheap silks and lace. Even wealthy local landowners supplied money for smuggling operations in exchange for a percentage of the profits.

Women were also often involved in smuggling in Dorset, carrying spirits in bladders under their petticoats, as well as a needle to prick the bladder if they were chased.[5] In *Dorset Smugglers*, Roger Guttridge adds some detail, referring to Thomas Creed as Mrs Moore's 'live-in partner'. He described the couple as making 'a good living' from the receiving and disposing of 'prohibited goods'.

On the Portland Museum website is a letter from a Mr Campbell to the *Free Portland News*, printed in issue number 162 dated May 1992, recalling his 'Granny Stone' who had told them about carrying smuggled goods when she was young. He said that

> as a young woman she would hide in the coastal quarries until she was secretly handed bags of spirits, which she would put under her skirts and tie around her waist. Skirts were very long in those days even for the younger women. She would then proceed on her arduous walk to Weymouth … When Granny was talking to us I believe her age to have been ninety plus, the date about 1916. If this was so she must have been born about 1826.

Another personal story features on artpal.com regarding Hannah Osment, born in 1793, who, in her mid-40s, was imprisoned in Sutton Poyntz Prison near the seaside hamlet of Osmington Mills for smuggling. It seems she was let out after six months for good behaviour!

A smuggler's wife who kept the customs men at bay was Betty Gulliver, whose husband Isaac was such a successful smuggler on the south coast that he came to control its length from Lymington on The Solent in Hampshire, through Dorset to Torbay on the Devon coast and was known as 'King of Smugglers'. Isaac (1745–1822) owned several farms and large houses in Dorset, among them 'Howe Lodge', in Kinson, Bournemouth, a 'purpose built smuggling stronghold', which had a secret room only accessible through a door which was ten feet up a chimney. One particular story featuring his wife, its date impossible to establish, alleges that she 'covered his face in white powder and lay in an open coffin'. When the customs men arrived to arrest him she told them he had died during the night and showed them the 'body'. An 1867 edition of the local paper *The Poole Pilot* carried a story about Gulliver landing a record amount of contraband from three luggers anchored near Bournemouth Pier.[6]

Another famous Dorset smuggler was the forementioned Jack Rattenbury (died 1844) whose wife, Anna, was similarly involved in his activities. One story is of his trying to evade being press-ganged into naval service, when his wife saw him being ordered aboard a vessel in Bridport Harbour. Rattenbury caught sight of her and asked permission to speak to her, which was firmly denied, but Jack managed to escape the impressment gang's clutches until his wife attacked the leading lieutenant, who threw her down on the ground. This caused the local townspeople in the vicinity to get involved, and, even though the impressment gang was made up of nine strong men, they managed to keep them away from Jack, who made good his escape, not for the first time. Smuggling was the main income for his whole family in the eighteenth and early nineteenth century and he wrote a small book about his life, *Memoirs of a Smuggler*, in 1837.

All the Dorset books and reliable websites such as the BBC refer to a Jenny Gould and her smuggling activities, her cottage a hiding place for contraband, but none mention dates. As there are a number of smuggling stories in the 1820s in the Purbeck area, Jenny's home patch and an area notorious for smugglers, it is a safe assumption that this was her century. In fact, Geoffrey Morley[7] brackets Jenny with other nineteenth-century smugglers such as Hampshire's Lovey Warne. He says that her house was at Godlingston Hill near the site of later waterworks and describes her as 'the smugglers' guardian angel' while others describe her as being a witch. Certainly any supernatural connections would have served her well as spreading tales of 'ghostly goings-on and witchcraft were a handy way of making customs men too afraid to go snooping around looking for contraband!'[8] But she was also apparently responsible for the accounting, storing, and checking of goods brought into her house as well as being important in its distribution – and, of course, keeping the preventers at bay. She certainly lived in the ideal location for a smuggler – the cliffs of nearby Ballard Down on Swanage Bay were a favoured landing spot where the barrels, or 'tubs' would be hauled up from the foot of the cliffs on Studland beach and taken along the top of the Down on farm wagons and hidden in her cottage. When the coast was clear, the local men preferred to land goods directly on a gentle slope with a smooth sandy secluded beach, not too close to the dangerous Old Harry Rocks which were responsible for a number of nineteenth-century shipwrecks. From Ballard Down a signal fire or flash could be seen out at sea miles away, so the risk of detection was slight.[9]

In *Smugglers' Trails* there are references to the 'Oxenbury women' in the early 1890s who 'used to carry tubs of spirits ashore hidden under their crinolines'.[10] Roadstead Farm in Chideock, a small village between Bridport and Lyme Regis, apparently featured a purpose-built secret room, ideal for hiding contraband. This is a seventeenth-century dwelling, now Grade II listed, its hidden room apparently a 'common feature' of smugglers' houses in many Dorset villages. There is a similar reference to 'women at Lulworth' in the 1800s carrying 'smuggled spirits in small tubs hidden in linen baskets piled high with clothes' or in animal bladders beneath the ever-useful voluminous petticoats. It seems that when these women were approached by a customs officer they would fold their arms and 'stand around gossiping' until he had gone. Smuggling, especially for women, was moving to a very different phase thanks in part to the changes in fashion, and partly by the involvement of a very different class of women.

Thomas Hardy, famous Dorset resident, born in a 'capacious safe-house for smuggled contraband that could accommodate up to eighty casks of brandy' in Higher Bockhampton, wrote about his father's and grandfather's links to smuggling.[11] He also wrote *Wessex Tales* in 1888, where one particular tale, *The Distracted Preacher*, features a young widow, Lizzie Newberry, who smuggled illegal liquor and was then involved in its concealment (in the singing gallery of the church) and sale. She simply 'couldn't give up smuggling' because 'It stirs up one's dull life at this time o' the year, and gives excitement, which I have got so used to now that I should hardly know how to do without it.' This pretty much sums up how women felt about smuggling in the nineteenth century, not only in Dorset.

* * *

Some sixty miles from Weymouth are the Channel Islands, which are known as Crown Dependencies, i.e. they are not part of the UK but belong to the Crown. They are nearer to France than to the UK with Guernsey, in particular, being a centre for the collection and distribution of goods for import and export.[12] Only in the 1850s were the Channel Islands brought into the ambit of UK customs laws. Even the Guernsey museums had no records of female involvement in smuggling – though this was not particularly surprising.

There was an interesting article, in *The Star* of 31 December 1896, however, a Guernsey newspaper. It is unauthored but reads as follows:

> There is little humour about the feminine smuggler. She does, undoubtedly, take a great deal of contraband ashore, and not uncommonly smiles rather defiantly at you as she walks past. No one, however, knows better that women are 'kittle cattle' than officers of Customs. Few of them are so bold as their vigilant colleague who, when the 'improver' [crinoline] had grown to its vastest dimensions, met two ladies landing from a foreign

> steamer at a great north-country port, and, begging to be permitted to escort them to the nearest female searcher, had extracted from their 'improvers' some ten or eleven pounds of cigars by that functionary's hands. Mostly, the lady smuggler makes hysterical protests against the indignity to which the horrid men in uniform are subjecting her, and, when these are disregarded, and the offices of the female searcher have made her guilt as clear as noon-day, she melts into such floods of tears as quite dissolve the sense of humour. Usually, she belongs to the second of the two classes into which smugglers now divide themselves – that of the passengers. It is a class embracing an immense variety.

Similarly, in another copy of *The Star*, 3 January 1874, an uncredited feature reveals that

> One libellous writer of last century, indeed, went as far as to say that 'most men and all women are born smugglers' and until within the last few years, when the abolition of duties on many articles of luxury removed most of the pretexts for smuggling, nine custom house officers out of ten would have … spun yarns hours long in support of the assertion ... Spirits are too bulky to pay in the long run for the risk of detection, and naturally the smuggling of spirits is dying away. But the desire to sweeten possession by secrecy still holds good as regards tobacco … tobacco passed secretly ashore from inward bound vessels, especially those flying other than the English flag … some of the watch smugglers went in for wholesale work. They made regular trips, and had secret pockets in various parts of their luggage; but women frequently brought time-keepers in vests and pockets under their frocks. One such vest, with a belt attached,

> contained when it was taken from its fair but Hebrew owner one silver and no fewer than 146 gold watches. Such a seizure must have taken the cream off the profit on many previous transactions of the kind, and yet it is clear that no such number would have been risked unless there had been a great encouragement from the lengthened impunity of similar frauds.

There was an account in the *Dorset County Chronicle* of 30 November 1848 which links Guernsey with Dorset's neighbour, Somerset, a really rare reference to a female smuggler in the latter county. The account refers to 'a poor woman, Elizabeth Langden, of Crewkerne, [Somerset] brought into Court on Friday, charged with having brought with her from Guernsey 6lb of tobacco. Mr Argent said it was by his order … that the woman was searched, for that she was in the habit of crossing for the purpose of smuggling.' His Worship asked whether she had crossed 'here' previously, to which the answer was 'No,' so he asked if there was evidence that she had crossed at other places. Mr Argent could not swear to this.

> The woman stated that she had been to the Island but once before, that her husband had died, leaving her with six children, and that she had been to Guernsey to see two of them, where someone advised her to take across a little tobacco for sale, to pay the expense of the trip. His Worship fined her in the small sum of £1 10s, but in default of payment she was sent to the house of correction.

So the Channel Islands remain a mystery, along with their women.

Chapter Four

Essex

THE GEOGRAPHY OF the Essex coastline was a major influence on the scale of smuggling operations and methods. This part of the UK in the nineteenth century was bleak, with miles of remote mudflats, sandbanks, saltings, and inlets where contraband was run ashore undetected. Horses and carts could carry contraband from the sea wall to roads close by, with the tide soon removing footprints and hoof prints from the sands. With more coastline than other counties plus its many tributaries and hidden creeks, it was the ideal location for illegal cargo arriving.[1] The land at the Great Clacton Cliffs, for instance, was not developed until 1871 so the desolate beach and the dangerous sand banks were idea for smugglers.

Then there were the packet boats sailing into Harwich, in particular, 120 miles from the Hook of Holland, where 'free traders' could sink cargoes in the shallow waters of its estuaries and creeks to be picked up later. Harwich, where cod smacks were used for some of the smuggling runs, figures specifically in *The Smugglers' Century*. Here is where James Scott was found to have 'bandanas on his premises' in 1817. Customs thought his wife was the 'villain of the piece', saying she had obtained the silks from a member of the crew of the packet *Lark* who had since left for Woolwich in London. The silks were thought to be part of an order given to Mrs Scott by Mr Duke, a shopkeeper then in Chelmsford gaol. Scott was actually imprisoned for a year as a result, and his wife had 'all her household goods seized and had to depend on the minimal support of the parish'. (At least Scott escaped the introduction of hard labour as a penalty, with the treadmill at Chelmsford gaol in use from 1833.)

However, it is probably Paglesham that could be regarded as the home of smuggling in Essex involving the entire community with so much gin landed that they (i.e. the women!) used it to clean the windows. It was also, interestingly, the place where Charles Darwin's *Beagle* ended her days when she was converted to a watch vessel giving accommodation to the local coastguards, its submerged mud berth on the River Roach now a protected and nationally important site. Tollesbury, at the mouth of the River Blackwater, near Maldon, was also a popular landing place for smuggled goods, which, even if customs officials threatened, could easily be dumped into one of the tidal pools to be collected later. Goldhanger, on the banks of the Blackwater, was the inspiration for Mary and Catherine Lee's 1887 children's book, *Goldhanger Woods*. This is a story of the adventures of a young girl 'among a band of desperate smugglers'. It seems that the authors had connections with, and stayed at, Tiptree Priory on the edge of Tiptree Heath, also known for its smuggling activity.

Essex featured some particularly notorious female smugglers in the nineteenth century. For instance, in the 1840s, Sarah Gregson kept a chandler's shop and tobacconists in the churchyard of St Margaret's at Barking, not far from the Creek. It seems she employed a number of young lads, all angelic youngsters under 16, their ages and appearance possibly rendering them immune from prosecution. These lads, known as Mother Gregson's Gang, were paid 4d for every pound of tobacco they brought her, mainly retrieved from fishing boat crews who were smuggling it in. Graham Smith in *Smuggling in Essex* describes her as a 'female Fagin'. Barking then had, perhaps surprisingly given its inland location, the largest fishing fleet in the country with 200 smacks owned by one family alone. Gregson has also been linked with Leigh-on-Sea, a more 'obvious' location for smugglers on the coast, and there was a programme on Phoenix FM some years ago in this regard, but there appears to be no confirmed evidence of this particular connection.

Mrs Gregson supplied large tobacconists and City merchants with her smuggled goods. On several occasions, she was able to produce official-looking (fraudulent) receipts for duty paid to Customs officers when her premises were searched – her contacts in London came in useful for this. But she was not always able to pull in favours, for there are newspaper records of her being arrested and fined for her smuggling activities.

For instance, in the *Surrey and Middlesex Standard* of 20 May 1837 there was a story of Mr James Jordan, a custom-house officer, accompanied by a customs' locker (a customs official responsible for the locks of bonded warehouses), who proceeded to the London house of James and Sarah Gregson,

> well-known dealers in contraband goods … for the purpose of apprehending the woman on a warrant granted by the city magistrates, for non-payment of a heavy penalty for running smuggled goods, which were found by Jordan and other officers, at her late residence, No 2, Barking Churchyard. The officers succeeded in capturing Mrs Gregson … and proceeded to search the house for other contraband property. Their search was not unsuccessful: a discovery took place of forty-one papers of loose foreign manufactured tobacco weighing 31lb, a pillow-case containing 81b of leaf tobacco, a pillow-case filled with mixed tea, several pound papers of green tea and green tea-dust, five glass bottles of brandy, and a stone bottle of brandy, in all ten gallons and three quarts, and several other articles, the whole of which they seized. It appears that the Gregsons, who have been several times convicted of smuggling, are connected with persons who smuggle tobacco, tea, lace, and other goods, from the foreign steamers, and conceal the contraband articles in bustles, and about their legs. Several men have been recently stopped by Jordan and other revenue officers, with property concealed in this manner, and the bustles of many women filled with tobacco have been lately taken

> from them. The pillow-cases found in the house of the Gregsons had been used for this purpose.

Sarah Gregson was sent to the Giltspur Street Compter – a small prison in the City. A few years later, she was in the news again. The *Morning Herald* of 5 January 1843 carries the following account:

> Sarah Gregson, a woman who has been long known to the revenue officers as a person well acquainted with smugglers of all nations, and who keeps a shop for the purchase and sale of all sorts of goods, in Barking Churchyard, in the city of London, was brought before the Mayor and Sir James Duke, upon the charge of having had in her possession 20lbs of tobacco, five gallons of brandy, 161b of window glass, and 14lb of tea, all liable to duties which had not been paid, and which had been smuggled into her house. This excited much interest, and occupied a great deal of time … upon being asked whether she was guilty or not guilty, said she was not guilty, but admitted she had had the articles specified in her possession. Davis, a vigilant officer of the customs, stated that on Tuesday, the 6th of December, he watched the premises of Mrs Gregson, from Barking Churchyard, accompanied by a brother officer, and saw a person who was well known to him as a smuggler enter her house with a white bag upon his back. He was not able to get over the rails in time to seize the man, whom he saw put the bag upon the counter, but he went to the premises as soon as he could, and the man quickly disappeared leaving the bag behind him, Mrs Gregson having, with as ready a hand, slipped it under the counter… The officers went into the house, and asked Mrs Gregson's leave to look about the premises, to which she readily consented. They saw her daughter in the back yard washing the

> sink, and with her finger, thrusting pieces of paper down, two of which they snatched, and which smelt of tobacco [plus] found near the sink two bottles of brandy, and one broken bottle, which had contained brandy … also found on the spot a quantity of loose tobacco spread out on two sacks. There were more discoveries upstairs: two large jars and 11 bottles of brandy, and a letter directed to Mrs Gregson giving an order for eight gallons of brandy to be supplied to a dealer, and two pounds of gunpowder tea. The letter stated that the writer felt disappointed at not having received other articles which had been ordered, and concluded by mentioning that Mrs Gregson should have a good order next week. The articles seized were all foreign.

Sarah's solicitor, Mr Langham, asked 'Is not Mrs Gregson a licensed dealer in tobacco and in tea?' The witness, Mr Davis, the customs officer, confirmed this information and was then asked why he had not seized the man who saw her going into her shop, to which Davis responded that he could not get over the railing 'soon enough'. The revenue officer, William Allen, corroborated the statement made by Davis, and added that 'he found a bag under a lot of rubbish containing a quantity of tea, and also a bag containing some raw tobacco'. The Mayor then said he had heard a good deal about Mrs Gregson's shop and asked 'what sort of shop is it?' The witness told him it was a chandler's shop, for the sale of every sort of article.

James Jordan, another revenue officer, stated that he found in the house 14lb of foreign glass, and he was asked by Mr Langham whether he had not heard from a respectable tea-dealer that Mrs Gregson dealt with him for tea. Jordan replied that he had heard a tea-dealer make a statement to that effect. Edward Wood, a Queen's warehouseman, stated that he had examined all the articles, and believed them to be foreign. Mr Langham submitted that the charge of having 'knowingly in her possession smuggled goods' had not been proved against his client. 'The fact was, she dealt with a tea-dealer for tea, and with a tobacco-dealer for tobacco, for the supply of her customers.'

The article goes on to mention that Langham produced a bill of parcels from a tea-dealer, to Mrs Gregson, for gunpowder tea, to the amount of £5 4s. As for the glass, the evidence that that article was of foreign manufacture was not, in his opinion, sufficient to affect the decision of the magistrates against her; and as for the brandy, it happened that Mrs Gregson kept a lodging-house for seafaring people, 'who might have brought in brandy now and then to the house, and as they were not punctual in their payments, she had no alternative for the security of her rent but the appropriation of the spirit they got possession of. There was no evidence of guilty knowledge in all this.' However, Sir James Duke pointed out that there were 'five gallons of brandy'. In her defence, Mr Langham said that 'The lodgers might have brought it in a bottle at a time.'

Langham then called a man named Stubbing who stated that he was 'shopman and traveller to a Mr Groves, a tobacconist' and was then closely interrogated by the Lord Mayor. Mr Langham asked the witness whether he thought that Mrs Gregson was in the habit of having goods at the house of Mr Groves, the tobacconist. Stubbing denied any such knowledge: 'The porter took the goods to Mrs Gregson.' The Lord Mayor wanted to know if the porter was present but he was not. Stubbing was then asked, 'Pray whom does Mr Groves deal with for tobacco?' but the witness did not feel this was a fair question. Asked why the question was unfair, Stubbing responded that: 'There might be some of his customers here, who if they knew, would go to the person he deals with', which provoked laughter in court. Asked if he travelled for Mr Groves, Stubbing admitted that he did 'all over the town'. But when asked if he had ever served Mrs Gregson with tobacco he denied it and denied ever having received an order from her. The witness was then asked to look 'at that tobacco which lies before you, and tell me, on your oath, whether Mr Groves has, to your belief, sold such as that to Mrs Gregson'. Stubbing could only say that he believed Groves to serve tobacco 'like this'. The next question was: 'Have you ever been to solicit Mrs Gregson to purchase of Mr Groves?' Stubbing said he had never done this. The Lord Mayor then spoke to Mrs Gregson in a loud voice, as she 'appeared to be rather deaf'. He asked whether Mr Stubbing had ever given her any order and she said he had. 'Yes, my lord, he called on me with Mr Groves and gave me an order for tobacco.'

> The fact is, this woman is a most notorious smuggler and receiver. I convicted a man here the other day for smuggling, and this woman came forward and swore that he gave her £9 for cigars, which Mr Roberts, a most respectable man, his master, declared were worth little or nothing. She is ready to swear anything to get the rascals with whom she is in league out of difficulty; and Davis, the officer who has pounced upon her, was the very man who apprehended the smuggler of whom I speak. I am very happy that we have got hold of the smuggler of Barking Churchyard. Mr Langham said the unfortunate woman was in an ill state of health and had a very large family, and prayed that his lordship would mercifully convict her the lowest penalty.

The Lord Mayor consulted with Sir James Duke and concluded with:

> My brother magistrate and I are induced by the representation that she has a large family, and by the palpable evidence that she is in an ill state of health, to inflict the lowest penalty, where, under other circumstances, the highest ought to be insisted upon. We have no doubt that she has been long a dealer in contraband and stolen goods, and we caution her to reform her ways altogether. She shall be watched both by the revenue and the police, and if detected again in any dishonest dealing she shall

> pay the full forfeit. We adjudge her to pay the penalty of £25. The tea, as no evidence has been adduced to show that that was not furnished to her by the tea-dealer whose bill of parcels has been produced, shall be returned to her.

A similar account of a trial was detailed in the *Morning Advertiser* of 3 December 1844, apparently exciting a great deal of interest with another high attendance. This time, both James and Sarah Gregson were charged with smuggling, both pleading 'Not guilty' to the charge of having had 'in their possession, on the 25th of October, a quantity of tobacco and cigars and a gallon and seven pints of brandy, and six bottles of eau de Cologne'. This time, Davis, the customs house officer,

> stated that he observed a child leave Mrs Gregson's shop with a bundle under his arm. He followed the boy … who said he came from Mrs Gregson's, and accompanied him back to her shop … the boy then said in her presence that she had given the bundle to him, and that he was delivering it to a man in Seething Lane [in the City of London], and she did not deny the statement. The bundle contained two paper parcels of tobacco, containing eight pounds weight, and two bottles of French brandy. The tobacco was full of lumps and compressed; part of it was quite warm.

Someone else then entered the shop, carrying 'something bulky' so Davis followed and tried to search him, but he was a 'powerful man' and ran out, pursued by Davis. He was brought back, and found to be carrying 'two pounds of foreign cigars'. Mrs Gregson's brother, who had endeavoured to prevent Davis from his search, was fined £5 for the obstruction, while the carrier fined £2 10s for possession.

The house was then searched, revealing a locked door which was accordingly forced. Mrs Gregson 'ran with bundle which she had in her apron to the water-closet, and Davis followed, but could not prevent her from putting something down'. In the scuffle they tore up the seat between them. She then took a bucket of water and emptied it into the water-closet, saying 'Do your worst and your best now.' Davis took a candle and

> looked down ... and saw some pieces of tobacco about the seat ... assistance having arrived, he proceeded in the search. Upon the fire he found a saucepan with boiling water and steamer, and some tobacco ready for steaming, a process used to prevent the article from breaking. Upstairs he found a jar containing a gallon of French brandy, and his assistant found six bottles of eau de cologne.

It was stated that the duty on the tobacco was £13 2s 3d, and that upon the spirits was £2 5s.

On the witness stand, Davis stated that he had been 'nine years an officer, and had known Mrs Gregson the whole time'. Mr Hobler, who was defending the Gregsons, asked Davis whether he had been in the habit of smoking and drinking in Mrs Gregson's house, and he admitted to smoking in the house just once in his life and produced a book from his pocket which documented this one-off event. He read from the book as follows:

> It was on Monday, the 19th of September, 1843, about ten o'clock in the evening. I had been watching it from seven till ten, and I went in and paid for a cigar and lighted it. Mr Gregson was there, and there was bottle and glass on the counter. He said 'Will you take a glass of wine, Mr Davis!' I was surprised by this invitation, and I took the glass. At that moment in walked two men... and I said to them, 'What have you got there?' They replied, 'Only a little leaf.' I told them I was Davis, and I called

> on Mr Gregson in the Queen's name, to go for the police, which he at length reluctantly did. The men had about 3lb of leaf tobacco, and I had them convicted in the penalty of 20s each. I went into the house to smoke the cigar for my own purposes.

Mr Hobler's next question was to ask Davis whether he had ever sent anyone to the Gregsons' house to purchase brandy and tobacco, which Davis denied. Although Mr Hobler suggested that Davis 'could be proved to have been on terms of intimacy in the family of the Gregsons, and was seen frequently to smoke and drink in the house', the prosecutor, Mr Potbury, said the officer's character was too well known to the custom house authorities to be in the slightest degree affected by accusations of such description. Hobler was not giving up that easily, however, and went on to ask Davis if he knew 'one Mrs Rose'. This time, Davis confirmed that he knew her 'Perfectly well. She threatened to knife me. She is one of the party.'

Mrs Rose was then called to the witness stand and stated, in answer to questions from Mr Hobler, that she knew Davis, and had seen him several times at Mrs Gregson's, before that defendant was fined. The witness had been servant to the Gregsons, and had known Davis to be 'as one of the family, drinking brandy and smoking cigars … she knew seafaring people very frequently to call, and whether they bought tobacco, and … they said Davis had sent them. She knew Davis to bring parcels of tobacco. She did not examine the parcels, for she had no right to interfere with what belonged to Mr Davis, but they smelt of tobacco.' The Lord Mayor asked the witness several questions, the answers to which gave the lie to her previous declarations, and convinced every person that 'every word she uttered against the principal witness for the prosecution was a fabrication'.

Another female witness, not satisfied with denying the truth of Davis's evidence, swore that he had used Mrs Gregson in a 'most indecent manner'. When the Lord Mayor asked her to be more specific, this witness said that he had 'knocked her head against the door, and she was black about the place for a fortnight afterwards. So help me, God.' The Lord Mayor then asked whether the witness's husband was not one of the persons who had been convicted in penalties elsewhere to which she replied that he had been fined for an assault, but not for smuggling. The woman went on to say that Davis had searched the house 'without showing his warrant, and had no right to do so'. However, judgement went against Mrs Gregson who was fined £100, James was released, and Davis was assured that no one had believed the accusations made against him. The detail available regarding Sarah Gregson is remarkable – but welcome!

One Essex woman, Ann Bacon of Brightlingsea, ended up in Chelmsford gaol in 1835. Her family, particularly her two sons, were apparently well known in smuggling circles, utilising their false-bottomed boat the *Speedwell*, the only known Essex vessel at the time to be adapted in this way. These sons (John and Thomas) were apprehended with Ann standing as surety for the £170 bond on the *Speedwell* which her late husband had bequeathed to her for life.[2] However, she was unfortunately unable to pay and was taken to prison as a Crown debtor, declaring that she was unaware of her sons' activities 'but the Collector clearly did not believe her' although it is not clear how long she was imprisoned for. It certainly seems likely she was involved, directly or indirectly, in their enterprise.

A story from www.clactonhistory.co.uk features a Mrs Dawson who lived with her husband in Brook Villa, a 'splendid house in Great Clacton with a brick front and weather-boarded rear'. In December 1832, revenue officers knocked at the door and wanted to search the building which was in Old Road. Dawson quickly hauled his smuggled goods up the ladder to the bedroom above, where he 'hid the barrels under the bed and told his wife to wet her face and start groaning'. Having searched the downstairs and outbuildings, the revenue officers were about to go up the ladder when Mrs Dawson 'wailed and shouted out'. According to Stan Jarvis in *Smuggling in East Anglia*, Dawson declared his wife was dying and that he 'must go up to her at once' the revenue men then making a 'discreet departure'. This may have been connected to Essex having a reputation for being a source of malaria, a fact known to have kept authorities away.

Brightlingsea was also the home of another well-known smuggler, George Orman, who lived with his wife and son. Jarvis writes of them being convicted of smuggling 'just two gallons of geneva' (the forerunner of modern gin, originating in Holland and Belgium). They were fined £100 initially, but it was later reduced to £25 when the magistrates decided this was a 'minor infringement'. This case was reported in the *Essex Standard* on 8 March 1878:

> George Orman, smack-owner of Brightlingsea, Mary Orman, his wife, and Arthur Orman, their son, were charged under the 187th section of the Customs Consolidation Act with having on the 11th February rescued and been concerned in the rescuing and destruction of certain seized goods, to wit, two gallons of geneva gin.

The defendants all pleaded not guilty.

It appeared that James Frost Smith, an outdoor officer of customs belonging to the Port of Colchester, and stationed at Brightlingsea, had gone to the house of the defendant, George Orman. He met the defendant leaving the house and asked him if he had got any spirits, which he denied. Smith then went to the back of the house, and after staying there a minute or two

> he heard the front door open and close and he saw Mrs Orman going up the road with a shawl over her head and something bulky, covered by the shawl, under her arm. He followed her, and on overtaking her about ninety yards from the house he told her it would not do for her to take anything out of the house unless he saw what it was and added 'give it to me, and I will take it back.' She said

> 'You shall have it, but let me take it back.' Smith allowed her to do so, and on reaching the house she took from under her arm a two gallon wicker jar and said 'There it is, come in.' He did so, and took possession of the jar and set it against the door. Mrs Orman went out of the house, and he then took out the bung and found it to be nearly full of geneva gin … She returned to the front room and brought out two half-gallon jars and asked him if they would take any notice of a little brandy. … 'This is some brandy my husband brought home, and (pointing to the jar against the door) that is gin.' … She shortly afterwards went into the yard and broke a bottle in a field, and the breaking caused a strong scent of geneva gin … Smith told her she had better break no more bottles as they caused such a scent, and she said it was empty. He told her it could not be so. She then broke two other bottles, witness remaining with the wicker jar close to the back door.

Whilst Smith was there the defendant Arthur Orman came in, followed by George Orman 'in an excited state' and a scuffle developed until help arrived.

This help came from a Mr T. M. Johnstone, who said he went to the house of the defendant George Orman, about three o'clock on the day in question.

> On seeing him the defendant said 'How do you do, sir?' and Johnstone asked where the jar was that Smith had seized from his wife. The jar produced was brought from a press in the same room. Finding it smelt of paraffin, witness said that stuff had been put in to deceive. … When the jar was produced … Smith said it was not the jar he had seen. Orman said it was, and on Smith saying it had basket work round it, Orman said 'Yes, it had, and I burnt it' and he produced from the fireplace a piece

> of the wicker work. Witness then asked for the two jars that Mrs Orman had taken out of the front room, and be produced two empty jars which had previously contained brandy, and when asked where the spirits from the three jars were he said 'I have spilt some and drank some.' If it was geneva in the jar Mrs Orman was carrying it would have been liable to duty at the rate of 10s 5d per gallon. Orman produced two decanters, one containing a little brandy and one a little geneva, and said that was 'what was formerly in the jars'.
>
> Thomas Collis, examining officer of Customs stationed at Brightlingsea, said he went to the defendant's house about noon, and … while he was there he saw something burning and looked in at the window and told Orman not to destroy anything. He said it was nothing, only an old basket. Witness saw a large blaze which set fire to the soot in the chimney. About that time he saw Mrs Orman come out with a paraffin lamp which she said she 'might as well fill up.'

It was pointed out that no explanation had been given why Mrs Orman should be 'ninety yards away from her house carrying a jar containing the dirty water which was afterwards found in the jar'. The magistrates retired to deliberate, and on their return into court fined George Orman £100 and the costs, £1 2s 6d, and in default he was imprisoned till the amount was paid. Mary and her son Arthur were acquitted.

Some stories are based on oral history. For instance, the River Colne en route to Colchester Hythe Port was ideally placed for smuggling, and the story goes that one young captain, John Pim, would navigate his cutter on a moonless night, looking out for the signal from his lover, Miss Molly, apparently in the nineteenth century. She was described as a lovely young woman with clear blue eyes like cornflowers and flowing golden hair like buttercups, a veritable garden of beauty. If the coast was clear, with no signs of customs men, Molly would lift the blind in a front window of the attractive Georgian house where she lived with her mother. Molly's fat cat, The Bosun, would sit alongside the lighted candle she placed on the windowsill, and Molly would receive a kiss for her efforts from the captain after his contraband had been unloaded. It seems that even after the couple were married, living in the same house – called the Darkhouse, on the corner of Darkhouse Lane at Rowhedge – they continued to indulge in a spot of smuggling to boost their income.

The most successful petticoated smuggler in Essex seems to have been Elizabeth Little of Leigh-on-Sea. She had a shop where the Peter Boat car park is now, selling all kinds of goods, much of it seemingly contraband. Her speciality was in luxury fabrics such as lace and silks, but she also sold perfume and gin, all of which were subject to heavy taxation at the time. She was listed in the *History Gazette of Essex* of 1848 as a Draper of the High Street, Leigh. In a world when most lady smugglers were not particularly ladylike, and would often have been indistinguishable among their male counterparts, she was educated and intellectual with a fondness for lavish dinner parties with the best food, wine and conversation. However, she was also well able to handle a boat and willing to get her hands dirty.[3] In fact, Elizabeth and her brothers visited France on a regular basis for their booty, picking up French wines for Elizabeth's dinner parties en route, prepared by her French housekeeper Madam le Gryse. Elizabeth was the apparent organiser behind these trips, and her knowledge of local tides came in very useful.

Of course, the coastguards at Leigh in the mid-nineteenth century were always trying to trap their suspect. On one trip to Ostend, they were delayed upon their return, with the Thames tide against them, and a coastguard cutter lying in wait, which let go 'a shot across their bows'. It was Elizabeth herself who put on 'more sail and made a run for it' resulting in another shot which wounded her younger brother, Bob, in the arm. They headed for Shoebury point and from there to Barling Creek, where the shallow waters meant the cutter could not follow them. Elizabeth and Will, her elder brother, knew they would be trapped when the tide went out, so Elizabeth decided to take Bob and the contraband overland, while Will took the empty boat back to Leigh under the noses of the coastguard. However, Will had to go to Little Wakering first, under his sister's instructions, to borrow a coffin and hearse from Benneworth the undertaker. The transaction was completed with Bob secured in the coffin, the loot on the floor, with Elizabeth in mourning-wear on the front seat next to Benneworth. At one point on this journey, a customs officer had stepped out into the road just past Leigh Hill, raising his hand to apprehend them, or so it seemed, but all he wanted to do was raise his hat and cast his eyes down in respect to Elizabeth, a story that the undertaker and Elizabeth related to Will later when they relaxed with a glass of rare French brandy, having attended to Bob and put the hearse and horse securely away in their stables.[4]

At the end of the century, smuggling was changing from its traditional association with rough types in small fishing boats. Contraband became more likely to be smuggled by 'respectable' passengers, often women, in passenger vessels from Europe. Hence this story reported in the *Dundee Courier* on 29 September 1899, headed 'Lady Smuggler Fined'. It refers to

> a well-dressed woman, who stated her name was Margaret Good, and her address St John's Wood, London, was charged with smuggling 1.5lbs of cigars. At Parkeston Custom House [built in 1798 less than 1 mile from Harwich and continuing as a custom house until 1935] officials said accused declared a few cigars, but on being searched cigars were found concealed in her hat, under her arms, and in her dress pocket. Defendant said she was told by an agent at Antwerp that she could take a few cigars home. She was fined the single value, duty, and costs, amounting to £1 10s 7d.

One more name that often cropped up when researching this Essex chapter was Bessie Catchpole, but as she was born in Suffolk and divided her smuggling activities between Suffolk and Essex, she features in Chapter Nine. Certainly there was no shortage of female smugglers in Essex, the county being ideal for smugglers (of both sexes) as Herbert W. Tompkins put it in his 1904 book *Marsh Country Rambles*: 'Examine a large map of Essex and you will see how truly the county was made for smugglers … There are at least fifty well defined rivers, creeks or outfalls.' Fortunately, unlike the research into many other counties, some of these women have been named, and have at least some of their stories written down and documented.

Chapter Five

Hampshire and the Isle of Wight

WHILE, AS ELSEWHERE, the eighteenth century was the dominant time for smuggling, one incident at the end of the century indicates that it was certainly not at an end, and certainly not in this part of the United Kingdom. A report from the *Hampshire Chronicle* of 25 March 1799 stated that

> A woman of the name of Maclane, residing at Gosport, accustomed to supply the crew of *Queen Charlotte* with slops, went out in a wherry to Spithead, when a sudden squall coming on, the boat sank; the watermen were drowned, but the life of the woman was providentially saved by being buoyed up with a quantity of bladders, which had been secreted round her for the purpose of smuggling liquor into the ship, until she was picked up by the boat of a transport lying near.

A case of being buoyed up by good spirits, no doubt!

Author Jan Toms writes of the Isle of Wight in 1822 as having more contraband traffic than at any time in the past, with ships being carved into the stones of houses to indicate their availability to assist the smuggling fraternity. Only the smuggling of salt diminished when in 1824 the Salt Tax was removed. Certainly, there is more material available with regard to smuggling cases on the island than on the Hampshire mainland. Perched on the cliffs above the shore near Bembridge Harbour, the Crab and Lobster public house was the perfect spot for covert night-time operations. Once the goods arrived on the beach, the local community helped to shift the goods, ready for concealment, redistribution, and sale on the mainland. Many of the village's women were tried for smuggling. There is a reference to a nineteenth-century 'grog shop' in Oyster Shell Cottages in Newport (since demolished) with a landlady who took regular delivery of smuggled tubs of spirits for her customers. As deliveries had to be accomplished at night, the fee for whoever made the delivery was one of her 'renowned square meals' and a bed![1]

Another inn, now listed, is the Wheatsheaf in Yarmouth, Isle of Wight, which had a landlady in the nineteenth century called Susannah Plumbly who had 'not been averse to taking in illicit liquor', but found herself in a difficult position when called as a witness in a smuggling case because she was thought to be aware of local smuggling activity and/or to have overheard gossip in the bar. She attended the lengthy inquiry which took place at another local inn, The George, alongside a barmaid called Maria Bright who admitted buying brandy from local people, some of which may, she said, 'be smuggled, I wouldn't know. But as you are aware, Sir, it might be illegal to smuggle brandy, but it is not illegal to sell it … I would only buy from respectable people.' She admitted that she had heard many conversations about smuggling, and was aware of successful landings because of the celebrations that took place in her bar. The evidence of both women was very similar, and there was no evidence given against them or any case initiated. The results of this inquiry, several weeks later, cleared all the defendants.[2]

One famous name you might not expect to link with the smuggling fraternity is the author Jane Austen. However, after a ball at the Dolphin Hotel in Southampton in December 1808, she it was – proficient as ever in summing up a gentleman's potential as a spouse – who noted that Corbet James D'Auvergne was both a captain in the Royal Navy, a ship owner, and single. However, he had his hands in large-scale smuggling. When Jane Austen lived in Southampton between 1807 and 1809, the town was a hive of wartime activity – and smuggling. Jane was in contact with officers of the Royal Navy, and would dance with them at balls. She admired the 'striking black eyes' of one in a letter to her sister Cassandra. Captain D'Auvergne (of the striking black eyes?) must have been a close acquaintance because Jane mentioned him twice in her letters to Cassandra, without further explanations, indicating that the captain was well known to the Austen family. Whether Jane and/or Cassandra condoned his smuggling activities is, however, not known, but is certainly food for thought.

In the early decades of the nineteenth century, a number of women on the Isle of Wight were prosecuted for conveying and concealing contraband liquor, which they hid in their baskets or under their voluminous skirts. In February 1830, for instance, Mary Sweatman of Ryde was convicted of smuggling brandy, along with her partner John Stagg. Both were prosecuted for identical crimes, yet Mary received a fine of £50, whilst John only had to pay £25. There was no mercy for any women (or men) who defaulted on fines, and many of the female culprits ended up behind bars for a while. Another female smuggler was Elizabeth Cooper, who was convicted of concealing spirits. When her brother faced a similar charge, a local news reporter said, 'Although the family of Cooper is not an extensive one, our bridewell [archaic name for a prison] is seldom without one.'

The customscowes.co.uk website also has details of Harriett Harbor, who, on 9 February 1833, was caught transporting a half a gallon of brandy in two animal skins and a bladder, without paying the tax. She was fined £25 but was unable to pay, and so spent a month in prison, not for the first time.[3] Harriett had two accomplices, Mary Ann Fagan and Mary Ann Fry, who were also found to be concealing brandy, but they managed to abscond and were never captured. According to the Isle of Wight Society's website, 'between 1830 and 1851 twenty seven' women were prosecuted for smuggling.

In *Blackgang 1835*, Keith Dyer writes regarding a Mrs Bennet who once owned the Jacobean North Court in Shorwell Shute near Blackgang Chine (now Grade II listed). He writes of her being a 'genteel lady' even when dealing with smugglers delivering brandy to her grand house, located not far from Niton Smugglers Tunnels, built from local stone and nestled just above the rugged coastline, known for its clandestine smuggling activities. The book is a fictionalised account of the activities of a smuggler called John Wheeler, but what is interesting where the women are concerned is the account of John's wife (Frances) and how she tried to befriend the lonely wife of Lieutenant Bulley, a local revenue officer, who prevented her from doing so because he felt the Wheelers would be a 'contaminating influence'. This must have been the case for many innocent women who were tarred with the same brush as their husbands, a problem for those upholding the law.

The female islanders were

> mainly responsible for decanting liquor from barrels and casks into smaller receptacles, such as bottles and pots. They removed the French identification stamps by burning and then hid the goods in places such as chimneys, under false floors, hedges and even in tombstones. Children didn't miss out on the action either, and they were used as go-betweens, passing messages from one family member to another.

On the Isle of Wight, smuggling was a real family affair! The now defunct website www.victorian-supersleuth.com had suggested that, at its height, it was estimated that in places like the Isle of Wight two-thirds of inhabitants were involved in 'free trading' (smuggling). This included fishermen and sailors who shipped in the contraband, and the women who did the decanting for its ongoing trade journey. Tobacco was one of the most popular 'imports', as well as brandy, gin, tea, fruit, and textiles. In 1847, a couple of bumboat women (women in small boats ferrying goods to and from larger boats) were 'interrupted' in Portsmouth by 'Mr Witt, a tide surveyor' smuggling 70lb of tobacco. The *Montrose Standard* of 3 December says that he was 'immediately attacked in a savage manner, one of the women actually seizing his left ear with her teeth, with which she nearly severed the ear'.

There is a reference to a very young – aged 9! – Caroline Tizzard of Portsea (at the mouth of the Solent) being arrested for carrying six gallon tubs of brandy in April 1837, a heavy load indeed. She was fined £5 for carrying and conveying foreign spirits and for non-payment jailed in Newport Common Gaol on the Isle of Wight for one month.[4] Additionally, there is quite a comprehensive listing on the www.customscowes.co.uk website of smuggling cases on the Island in the 1820s and 1830s. The following, although detail is minimal, gives an idea of its prevalence among the women, and is not even complete:

- Diana Hudson of West Cowes, April 1824, possessing 15.5lb of coffee on which no duty had been paid, being her first offence, the accrued penalty was £6 15s but reduced by two-thirds which she paid a week later.
- Sarah Wright of St Helen's, March 1825, possessing three skins containing one and three-eighths gallons of foreign spirit liable to duty value £2 1s 3d, full penalty, triple value £6 3s 9d.
- Ann Dyer of St Helen's, March 1825, did not turn up in court, convicted of possessing one skin containing one-eighth gallon of brandy and eight skins containing more than one gallon of foreign geneva, liable to duty, value £1 10s, penalty treble value £4 10s.
- Elizabeth Tribbick of St Helen's, March 1825, convicted for possessing eight skins containing 1.25 gallons of foreign geneva liable to duty, value £1 10s. Did not turn up in court but penalty treble value £4 10s.
- Elizabeth Wright of St Helen's, possessing two skins containing 1.5 gallons foreign spirit on which no duty had been paid, March 1825. Having children at home, convicted and given time to pay £6 15s.
- Elizabeth Knapp of Ryde, May 1825, convicted for possessing half gallon of foreign geneva, fined treble value of £1 11s 6d.
- Elizabeth Harbor, March 1826, carrying and conveying foreign spirits, penalty £100, mitigated to £25 but not paid so jailed at Winchester for six months.

- Elizabeth Taylor, convicted of possessing smuggled brandy, August 1826, fined £25 but jailed at Winchester for non-payment.
- Hannah Scovel of Brading, mitigated fine April 1830 concealing 1.25 pints brandy.
- Ann Southcott, Jemina Stallard, Ann Skinner December 1832 found guilty of concealing a quantity of spirits in tubs in each of their dwelling houses. Southcott's and Stallard's penalty mitigated to £25 from £100, and not being able to pay were committed to prison. Skinner did not appear and full penalty was inflicted.
- Mary Ann Matthews May 1835, fined £100 for conveying and carrying four gallons of brandy, and in default of payment was committed to the House of Correction at Winchester for six months.
- Elizabeth Stone, September 1835, carrying and conveying fifteen skins containing 2.8 gallons of foreign geneva, fined £100, not paid so jailed for six months at Winchester, without hard labour (so many Elizabeths!).
- Matilda Green, September 1835, carrying and conveying fifteen skins and one bladder containing four gallons of foreign geneva, £100 fine not paid, so jailed at Winchester for six months without hard labour.
- Matilda Street, October 1835, carrying and conveying twenty-one skins containing 2.75 gallons of brandy, fined £100 not paid so jailed at Winchester for six months without hard labour.
- Matilda Street, second offence, September 1836, carrying and conveying certain quantities of foreign brandy in the parish of St Helen's on which the duties had not been paid, nine months imprisonment.
- Mary Gutteridge, December 1838, carrying and conveying three-eighths of a gallon of brandy, defaulted on penalty payment of £5; committed to the Common Bridewell at Newport for fourteen days' imprisonment.

Another source refers to tubs of liquor smuggled across to Portsmouth, in ordinary packet boats, this work 'carried out by the women folk' with tubs concealed under their crinolines. Another trick mentioned was for them to 'carry the tubs wrapped in shawls so to all outward appearances they were carrying infants'. It seems that one of the best known at this particular role was a Bembridge woman called Nancy Smith, who for a great many years 'carried on' under the noses of the revenue officers, but was 'never once found out'.[5]

Author Richard Hutchings interviewed a Gertrude Turner in the early 1970s regarding her smuggling memories. She told him about her grandmother and great-aunt Sarah, living in West Wight in the nineteenth century. Her grandmother diluted and coloured smuggled alcohol brought in from France, and her great-aunt burned the ropes which the smugglers had used when carrying the heavy tubs up the cliffs. Gertrude's cousin remembered seeing them do it though had not connected their activity with smuggling. Hutchings is one of the few authors of books about smuggling that bothers to include the involvement, and importance, of the wives, female relatives, landladies, and female supporters of the smuggling fraternity.[6]

The same book gives an account of George Osman's grandmother who, also in the nineteenth century, was strong enough to carry the smuggled tubs brought in at Alum Bay on the island. She also 'watched for the approach of the Coast guards and warned the men below'. Apparently there was a cave halfway down the brow of the chalk cliff known as Main Bench Cliff, large enough to turn round a horse and coach inside, and unapproachable 'except by ropes or rope ladders', a perfect hiding place for a large number of tubs of contraband brandy. Hutchings also accessed the scrapbook of the Totland Bay Women's Institute which includes details of a Freshwater carrier who was hiding two kegs of brandy in sacks of potatoes and other vegetables, while awaiting transport to distribute the contents, but was faced with an unexpected visit from the excise men. His wife 'hastily prepared a tub of washing, put the kegs underneath her crinoline dress and continued washing while a fruitless search was made of the house and outbuildings'.

Then there was well-known smuggler Charlie Kingswell at Luccombe, another who received an unexpected visit from the excise officers, the men arriving to find his wife, Hannah, seemingly suffering 'from spasms and groaning loudly as she rolled in her chair from side to side'. She explained away the odour of brandy as being for medicinal purposes, and the officers found nothing. They had not noticed the trap door under her chair, 'leading to the underground cellar'. The final female that Hutchings features in this period is Fanny Wheeler, the Wheelers being an established smuggling family on the island. She married John when she was 17, and her honeymoon was a smuggling expedition to France. On their way back to Portsmouth 'on a big sailing vessel' she went down below but her husband encouraged her back on deck because he knew customs were watching and would be 'less suspicious' if they saw a woman aboard. So Fanny agreed and waved a 'small hand-towel' at the customs vessel – she got a wave in return and they moved away.

Any public house perched on the cliffs on the island above the shore was perfect for covert night-time operations. Once the goods arrived on the beach, the local community helped to shift the goods, ready for concealment, redistribution, and sale on the mainland. This included the Crab and Lobster near Bembridge Harbour, where many of the village's women were tried for smuggling.

Some accounts in local newspapers on the British Newspaper Archive show how many women, especially those married to smugglers, escaped the strong arm of the law just by being women. For instance, in the *Hampshire Telegraph* of 5 December 1866 there is an account of the County Petty Sessions a few days earlier, headed 'The Seizure of Contraband Spirit at Newport'. This refers to George Jones, of Wroxall (a small village near Ventnor on the Isle of Wight), a carter, and his wife, Susannah, plus a labourer named John Toogood, all charged by 'William Dear, Esq., collector of customs at West Cowes, with having a quantity of contraband spirits in their possession'. Mr Beckingsale appeared for the defendants. The case started with the evidence of George Wade, commissioned boatman of the coastguard at Ventnor who had been to Wroxall on 25 November. 'He went to Jones's house, which is close to the railway; it is a double house, and … went upstairs where he found a tub of spirits near the head of the bed. Mrs Jones was in the house. He delivered the tub to the chief boatman who was present. The tub contained white brandy.'

James Wade, chief boatman, then gave evidence that

> he went over the Down to Wroxall, and went with the last witness to George Jones's house, and … found a tub of spirit in the bed-room. It was not quite full; he tasted it and found it to contain strong spirits. They then searched the outhouse, and Thomas Pill, boatman, found one tub of spirits there, which was full. William Pill afterwards found five more tubs in the outhouse, covered with furze.

(Two Pills and two Wades could be reporting errors.) Yet another boatman, William Nosworthy, said he was ordered to go to George Jones's, 'and found five tubs in the shed and passed them out to James Wade. They were perfectly full, with slings, under some furze. He took possession of them, and sent them to Cowes with James Wade.'

Further evidence was provided by P. C. Skeats who had gone with Pill to Jones's house, 'and from information received apprehended him'. The prisoner said he had done wrong, and acted against the law, and he must get out of it in the best manner he could. A second P. C. (Rossiter) said he went to Jones's house at eleven o'clock on Sunday morning and 'first saw Toogood standing by the pigsty, and then saw Mrs Jones go from the woodhouse door into the house … carrying something. He did not go into the house, but went down the village, and when he came back he saw the tubs handed out of the shed.'

This account does not reveal what happened to George Jones, but does add that both Mrs Jones and her brother (Toogood) were 'discharged there being no evidence against them'. Unlike the evidence against George Jones …

The same newspaper, dated 4 September 1878, has another detailed account involving a husband being sentenced rather than the wife. This time the case is described as a 'Serious Charge of Smuggling Against Tradesman', being George Cooper, grocer and butcher of Brixton (now Brighstone on the Isle of Wight). He was 'charged with having smuggled foreign manufactured tobacco in his possession'. The Collector of Customs for the Isle of Wight, Mr Henderson, prosecuted, and Mr Joyce defended the prisoner.

Initial evidence was given by George French, the Chief Acting Boatman at St Catherine's Coastguard Station who

> last Thursday had occasion to consult his commander, who instructed him to … search the shop of Mr Cooper. On entering the defendant's shop he found he was absent, but he asked Mrs Cooper if she had any smuggled tobacco on the premises and when she said there was no smuggled tobacco on the premises, he asked her to show him all the tobacco there was on the premises, when she produced some English tobacco, and afterwards she took out from the lower drawer

foreign-manufactured tobacco weighing 13lb. The defendant returned home at 2 p.m., and on speaking to him about the tobacco, he said he 'bought it of a dealer at Ventnor, but would not give the name of the person of whom he bought it'. The prisoner was charged 'with being in charge of foreign manufactured tobacco', and taken into custody.

Mr Joyce claimed that Mrs Cooper had some rolled tobacco of English manufacture in her possession, which she readily produced, but 'she was rather reluctant to produce the smuggled tobacco'. Then Mr William Dibble, a commissioned boatman stationed at Reeth Coastguard Station, said he had accompanied the witnesses to the shop of the prisoner, which they searched, and 'found the 13lbs of smuggled tobacco produced'. Mr Henderson said that as the tobacco in question was valued at £5 4s the prisoner was fined £10 8s, double the value, and £2 9s costs, a total of £12 17s which seems to have been promptly paid, with no charges made against his wife.

As for mainland Hampshire, in the mid-nineteenth century there was a boom in the construction of railways which meant more passengers travelling abroad. The customs officers in Southampton commented that 'lady passengers are dressing themselves in valuable dresses and jewels, more calculated for their entry into a drawing room than merely to come ashore. They are all items newly acquired abroad.'[7] Trevor May pointed out that as early as 1846 'the Collector of Customs at Southampton reported that the extent of smuggling by the steamers was most extensive'.[8]

The most famous female associated with smuggling in Hampshire is Lovey Warne of Burley, born *c.*1796. She grew up in the Regency era when, according to www.hhhistory.com, smuggling conjured 'images of darkness, moonless nights hiding the illicit acts of free traders loading and unloading casks of brandy washed up on English shores by the tide, or hauling contraband like laces, silks, and tea through secret, underground tunnels'. However, while smuggling was best achieved at night, it wasn't always carried on as a nocturnal activity, at least, not for the Warne family. Lovey, or Loveday, was one of the three children of Peter Warne and his wife, all born before the end of the eighteenth century.

She is described by Geoffrey Morley as 'an ingenious smuggler in her own right when she was young'. While her brothers kept watch on the cottage and route-junction at Knave's Ash, their house just outside Burley in the New Forest, she would trot off on her pony down to Mudeford on Christchurch Quay to indulge in her very 'specialised form of smuggling'. She would board a vessel tied up at either of the two quays where she would enter the captain's cabin, 'take off all her clothes and proceed to wind her body in rich silks and priceless lace handed to her by the smuggling captain. She would then carefully dress again smoothing the fabrics so that they followed the contours of her body as closely as possible, spring on to the cobbles of the quay and trip back to her pony, past the smiling

Revenue men', who were unable to 'rummage' women, and then back home. From here the smugglers would take the goods up what was known as the Smuggler's Road to Ridley Wood, the marketplace for the finest specialities including Lovey's fabrics, 'or across the great turnpike road to Winchester and London and on to Wiltshire'. The Warne family were innkeepers, but made ends meet with their smuggling activities like many others at the time, with people of all classes engaged in the buying or selling of smuggled goods.

There are several stories from the Regency era when the Warne sons, Peter and John, would haul wagons of contraband along the chalk Smuggler's Road in broad daylight. Lovey helped them in more ways than one. For example, if a revenue agent happened to be making rounds on the days when they went about their illegal business, Lovey would don a red cloak and climb Vereley Hill in Burley to stand as a human signal, warning them to take another path.

According to one story, she was almost caught on one occasion, when an unsuspecting revenue agent liked the look of her and tried to embrace her.

> She had been invited to join a Revenue Officer for a drink at the *Eight Bells* in Church St and she accepted the invite to avoid suspicion, the two of them enjoying the gin to the surprise of the customers – until she felt his hand on her knee … now alarmed, she swore at him, dug her elbow into his eye and made for the door. The landlady held the man back on the pretence of concern over his eye, her maid producing a cold compress, and by the time he had freed himself from her grip, Lovey was gone.

When she told her brothers, they warned her off smuggling on her own account any more, although she continued to ride her pony leading the pack-pony trains across the moors, and could help them more by being a human signal with her voluminous scarlet cloak.[9]

The legend of Lovey has endured, and now there's even an ale named after her. But what happened to the real Lovey Warne? She certainly continued with using the scarlet cloak into old age to warn her smuggling friends. Lovey never married, but lived with Peter, a maltster, until his death in 1870. She died in 1873, leaving £6 in her will, and was buried in the Church of St John the Baptist in Burley, one of the first parishioners buried there. Apparently, she wished for her beloved pony to be buried with her, but officials did not grant her request and her pony was buried near a ring of fir trees outside the churchyard.

Geoffrey Morley tells of local Sowley smugglers who landed their goods at nearby Pitts Deep and used Sowley Pond, on the southern edge of the New Forest, as the site of an underwater cache. The Forge Hammer Inn (on the site of an earlier ironworks but no longer a hostelry) was used for the storage of illicit goods until the mid-nineteenth century. The inn was on one occasion approached by a group of coastguards when smuggled goods were hidden in the huge chimney. Alert to the dangers of discovery, the landlady came out and harangued one of the guards, loudly accusing him of not paying his bar bill. A pre-arranged signal, given when the smugglers had safely removed the contraband and made off with it out of harm's way, told the landlady when the coast was clear so she ceased her tirade and let the coastguards into the inn where they found nothing untoward.[10]

The Hampshire Telegraph and Sussex Chronicle for 12 February 1858 contained a report of a 'seizure of contraband from a small cottage to the East of Farlington Church, within the parish of Bedhampton [near Havant]. A suspicious police constable found 21 kegs of brandy in the cottage.' When a police sergeant arrived to help the constable, they forced open a door and found more brandy, a still, empty kegs and 'colouring matter', all of which were removed to Havant Police Station. 'The only occupant of the cottage at the time was a woman called Mary Cole who said that the room in which the kegs were found was occupied by her lodger, whose name she did not know.' The newspaper report went on to say that it was believed that many people in Havant and Bedhampton were involved. 'The woman stated that someone knocked at her door and asked to leave something, to which she consented, and not having a candle the light was insufficient for her to recognise them. It certainly seems strange that a lone woman should open her house to strangers at 4.20 on a dark morning.' What happened to Mary Cole, however, frustratingly, is not reported but presumably she was not prosecuted.

A very different form of smuggling features in the *Norfolk Chronicle* (and elsewhere) on 17 August 1861, headed 'Lady Convicted of Smuggling'. This relates the case of Caroline Bennell, a 'lady of independent means, of good family, and of extremely genteel appearance' who was placed at the bar in Southampton, charged with smuggling '4lb of cigars and 1lb of tobacco, the single value and duty of which was £3 12s 4d, and the treble value and duty £10 17s'. It was John Yeoman, customs officer, on duty the previous day on board the *Southampton* from Jersey, who saw the defendant, and asked her if she had anything liable to duty. He gave evidence that 'She replied in the negative, but on the officer searching her cabin he found 4lb of cigars and 1lb of tobacco.'

The defendant was then asked: 'You have heard the charge preferred against you, a very serious one, that of defrauding her Majesty's Customs; what have you to say?' Her response was that she did not know she was 'doing anything wrong; I brought it over with the intention of giving it to some friends.' She went on to tell the court that she was of 'small means, which enable me to live independent' and that she lived in Belgrave Terrace in London. She was given a fine of £5 11s 6d and the costs of the proceedings, with the customs officer advising that he had 'the lady's money in my custody'. On being told that she needed to be 'more careful for the future, and mind you do not come here again, or you will be more severely dealt with', she replied: 'I should not have been here at all if I had known that I was doing wrong at the time' and she then left the court.

Another variation on smuggling featured in the *Essex Standard* of 30 December 1863 involving two German women who were attempting to smuggle goods out of Southampton, rather than into it. They were heading out in the *New York* steamer a week earlier and 'were detected in endeavouring to smuggle 22lb of cigars' into the US from 'the steamer which lay in the dock, and which had just come from Bremen' (in Northern Germany). The cigars were in

> ordinary boxes, each containing 1lb weight. Each of the women had eleven boxes strung round her person inside her dress, and fastened to her crinoline. Although the women walked very carefully, the boxes rattled one against the other, and a custom-house officer hearing a strange noise as the women passed him, suspected that it had a contraband origin. The women had got outside the dock gate before they were detected.

Some years later, the *Yorkshire Gazette* of 19 January 1884 gives an account of two 'respectable women named Everett and Johnson, residents of Southampton' having been charged with smuggling. The two women had been stopped at the dock gates and 'in pocketed petticoats specially made' was half a hundredweight of tobacco. They were remanded in custody, liable for a penalty of £100 each.

Another case illustrates the variety of females involved in smuggling. This was in the *Hampshire Advertiser* of 23 January 1886, headed 'Extensive Smuggling by a Woman'. The account confirms a case at Portsmouth Police Court in front of 'Captain McCoy (in the chair), Mr J. Griffen and Alderman Whitcombe'. The woman on trial was Eliza Evans, the wife of 'a naval pensioner at present serving on board the *Duke of Wellington*' who was charged, on remand, with having 'unlawfully concealed about 28lb of tobacco stems, with intent to defraud Her Majesty's Customs'. Mr G. H. King defended. Although the seizure had been proved, Mr King 'contended that the revenue was not defrauded as the stalks were merely the refuse of the tobacco served out to the men which they threw away; they were barely worth sixpence a pound'. The captain, however, disagreed, saying that 'they were sold for the manufacture of snuff'. As a result, the Collector of Customs said he was 'instructed by the Commissioners to ask that the full penalty of £100 be inflicted', although the bench, after some consideration, fined the defendant £10 in addition to costs.

Finally, Blackgang Chine, once a notorious landing spot for contraband on the Isle of Wight, became Britain's first 'theme park' in 1843 while many parts of the Island were still very much involved in smuggling. In fact, gangs of smugglers were known to operate in this very area (possibly including a 'Black Gang'?) so that it became the theme of the park, and there are still giant figures of smugglers at the entrance!

Chapter Six

Ireland

IN THE EIGHTEENTH and nineteenth century smuggling was rife along Ireland's rugged coastline with somewhere between 30 and 50 per cent of some goods (such as tobacco) being brought into the country illegally. At the beginning of the nineteenth century there were fifty smuggling vessels based in Ireland, dominating trade in the Bristol Channel.[1] Waterford (in Southern Ireland), Ireland's closest deep-water port to mainland Europe, required a particularly significant force to patrol the coast and the harbour entrance. However, a report by the revenue to the British Parliament from 1824 mentioned that 'every available house in the area was under the control of local smugglers and no house was available to rent while they built a coastguard station'. The coastguard had to resort to anchoring a ship off Ballymacaw bay while construction of a station could take place.[2]

There were women involved in traditional contraband, i.e. spirits and tobacco, especially the former given that illicit distilling was a major cause for concern, as in Scotland. One features in *Jack's Strange Tales Collection* – an unnamed (as usual) Irishwoman who smuggled 'three large pieces of window glass, 13in x10in, under her skirts'. One piece hung down by 'each thigh' and one at her back. Certainly strange! She was caught, but this was a risky exercise and must have meant she had to remain standing while travelling.

The Evening News of 8 April 1886 gives an interesting account of the Rational Dress Movement and its effect on smuggling. The article suggests that

> If the rational dress movement were to achieve its purpose, there might possibly be less illicit drinking. This may

> seem a strange saying, but the explanation of it is afforded by a case heard at the Belfast Police Court. A police sergeant, in giving evidence respecting the sale of liquor on certain unlicensed premises, stated that a female whom he apprehended there kept the stock upon her person. She was in fact a walking public-house. Her petticoats were so artfully constructed that in them she was found to have carried thirty-six bottles of porter and two pints of whisky … when a less bulky style of dress is worn these ingenious ladies will find their occupation gone.

Indeed!

The mother of Irishman Will Watch, an early nineteenth-century smuggler, features in *The Compleat Smuggler*. When he was in prison for the murder of an excise officer, she is said to have gathered 'a crowd of sympathizers' and to have 'stormed the prison, climbed a ladder, and smashed a way in through the roof', rescuing him successfully. His sweetheart, Sue, no doubt also condoned his smuggling activities; she features in a ballad about him.

The one name that features prominently when it comes to Irishwomen involved in smuggling in the nineteenth century is that of Jenny Watts who lived in a cave believed to run for miles under Bangor town to avoid capture by the excise men. Jenny was the youngest daughter of Jack Watts, owner of The Jolly Fisherman, a tavern to the west of this County Down town[3] and was known to smuggle contraband 'under the noses of the local militia'.

As well as being the proprietor of The Jolly Fisherman, John Watts was also involved in smuggling coffee, tea, silk and brandy from the Isle of Man and selling them in the expanding town of Belfast. The Isle of Man was widely used as a base for smuggling contraband into Ireland and Scotland as they did not pay the high duties levied in Great Britain and Ireland. While Jack Watts may have not taken a hands-on part in the smuggling, he did encourage and assist his daughter Jenny who was an excellent sailor and skippered her wherry regularly to the

Port of Peel in the Isle of Man to obtain duty-free wine and brandy for the growing population. This illegal trade continued for some years and Jenny became a local hero as she shared the proceeds of her activities among the poor in the local community. It is even rumoured that she was a founder member of Ballyholme Yacht Club in Bangor in 1900, although as she was apparently born in 1790, this seems unlikely. However, what is a fact is that she had a number of close encounters with the excise men, but because of her local popularity always managed to avoid capture, particularly fortunate when the penalties for smuggling for both sexes was severe, ranging from long periods of imprisonment to hanging.

It is not clear exactly when and how Jenny Watts' smuggling career ended, but rumours have it that one 'dark November night' while Jenny and her crew were storing kegs of brandy in what is now known as Jenny Watts' Cave they were surprised by a large number of excise men. It was suggested that Jenny had been betrayed by a local squire whose advances she had rejected. The crew managed to escape at the time, but Jenny, who was deep in the cave when the excise men arrived, decided to hide rather than face a long term of imprisonment. Jenny was never seen again and the locals believed she may have drowned when the tide came in and flooded the cave. It is also rumoured that she can be 'seen' on Brompton Harbour on the last Friday of November every year.

An interesting postscript to the Jenny Watts story is that she had apparently anticipated that she might one day be caught and had hidden a map to show where she had stored her fortune. However, despite many searches over the years, no one has been able to find it. A number of local boys playing football in Bangor Castle Park in 2015 did find a leather container which experts think may contain details about the long-sought Jenny Watts treasure. The boy responsible for the find was 10-year-old John Small from Silverstream Mews and, in an interview published online, he explained how the find came about:

> We were playing in the woods beside the Town Hall and Dave booted the ball into the trees. When we were

> searching for the ball I found this hole under the root of a dead tree. It was quite a deep hole but at the bottom we could see a leather tube about six inches in length. It was very old and dirty and badly damaged. We pulled it out and saw it contained some old papers and a map. We decided to take it round to Dave's house to let his dad see it. Dave's dad could not read the papers as it was old and torn and damaged by weather but his mum said that it looked important and we should take it to the Museum. We took it to Bangor Museum and showed it to Ann Teekes who said that despite the damage it was clear that the documents dated from the early 19th Century and related to Jenny Watts a well-known smuggler in these parts. It would appear that the papers show that she has buried her loot in the Bangor Area.

The documents were sent to the Central Museum to be restored.

Jenny Watts' Cave is located next to Brompton Bay just under the North Down Coastal Path but is only accessible at low tide by boat unless you are a rock-climber. Her legend lives on in many ways – there is a pub named after her in High Street, Bangor, there was a children's story and a poem published in recent years, there are images on YouTube, and there are even (as at 2023) Jenny Watts Boat Tours.

Earlier and more violent is the story of Margaret Jordan, wife of the Carlow-born pirate and smuggler Edward Jordan, who escaped prison (or worse) in 1809, because the court were sympathetic to the needs of her children. Her husband was executed, although in fact his final trial was for murder as well as piracy after the family had moved from Ireland to Nova Scotia in Canada at the turn of the century. He got involved in a very violent dispute with the financers of his mortgaged schooner *The Three Sisters* (the name because of his three daughters). There seems to have been no doubt that Margaret assisted Edward in his piracy, but she was cleared of murder. She stood trial alongside her husband and even though she also took part in the attack on Captain Stairs (the new owner of the schooner) she claimed she was doing so 'under duress as she had suffered years of abuse at the hands of her husband'. The court believed Margaret's story and she was granted a pardon because she 'acted out of fear of her husband'. After the trial, local residents raised money for the destitute Mrs Jordan and her four children to pay for a passage for them back to Ireland.[4]

In Donegal, in Ireland's north-west corner, women in the 1820s had pockets made from tin and 'a breast and a half-moon, that goes before them … with a cloak round them they will walk with six gallons, and it shall not be perceived'. One Irish distiller even went so far as to have a tin vessel made with a head and body in the shape of a woman which 'he dressed to resemble his wife, and rode to market, his poteen [i.e. illicit alcohol] on the pillion behind him'.[5] Much later in the century, there are a number of cases reported in a variety of Irish newspapers. In the *Cork Examiner* of 25 January 1858, for instance, a Mary Williams, 'native of Patrick Street, Queenstown, Co. Cork' was in court for selling a large quantity of Cavendish tobacco, 'the possession of which she was unable to account for satisfactorily'. She had been arrested by sub-constable O'Brien and brought before Mr Besnard, the police officer, who 'conceiving that the tobacco had been smuggled, directed the complainant to put the case into the hands of Mr John Bennett, solicitor to the Customs'. Rather frustratingly, however, the story is not followed up in available resources.

The *Cork Examiner* did a slightly more comprehensive account in 1870. They reported on 8 September that a woman named Ellen Dennehy was arrested on board the troop ship HMS *Himalaya*, by William James, custom house officer, and brought before Mr H. H. O'Bryen, JP of Queenstown, charged with 'carrying and concealing 3.5lb of leaf tobacco contrary to the Customs act'. She pleaded guilty, and was ordered to forfeit the tobacco and pay for single duty, single value and costs in the sum of £1 1s 6d, or in default, to go to gaol for fourteen days. At the same time, James Higgins, custom house officer, brought up 'Anne Butler, a child of eleven years of age' charged with concealing 4.5lb of stalk, and 2.5lb of tobacco leaf. She stated that she 'got the tobacco from a sailor, who gave her a shilling to take it to Cork for him, and she thought there was no harm in doing so'. In consideration of her extreme youth, Captain O'Bryen let her 'stand out her own recognizance the sum of £10, to come up for trial when called on'. (Queenstown was named after Queen Victoria, but is now Cobh in County Cork.)

Another Cork newspaper, the *Cork Constitution*, reveals that smuggling was by the 1880s featuring contraband from the USA as well as from Europe. Their issue of 5 March 1888 refers to a 'Novel Smuggling Case in Queenstown' as follows:

> A case of smuggling was discovered today which caused much gossip and considerable amount of amusement amongst the public. Two young girls, passengers per the Royal Mail Steamship *Celtic* from New York, after landing at the Deep Water Quay, fashionably dressed, and adorned with rather large improvers [cushion shaped bustles], were, as is usual, directed to enter the female searcher's room by the vigilant Customs' officers, who, no doubt, had their own suspicions of the two damsels referred to, for soon after the hand search was made the large improvers were found to contain 6lb of Cavendish tobacco, 3lb being discovered in each bustle, neatly packed. The ocean travellers protested their innocence, stating they had never placed the favourite weed in the secret places, and that they did not know even of the tobacco being there, but all to no purpose. The stern but courteous official informed the young women that they were guilty of smuggling and consequently should suffer the penalty, which was to pay treble duty and single value on the contraband and the forfeiture of the tobacco and improvers. The penalty imposed by law was complied with.

As a change from tobacco smuggling, there are two similar accounts of women smuggling ammunition – also into Queenstown. The *Birmingham and Aston Chronicle* of 22 December 1888 records the arrest of a Bridget Gallagher, who is described as an 'old woman … arrested at Queenstown on Saturday after landing from the *Umbria*' for smuggling into the country fifty rounds of ammunition. She 'appeared before the magistrates on Wednesday, and was ordered to pay a fine of £2 10s and costs, or in default to go to prison for a month.' The following month, in the *Aberdeen Evening Express* (18 January 1889) there is a heading 'Revolver Smuggling By A Woman'. This is about Kate Corcoran, who had landed at Queenstown from Baltimore, and was arrested for having in her possession a 'five-chambered revolver and thirty-seven rounds of ammunition'. There is a follow-up to this in *The Star*, a Guernsey publication, on 19 January 1889, revealing that Kate was a married American woman, travelling with her husband, and that she was fined 10s plus costs, having 'secreted' the revolver and ammunition 'in her luggage'. It would have been fascinating to know what the intentions of these two women were given that gun-smuggling into Ireland did not begin in earnest until the Easter Rising of 1916. Perhaps this is an early indication of how women were to become involved in even more intense levels of smuggling in Ireland as the twentieth century came around.

Chapter Seven

Kent and Sussex

WHILE MUCH OF the contraband smuggled into Kent made its way to London, there was also a need for local supply – until at least 1820 when preventive services began to make their presence felt. Before the end of the war with France (1815), revenue officers concentrated on seizing smuggled goods, but after that they seemed more interested in seizing the smugglers. The Stade in Folkestone has been described as being purposed to 'meet the exigencies of the smuggling trade, and for the more readily disposing of the kegs of spirits, and bales of other excisable goods'.[1] France was only thirty miles away, less than three hours in a 'fast vessel under full sail'.[2] While Kent smugglers were generally considered more violent than their West Country peers, they were actually less at risk because of their shorter haul to the continent.

Another author, Geoffrey Morley, refers to a 'stream of songs issued from the pens of minor composers in the first part of the nineteenth century' which featured male, and female, smugglers.[3] One example was 'The Smuggler's Bride', referring to a 'damsel fair that in Kent did dwell' – she dies, with her fugitive lover, after a 'firefight' with the coastguard.

There was a popular practice in vogue between Calais and Dover, in particular, around 1819 and 1820. This was rather an evasion of customs duties than actual smuggling. It was fashionable for ladies to wear Leghorn hats and bonnets of enormous dimensions. They were made of strong plaited straw, nearly circular, and commonly about a yard in diameter; often decorated with feathers, and sold in England at two to three guineas each, and sometimes even more. A heavy duty was laid upon them, amounting to nearly half their value. It was a concession made by the custom houses of various countries that wearing apparel in use was not liable to duty, so leaving a loophole for these to be smuggled in. Dealers would hire, cheaply, numerous women and girls who were in need of extra cash to travel daily to and from Dover and Calais, and would even enter into a contract with the owners of the steamers for cut-price tickets for a whole band of them. The sight of these women leaving the town in the morning with the most deplorable headgear and returning in the evening gloriously arrayed was for some few years a familiar and amusing one to the people of Dover.[4]

It is an indication of why women were involved in so-called fashion smuggling when looking at the kind of goods recovered by the local revenue officers in and around Deal, which seemed to have become a notorious smuggling centre. In 1814, 420 bandana silk-patterned handkerchiefs were recovered from the rear of the Hoop and Griffin, then a popular inn overlooking the sea; and in 1825 the customs recovered 1,249 yards of silk, 2,845 yards of ribbon and 461 handkerchiefs, all 'fashionable items in Regency days' according to Holyoake's book. Apart from luxury fabric, playing cards were also popular with local smugglers, the duty on them not abolished until 1960, although, of course, spirits, watches and tobacco were the main source of income for the smuggling fraternity.

Fashion smuggling into Dover featured in the *Belfast Commercial Chronicle* of 27 January 1823. It quotes an order 'received at the Custom House, Dover, to submit certain females, known [for some now unknown reason] by the nick-name of Duffers, on their arrival from France, to a rigorous search for contraband property'. When it was discovered that these females were indeed on board the arriving packet, 'the officers in consequence were on the alert'. As soon as the packet was moored, 'a general rush was made by these women to gain the quay' with more than 200 people assembled to witness the proceedings. 'They were opposed in their design by the officers, who were violently obstructed, and even assaulted. One female was so terrified, that she went off into strong hysterics, and was ultimately dragged on shore with her apparel much torn, and shrieking dreadfully.' However, the officers were said to behave 'with great moderation' and succeeded in detaining several women. 'Upon a general search of them, upwards of 80lb of lace, and several pieces of bandana handkerchiefs were taken from their persons.' Interestingly, 'among other novelties, one of these females turned out to be a man!'

An anonymous cynic in the *Ampthill and District News* of 1 April 1893 wrote that: 'Women always smuggle something across ... they can't help it. It is not in order to save the few shillings they would have to pay, but merely because they like to do something which they ought not to do. It is their nature.' This was evidenced, in their opinion, by one awful dark, wet, cold morning at Queenborough, its harbour conveniently situated where the rivers Swale, Medway, and Thames meet, with the discovery of undeclared Apostle spoons and eau de cologne. The writer also mentions a female friend importing an ancient silver christening basin while avoiding the custom house officer, but whose husband more honestly declared its presence, which meant a search which revealed 'many other contraband'.

In Elizabeth Grant's 1898 autobiography, she writes of a holiday visit to Ramsgate in 1811, when her mother began smuggling 'vigorously', much to her father's dismay. The well-travelled Elizabeth was on the side of her 'dear mother' because she was being criticised by a man who 'lavishes thousands on his whistle' but lifts 'his eyebrows at the cost of his wife's'. It seems her mother could not resist the 'melodramatic sailors with their straw hats smartly bound with ribbon' and their 'long, curled love-locks' with their irresistible 'silks, laces, gloves and other beautiful French goods so immeasurably superior to any in those days fabricated at home'. She was one of many who escaped the law, undeterred by the prospect of being stopped, searched, insulted, and fined which frequently happened to others of their acquaintance when their 'transactions were too daring'. Obviously buying smuggled goods was not just a cost-saving but added an element of excitement to the transaction.

However, there were women who were involved in smuggling more traditional goods (spirits and tobacco) as part of one of the Kent smuggling gangs in the nineteenth century. For instance, the Ransley gang were one of the smuggling gangs roaming the Romney Marshes and Kent villages at that time and many sources mention that the family of George Ransley, both men and women, led a great body of smugglers in the area. It has been said that the last UK skirmish when shots were fired was on Romney Marsh in 1821.

There are a number of other newspaper articles regarding smuggling by European women into Kent. For example, in the *Lincolnshire Chronicle* of 17 September 1858, which detailed a story of 'a French lady convicted of smuggling four bottles of brandy and eight flasks of Eau de Cologne, which she had concealed about her person' during a pleasure trip from Calais to Ramsgate. She was fined £3 14s 6d, although she had the option of gaol for fourteen days. Similarly, additional detail in the *Norfolk Chronicle* of Saturday, 11 September 1858 recounts this story, adding that she had arrived on the mail steam packet *Vivid*, along with 200 passengers. She (unnamed) was subsequently charged before the local magistrates and the case was proved by the custom house officers, with the assistance of a lady interpreter.

Interestingly, according to Anthony Lee, nearby Margate was 'well known as a smuggling town' which actually became an 'attraction for visitors'.[5] However, the north of Kent, particularly the Isle of Sheppey, also features. For instance, in the *Sheerness Guardian and East Kent Advertiser* of 18 June 1881, an article by 'a contemporary' has a descriptively worded account as follows:

> The energetic gentlemen who collect her Majesty's customs made a capital haul at Queenborough – Isle of Sheppey – last week. Amongst the passengers who arrived by the Royal Zeeland Steamship Company's vessel was a very stout lady, who wobbled along apparently under the pressure of about twenty stones of superfluous flesh.

> Possibly thinking that the party's body was rather too fat for the party's face, the officers politely detained her for a short time, and introduced her to the female searcher. The searcher at the first dive brought out about a pound of cigars from the lady's sleeve. This looked suspicious, as the woman could hardly claim that they were for her own smoking. In the course of time, by judiciously taking off one garment after another, the searcher managed to land 20lb of fragrant weeds. The lady had nothing on now but what our female friends roughly class as 'underclothing'. Still the lady had wondrous calves, exceeding those of the most pompous footman ever reared, and the female searcher was still inquisitive. She tapped the calves with her hand, she rolled down the – but it is not needful for us to go into further details. It is sufficient to say that these beautiful calves were simply Havannas, Cubas, and Manillas. Further investigation brought forth more weeds, and in the end, when the nymph was allowed to dress herself again, she was thirty pounds lighter. For three months she will not have the chance to smuggle again.

On 6 April 1872 the same newspaper wrote of the new service offered by Thames steamboats between Stroud in the west and Sheerness in the east, 'taking up and setting down in the impressive SS *Great Eastern* steamship', presumably en route to Europe. This route apparently resulted in 'a line of women which extended round the corner whenever a ship was about to be paid off. Each woman carried a bladder, and her business was to buy rum [from the local Fountain inn], and to smuggle it on board the man-of-war.'

The *Derby Daily Telegraph* of 21 September 1882 refers to two women being charged at Dover with smuggling 73lb of foreign tobacco, resulting in their conviction, with fines of £32 and £27. This same incident is featured in several other newspapers, with additional information, e.g. the *Hartlepool Northern Daily Mail* describes the women as 'respectably dressed Englishwomen', and *St James's Gazette* named them as Clara Dennis, aged 70, and Emma Thomas, aged 31, who 'begged for mercy' on being arrested on leaving the steamer from Ostend. *The Northern Evening Mail* explained that they were detected when they asked a policeman for directions on arrival and he could smell tobacco, which turned out to be in stockings wrapped round their bodies. Cigars were a popular product for women to smuggle as they could be discreetly hidden in muffs as well as in crinolines.

Author Graham Smith writes of customs officers at Dover in the mid-nineteenth century complaining about 'lady passengers dressing themselves in valuable dresses and jewels, more calculated for their entry into a drawing room, than merely to come ashore. They are all items newly acquired abroad.' Petty smuggling continued to rise during the century as foreign travel expanded for more than the nobility. It certainly seems that a superior class of women were waiting on Dover 'deliveries' judging by the records of 160 blockade seizures made at Dover in the three months to 30 June 1823. On one boat alone (the *Victory*) on 12 June were concealed 'gold rings, bead purses, strings of beads, a lace dress, five cotton dresses, swathes of material, twenty pairs of silk shoes, sixty-three pairs of leather gloves, twelve yards of crepe, eighty-seven yards of silk and 110 yards of silk gauze'. A similar stash was found in a house close to the water's edge at Dungeness in 1824, which was targeted when smugglers were seen running away from a bale of cloth left behind on the beach. The house was searched, and found to be storing '18,000 cambric and 173 silk handkerchiefs, 693 yards of tiffany, seventy-two yards of silk velvet, nine pieces of tulle, one silk dress, thirty-six silk scarves, twenty-two yards of crepe' and – harking back to earlier shortages – 220lb of green tea. Quite a sophisticated haul, aimed at a mainly female and sophisticated market who asked no questions.[6]

However, the women of Deal (according to Gregory Holyoake) could be much more violent and much more directly involved, as in 1816 when he mentions a mob of 300, mainly women and children, throwing stones at soldiers and customs men. The officials were part of the escort attempting to remove a smuggler called Foreman, but the mob rescued him, having 'closed in so tightly around the soldiers that firearms could not be employed'.

Another author (Charles G. Harper) wrote of a similar incident at Dover in 1820. He refers to a Lieutenant Lilburn, 'in command of a revenue cutter' who had captured a smuggler, and had placed the crew in Dover gaol.

> As they had not offered armed resistance to the capture, their offence was not capital, but they were liable to service on board a man-o'-war, a fate they were most anxious to avoid. These imprisoned men were largely natives of Folkestone and Sandgate, and their relatives determined to march over the ten miles between those places and Dover, and, if possible, liberate them.

When they arrived in Dover, a 'crowd of fisher-folk and longshore people swarmed out of the Dover alley-ways and reinforced them. Prominent among them were the women, who, as ever in cases of popular tumult, proved themselves the most violent and destructive among the mob.' Nothing less than the destruction of the gaol was decided upon, and

> the more active spirits, leaving others to batter in the walls, doors, and windows, climbed upon the roof, and from that vantage-point showered bricks and tiles upon the Mayor and the soldiers who had been called out. The Mayor, beset with tooth and claw by screeching women, who tore the Riot Act out of his hand, fled, and Lieutenant Lilburn exhorted the officer in charge of the military to fire upon the crowd, but he declined; and meanwhile the tradespeople and respectable inhabitants busied themselves in barricading their shops and houses.

The *New Times* of Tuesday 3 August 1820 covers the same story, referring to the violence of the women involved.

> Three of the party of smugglers taken on the coast near Birchington Minnis [a bay near Westgate-on-Sea] … by the men belonging to the Coast Blockade Service, and committed to Dover gaol, were yesterday morning removed from thence under a strong military escort, assisted by the Magistrates and a party of Constables … and put on board [HMS *Lively* captained by William Lilburn] to be conveyed to the guard-ship in the Downs. The time of their removal being known, a great number of women and boys assembled on the beach, and assaulted the guard by booting and pelting them with stones; the Magistrates, with the Constables, immediately rushed in amongst them, and succeeded in securing the most refractory, and committed them to prison, with a man who attempted to rescue them.

However, according to the Naval Database this skirmish happened in April 1807, which ties in with a report in the *York Herald* in 1812 of Captain Lilburn's death. So some confusion over the date, but not, it seems, the event, because in the 1888 publication *English's Reminiscences of Old Folkestone Smugglers and Smuggling Days* a riot of 1823 has the women involved charging 'like furies' and 'regardless of the consequences'. This particular account mentions that the liberated smugglers had their manacles 'removed at the blacksmith's near *The Red Cow* in Dover before making their way to Folkestone'. Another account is featured in the *Suffolk Chronicle* of 3 June 1820 referring to four or five hundred men, women, and boys armed with all sorts of weapons i.e. 'staves, bludgeons, pickaxes, scythes' who set out from Folkestone for Dover intent on attacking the gaol and freeing the prisoners, chiefly smugglers, eleven of whom had been imprisoned that week. The mob dispersed when military force was 'procured from the garrison'. So, a variety of accounts of the same riot, or more than one very similar riot? Perhaps this was a regular event at the time!

Whatever the explanation of the above, a folk song called 'The Breaking of Dover Gaol' celebrates the violent release of imprisoned smugglers, with the final verse being:

> And now they've gained their liberty
> The long wide world to range.
> Long life to the Dover women,
> Likewise to the Folkestone men.

An additional snippet from Harper referencing local women tells of one of the escapees (named elsewhere as 'Will West') returning to his home at The Black Bull (probably the one in Canterbury Road). A posse arrived outside at night, but Will's father threatened to shoot the first man who entered the house while the females were improperly dressed. While they waited, Will hid under a mound of bedding, with an 'old woman' (no doubt his mother) sitting on top, shivering, thereby avoiding a search.

English writes about the women who kept the revenue officers away from smugglers who were using six-oared boats (called cocktails) a few years earlier, bringing in tubs of spirits which had been sunk in the Channel. The smugglers had instructed the women to light a big fire 'on the Durlocks' (where St Peter's Church stands atop East Cliff) if they saw the officers approaching, and they had prepared plenty of straw and flammables. As soon as the officers were spotted, the fire was kindled, and the officers knew straightaway its purpose. Rushing to put out the fire, the 'result was a free fight, in which the women as usual got the best of it' and the smugglers abandoned their mission, temporarily. It is clear that women took a very active part in smuggling in the area, as lookouts, hiding the cargo, or disposing of contraband. Some were particularly young and saucy, like the two young women dressed as laundresses who walked into the pub in

Radnor Street favoured by revenue officers, carrying a laundry basket of clothes for the landlady – of course, under the newly washed linen were a couple of kegs of spirits.[7]

One woman who was apparently notorious in Folkestone for smuggling at the time is named (by English) as 'Fox', whose main role seems to have been finding suitable storage for contraband. It seems that when she was younger she earned her fitness to be a smuggler's bride by having 'a single-handed contest with an officer of the revenue'. When on her way to The Folkestone Arms in The High Street, with a keg concealed beneath her big cloak, she was confronted by the officer demanding to see what she was hiding, starting a tussle between the two. Her brother approached and she passed him the keg which he ran off with but she detained the exciseman to avoid her brother being pursued, giving the man a 'sound thrashing'.

Women of all classes would have been involved in smuggling in some way. For instance, in *Deal, Sad Smuggling Town*, the (unnamed) wife of the chief official at the Port Admiral's 'grand mansion' – in Queen Street until *c.*1850 – would have been aware of its importance as a place to store not only the fleet's pay but also the gold bullion smuggled into Deal. Although Royal Marines were employed to guard the stores, there was a secret room near the safe deposit, but she took the risk of keeping a wounded smuggler there and nursing him back to health until 'he was able to make his escape'. Lucky for her that her husband did not find out. The book title, by the way, is a quote from Fanny Burney's diary who had referred to Deal as a 'sad, smuggling town', her opinion shared by eighteenth-century author Elizabeth Carter who lived in the town and who was against 'the nobility' travelling from London to buy contraband. Deal was particularly suitable for the trade, with streets running parallel to the nearby beach, connected by alleyways, with wooden boatmen's sheds along the shingle to facilitate unloading.

Of course there were also women who became informants, for various reasons which we will never know. One such was a Mrs Everitt of Canterbury, featuring in Chris McCooey's *Smuggling*, who had been a smuggler's accomplice but, when the North Kent gang were involved in their lengthy trial of 1822, gave information against them in order to claim a financial reward then on offer to informants – she was paid £17 15s. But this was effectively danger money because for ever after she would have been looking over her shoulder following the death sentence dished out to four of the gang with fourteen transported to Tasmania. Women connected with the Aldington Gang were particularly low profile, given the gang's reputation for violence, and were more likely to be supportive than otherwise – like the unnamed woman who called out a warning to George Ransley (the leader) when she became aware of a force of 120 men, with the Bow Street Runners leading, marching on Aldington in October 1826. As they surrounded the houses of Ransley and his gang, she called out 'Warhawk' from an upstairs window; nevertheless, Ransley and six others surrendered when they saw the size of the force and were arrested.[8]

All parts of Kent saw a diminution of free trading once the Coast Blockade was established in 1816, closely followed by the coastguard for areas not protected by the blockade. However, smugglers of both sexes in Deal and elsewhere in Kent kept going for much longer than elsewhere, with coastguards seizing tobacco, brandy and gin well into the 1880s.[9] There is still a popular Smugglers' Trail from Broadstairs to Cliftonville confirming how the chalk in the area lent itself to caves and tunnels.

Sussex

When Rudyard Kipling wrote 'A Smuggler's Song' in 1906, he was thinking of Sussex. Living at Burwash, from 1902, he was right on the edge of smuggling country. Rye was not far away, known as a meeting point for the cut-throat Hawkhurst Gang some 150 years previously. The rest of Sussex was familiar to him as he had lived in nearby Rottingdean in the 1890s. Some of the words refer specifically to women:

Five and twenty ponies,
Trotting through the dark -
Brandy for the Parson,
'Baccy for the clerk;
Laces for a lady, letters for a spy,
And watch the wall my darling, while the gentlemen go by…
If your mother mends a coat, cut about and tore;
If the lining's wet and warm – don't you ask no more!
If you meet King George's men, dressed in blue and red,
You be careful what you say, and mindful what is said.
If they call you 'pretty maid' and chuck you 'neath the chin,
Don't you tell where no-one is, nor yet where no-one's
been! …

The county of Sussex had favoured landing places for smugglers including Pevensey Bay, Cooden Beach, Sea Lane in Bexhill (now Sea Road), and St Leonard's. Goods were usually landed at night between moons, and carried away on the backs of ponies and men. Temporary hiding places have been found, amongst other places, at Barnhorn Manor (behind a chimney breast), at Whydown Farm (behind a false wall) and at Sandhurst Farm. Cuckmere Haven, near Alfriston, played a pivotal role in the battles against the smuggling trade of the early nineteenth century – while opportunistic local gangs operated on a small scale, at Cuckmere Haven the flat, wide, shingle beach attracted the big organised gangs.

In February 1822, smugglers marched on Martello Tower 52 (at Little Common in Bexhill) to seize the Blockade Sentinel, one of whom was shot dead. One version of the story says there was a lady waiting in a coach with six horses, but she drove off when the boat set sail – perhaps a spy waiting to hand over (or receive) information? However, this story of the lady is also mentioned in another confrontation the same month when 300 smugglers from the local Little Common Gang gathered near the Star Inn 'to unload their boat the *Queen Charlotte*', battling the preventive customs men, who drove them off, with 'one smuggler shot'. So was this the same mystery lady at both confrontations, or neither?[10]

Bexhill Museum's website also mentions an account book from 1825 to 1827 written by George Gillham, the leader of the Little Common Gang, and part of a large smuggling family. There is a separate story of 'old Mrs Gillham sitting on a barrel of brandy', her skirt spread over it, knitting, while the revenue men searched her Little Common cottage, finding nothing.[11]

The Archives at the Keep in Brighton have a copy of Roy Philp's *The Coast Blockade 1817–1831* which refers to Mrs Anro, landlady of the Royal George on Shoreham, who vouched for the character of a smuggler ('Wilkinson') under suspicion. The prosecutor, Captain Mingaye, spoke of the inn as being 'nothing more than a pot house in a nest of smugglers'. The full report is in the Admiralty papers in The National Archives. A twenty-first-century musical called *Beware the Mackerel Sky* actually features Mrs Anro in the cast. The Keep also has details of a Mrs Leppard of Stanmer, near the Ditchling Road, whose home was raided before her husband had had time to get rid of his overnight cargo. She saw the excisemen approaching and sat upon the illicit tubs near to the glowing fire, concentrating (seemingly) on cooking the dinner. When the officers entered, announcing their intention to search for contraband, her response was 'go where you like' but their search proved fruitless, resulting in Mrs Leppard becoming something of a heroine among the smuggling fraternity (this story taken from a 1929 article).[12] Ironically, it seems that one of her sons was at some point a member of the local coastguard.

Smugglers were involved in a number of pretty ferocious battles in and around Hastings and Brighton in the nineteenth century, but it seems that it was often their women folk that suffered as a result. *The Carmarthen Journal* of 18 April 1838 refers to one young woman affected by 'madness' resulting in her death after her husband was dragged out of the marital home, and another becoming 'delirious' and narrowly escaping 'the jaws of death' following her husband's arrest. However, one smuggler who got his comeuppance, so to speak, in 1799 when he was deported (though not for smuggling, but for horse thieving) was a Jevington innkeeper known as Jevington Jigg (real name John or James Pettitt) whose female family members were associated with his smuggling activities, but escaped any form of prosecution. It was also not unusual (and this does not just apply to Sussex!) for smugglers to abscond, leaving behind their wives and children to fend for themselves, for example one called Foster in the Playden parish records for 1844 who was in Rye gaol for smuggling, having ditched his family in Newhaven. Similarly, Frances Peters of All Saints, Hastings, was abandoned by her husband, John, a convicted smuggler, in 1832.[13]

A more light-hearted nineteenth-century incident occurred when a smuggler was hiding in a cottage (now Grade I listed) near Market Cross, Alfriston, home of the notorious Alfriston gang, with the revenue men hot on his heels. There lived a woman who was expecting a baby. Friends hauled a pig from their sty and hid it with the man under the woman's bed. The officers searched the cottage and were about to enter the bedroom when the smuggler gave the pig a squeeze – it let out a squeal like a newborn babe and the officers discreetly departed.

The Beachy Head area was apparently notorious for smuggling in the nineteenth century, and the families of Osborn (Caroline and her husband John in particular) and Hills (Caroline's parents) are commonly mentioned. Caroline Souter Osborn apparently had links with Hastings and Eastbourne, all linked to smuggling activities. She was the only child of the village blacksmith, and lived as a child at the Forge in East Dean with its vaulted cellars, closely associated with local smugglers. (One of Caroline's children, Ellen, died in what some believe to be an 'overnight smuggling operation' in 1855, possibly at Beachy Head.) Incidentally, when the Forge Cottage was renovated in the 1960s the vaulted cellar was 'well preserved', and the window that once contained the discreet 'smugglers' signal lamp' was visible.[14]

Chapter Eight

Lancashire, Merseyside, and Cheshire

THE WIRRAL COASTLINE and Mersey Estuary were, in the nineteenth century, a treacherous region for vessels seeking a safe haven on stormy nights. Wreckers were known to control the rocks carrying lanterns which ships could mistake for a lighthouse and safety and head for the beam, only to be dashed to pieces on the rocks with loss of cargo and lives, then having to face the wreckers who were in waiting.

In 1863, James Stonehouse, author of several books about Liverpool and its environs, wrote of the Wirral area as being inhabited almost totally by 'wreckers and smugglers'. While not that many women may have been directly involved in either of these activities, they certainly assisted their menfolk in many ways. However, one woman, Margaret Boode of the sixteenth-century Leasowe Castle, the daughter of the rector of Liverpool, went against the grain and merits inclusion in this chapter for different reasons. She offered aid to wrecked mariners while her neighbours left shipwrecked crew and passengers to die after taking as much as they could lay hands on. The castle was close to Mockbeggar Wharf, notorious for the frequent amount of wrecking that occurred there in the eighteenth and nineteenth centuries. During her occupancy of the castle, it was often turned into a receiving house and hospital for the survivors of shipwrecks, which were then frequent along the local coast. Half-drowned mariners, who received scant consideration from the wreckers of the area who would rob them and then kick them back into the sea, found a good friend in Margaret Boode.

According to the History of Wallasey website, she was known as the 'kind old lady of Leasowe Castle' and was the 'local lady bountiful, the town's do-gooder-in-chief … the friend of the ship-wrecked, the fine lady with a heart to match'.[1] The widow of a West Indian planter, she had moved to Leasowe in 1802, and apparently made considerable additions and alterations to the old place including the gardens, described in 1816 as being 'disposed in terraces and alcoves, surrounded with a large fosse and mound…' Just how much she did for those who staggered ashore near her home is indicated in this description of the wreck of the schooner *Mary Betsy*, which sailed from Wexford on 24 October 1820. Two days later, 'they picked up a Liverpool pilot, and by 4 p.m. a dreadful gale had sprung up. Two hours later the vessel struck on a bank … and drifted ashore.' Although the crew tried to launch the boat they failed, 'so took to the rigging' where they were stuck for well over five hours, drenched by every wave. Cullen, one of the crew, said: 'I don't know how I held on as I was quite unconscious. Hearing a noise below, I looked down and saw a large crowd of 100 or more people with horses and carts. [Note: "people" not "men", suggesting "men and women".] It was just at break of day at a place called Mockbeggar.' He then described how two carpenters working at Leasowe Castle for Mrs Boode 'took him in a cart to the lodge, where restoratives were applied and he received every kindness'. The wreckers 'completely stripped the vessel, leaving nothing but the standing rigging and the masts'. There seems to have been little or no doubt that 'many committed murder to gain a few gold pieces of small items of jewellery'.[2]

There was one incident in November 1821 which resulted in her good deed assisting the local wreckers, probably unknowingly. While she (and only she) provided the crew of a cattle ship who had been driven ashore in bad weather with food, drink, and warmth, the wreckers had more time than usual to steal all the cattle and distribute the meat between local dwellings. Just a few years later, in 1826, these wrecked mariners lost their saviour, when Margaret Boode was killed in a carriage accident.

Just a few miles away, on the island of Hilbre (on the Wirral peninsula) was The Seagull Inn, whose patrons were 'the crews of some small vessels which find a harbour under one side of the island'. The islands had a dubious reputation for wrecking and smuggling and the innkeeper in the early nineteenth century was said to be unaccountably wealthy. Traveller Richard Ayton recorded in 1813 the local gossip about the Hilbre innkeeper and his wife that 'their riches have been gained principally by wrecking, for which business their situation is said to be admirably calculated'.[3] Similarly, Wood writes in *Smugglers' Britain* of the wife being an 'active partner' in the miscellaneous business of her husband, having 'hardihood enough to despise the privilege of her petticoats' with the 'miscellaneous business' including smuggling 'for which the island was well suited, as was Middle Hilbre with its tall, secluded, narrow cave known as the Devil's Hole, ideal for concealing smugglers and their contraband'. (Middle Hilbre is now known as Middle Eye, with the third island known as Little Eye.)

Far more widely known, this time as a friend of the smugglers rather than the wrecked mariners, was Mother Redcap, the source of many legends. It seems that her real name was Poll Jones. According to *Wirral Smugglers*, she ran a tavern friendly to 'smugglers and privateers' which became known as Mother Redcap's due to her red headwear. Over the years, this tavern, on the banks of the River Mersey from late in the eighteenth century, has been known by many names, including The Red House, Halfway House, Mother Redcap's, and Seabank Cottage. 'It was rebuilt during its lifetime as a hiding place for smuggled goods and a potential death-trap for customs officers.' It started life as a family home in the sixteenth century built with thick stone walls, and became a tavern 200 years later 'with a thick oak front door, which, if forced, meant that the bolt of the adjoining trapdoor would be activated, depositing the intruder into the cellar nine feet below'. The house was renovated and enlarged over the years, most noticeably in 1888 after Redcap's death when the new owner Joseph Kitchingham, a local lawyer, discovered the hidden side to the old building. Sadly, Kitchingham had 'many of the tunnels and secret rooms filled in and bricked up during the renovations'.

It became a café in the twentieth century and was demolished in the 1970s. At some point the internal walls were covered by thick planks of wood from wrecked ships, although these fell off early in the nineteenth century. Similar wood was used to make a seat outside, with an image of Mother Redcap holding a frying pan over the fire and the following words:

All ye that are weary come in and take rest
Our eggs and our ham they are of the best
Our ale and our porter are likewise the same
Step in if you please and give 'em a name. Mother Redcap.

A fake weathervane was used to signal it was safe for pirates and privateers to enter, turned a different way to indicate danger from the authorities.[4] At the side of the dwelling was a cave leading to a lookout post and a choice of escape routes on the Wirral peninsula. Author Gavin Chappell describes Poll as 'a handsome woman' in her youth, believed to be a widow with a beautiful niece attracting young mariners and who, unexpectedly, married a revenue man. The website smuggling.co.uk describes Poll as 'a comely, fresh-coloured Cheshire-spoken woman … a great favourite with the sailor men'. It certainly seems that Mother Redcap was a likeable individual who acted as a banker of sorts for sailors, 'minding their earnings while they were at sea', presumably charging a handsome fee for the service. There was an anchorage known as Red Bets just opposite the tavern with privateers able to row over to drink and gossip. They were able to hide 'in the cottage' if the pressgangs were seen approaching and until their ships were ready to sail. Contraband was hidden in the walls and ceilings of the lower rooms and there was even a secret room which could hide a man, with smaller cavities for concealing the crews' cash. Goods could be moved over Liscard Moor behind the cottage when the coast was clear, and usually at night, sometimes using a donkey cart.

It seems that the tavern was also used by local customs men who may have turned a blind eye in return for generous rations. Because the inn was popular with smugglers and with lonely revenue men, they were entertained with the same hospitality as any other customer to avoid suspicion. However, the general prosperity of locals during Mother Redcap's time must have made them suspicious to say the least. In fact, smuggling was a major business for this small neighbourhood and could sometimes involve 'the whole community'. Chappell gives a number of entertaining stories about Mother Redcap's run-ins with customs men, but without dates, so they are not included as they could be eighteenth rather than nineteenth century. Bob Burrows, in *Infamous Cheshire*, however, mentions a 'highly profitable cash deal' she made before her death, leaving her without the opportunity to 'dispose of the cash' – so the location of this profit has been a source of speculation ever since. Burrows also mentions a 'cargo of rich silk' which had been salvaged or smuggled, with local women seen subsequently walking around in dresses of 'high quality'. However, and remarkably, Mother Redcap was never arrested.

The proximity of revenue officers with smugglers in the inn could obviously cause difficulties. There is a record of a single officer there 'on one occasion when the smugglers were desirous of getting a cask of rum or some other merchandise away from one of the hiding places' but were prevented by his unwelcome presence. So it was arranged that one of the smugglers was to creep down to the shore, and lie down in the water, at the edge of the receding tide. The attention of the solitary officer at Mother Redcap's was called to the supposed body which had been washed ashore, and he quickly made his way to it. He had removed the watch, and was searching the pockets when the corpse came to life, sprang up, and laid out the surprised officer. By the time he had come to, the rum had been removed from Redcap's, and started its journey to the Moss (now known as Bidston Moss). No blame could be attached to the 'drowned man' who said he was walking along the shore, when he must have had a fit, for the next thing that he became aware of was that he was lying in the sand with his pockets being rifled.[5]

The *Liverpool Mercury* of 23 June 1854 describes Mother Redcap as 'an old woman … wearing a sort of red coif, or cap' living in a house which 'stood by itself, no other being near it for some distance' where she 'drove a thriving trade. Her house was the resort of smugglers, fishermen and others of the like employment; but the house was especially noted as a place of refuge for runaway sailors, and those who were in hiding to avoid the pressgang, which in the time of the first American war was very actively employed in this neighbourhood.' The article goes on to describe Mother Redcap as 'the sailors' friend' who 'like an old hen with a brood of chickens, spread the wings of her protection over them and defied the hawk to the death.' It refers to her being trusted with large sums following profitable 'voyages' and it was well known that she had 'accumulated a considerable amount of wealth'.

Stonehouse records the tradition that 'the caves at the Red Noses [cliffs at New Brighton] communicated in some way and somewhere with Mother Redcap's'. He and others also suggest that there were two tunnels leading from Birkenhead Priory, one leading from beneath the current church under the Mersey to Liverpool and another to Mother Redcap's. Even now, locals search for the treasure of Old Mother Redcap, believing the tunnels beneath what is now a nursing home in Egremont Parade to hold a pirate's hoard. There is a statue to her in Liscard Village and local companies have arranged treasure-seeking tours in the area in recent years. Apparently there was also a performance of a play in 2004 called *Mother Redcap's Tales of Tempest and Treasure* but this has proved elusive. She has her own Wirral 'song':

Old Mother Redcap
Wicked old witch.
Ill-gotten gains
Once made her rich.
Host of a tavern on the Mersey Sands.
Blood of the mariners
Red on her hands.

The date of her death is unknown, other than its being before 1888. That was the year that a Mr Kitchingman, who was born in Wallasey in what became the Horse & Saddle Inn, retired from legal work in Warrington and bought Mother Redcap's, insisting that the land in front would not be allowed access to carriages. When an extension to the Navy League premises was built carriages did indeed use the promenade and this so enraged Mr Kitchingman that he left the house for use as a Convalescent Home for the people of Warrington. Being unsuited for this purpose, powers were obtained to set aside the wishes in his will, and the next purchaser opened it as a café called Mother Redcap's. But the fact that since its demolition in 1974, it has been rebuilt as Mother Redcap's Nursing Home – at time of writing – is pretty ironic. The remains of the original stone arched gateway remain.[6]

One of the ports of call of the smugglers transferring contraband across Bidston Moss was the Ring 'o Bells, now Stone Farm, in Bidston. This was owned by a local family, some say the Radleys, others the Pendletons. In the mid-nineteenth century, Mary Radley (or Pendleton) married a Simon Croft and the Ring 'o Bells became as notorious as Mother Redcap's, with Mary not quite as involved as Poll perhaps.[7] Bidston Moss was also the location for Hannah Mutche's Farm, surrounded by a moat. This old farm was the haunt of smugglers and a noted hiding place from the press gang, the sailors escaping there from Mother Redcap's. It is thought by some that the old Moss holds Redcap's lost or forgotten money and valuables. Chappell has written about Hannah Mutch(e) being prosecuted in March 1839 for being in possession of contraband, her husband William already having been arrested when bolts of printed cotton, merino, and other materials were found in his home along with bottle stoppers marked 'Madeira', all supposedly the property of a wrecked vessel.

Also in the 1830s is a story in *The Liverpool Underworld* of when *The Grecian* went down (in 1832) off the Cheshire coast. The ship's master was drowned and while his body lay on shore awaiting transport to the inquest, wreckers stripped him naked. 'Not content with his clothes, they hacked off one of his fingers to steal his ring. A woman from Moreton [at the north of the Wirral peninsula] also chewed off the earlobe from a female corpse to take her ear-ring. Each winter, the women prayed for a rich harvest of shipwrecks.' Following this particular wreck, twelve cartloads of booty were found in local marine stores.

Another female features in the *Liverpool Standard and General Commercial Advertiser* of 19 March 1844. This was Mary Evans, who was

> brought before Mr Rushton on a charge of having in her possession four brown bottles of whisky, supposed to be smuggled, and with which she had been stopped by a police officer in the street. An excise officer stated that the bottles contained a little short of a gallon of raw spirit, and that the prisoner was in all probability the distiller of it. The prisoner, on being asked what she had to say, for some time affected to be unable to speak a word of English, though she had spoken readily enough in that language the same morning in *The Bridewell* [the name of a Liverpool pub]. She at length said, 'A man gave it to me.' She was fined 40s, or, in default of payment, ordered to be imprisoned for twenty-one days.

Two years later, the same newspaper (9 June 1846) featured 'An elderly female, apparently in humble life, named Catherine Collier'. She was

> yesterday brought before Mr Rushton, on a charge of smuggling whiskey. An officer of excise stated that on Saturday he observed the prisoner coming from on board the *Waterford* steamer with something bulky under her cloak, and on searching her found three gallons of whiskey

> contained in bladders in a basket. The prisoner said that it had been given to her by a man who had promised her half-a-crown to carry it. It appeared, however, that she had, in the first instance, told the excise officer that it was her own. Mr Rushton said she was liable to a fine of £100, which he should mitigate to £25, and in default of payment she must be imprisoned for three months.

Spirits were also being smuggled into the area (particularly Liverpool) from Ireland, as per this account in the *Drogheda Argus and Leinster Journal* of 14 September 1850. Two excise officers, named as Dodd and Chadwick,

> preferred a charge of smuggling against a respectable looking young woman, who stated her name to be Bridget Loftus. The prisoner had been a passenger on the *Duchess of Kent* from Dublin, that morning. The rotundity of her figure attracted attention, and on examination it was found that seven bladders containing six gallons and a quart of whiskey, were concealed around her person. The prisoner was ordered to pay ten pounds [or face imprisonment].

Less respectable perhaps were the women on the shore of New Brighton and Wallasey when the *Elizabeth Buckham* was wrecked in November 1866, spewing large quantities of coconuts and rum on the sands. *The Albion* of 3 December referred to 'frightful depravities on the shore … consequent on large quantities of rum having been cast up on the coast from the *Elizabeth Buckham*, wrecked on Burbo Bank on Tuesday last. The Wallasey wreckers seem thoroughly to have maintained their olden character', while the *Liverpool Daily Post* of 29 November mentions the involvement of local women:

> All through Tuesday night and yesterday morning men and women, and even children, were found in a state of

> unconscious intoxication among the sand-hills, and were removed as soon as possible to their different homes, where they were attended to by stomach pumps. These are not the only disgraceful features connected with the wreck of the *Buckham.* Several females, one especially who is respectably connected, went down to the remnants of the brig … they were induced to take some rum, which appeared to be the order of the night. They soon became helpless, and while in that state were treated in a most foul and atrocious manner. One of them was found lying on her back in the sand-hills, quite insensible, and in such a state as to show that she had been unfairly treated.

The next day's issue of the *Liverpool Daily Post* mentions two women who were 'found lying in the Sandhills at Hoylake in a state of insensibility, and their condition testified to them having partaken of the fiery spirit'. At this stage, none of the bodies of the crew of the ill-fated vessel had been recovered, and 'all traces of the unfortunate vessel vanished' apart from much of its illicit cargo. Chappell mentions one woman who could not find a cup or container to fill with rum so 'used her shoe' to drink from.

The York Herald of 16 December 1875 has a heading 'Smuggling by a Woman'. This is with regard to 'an important seizure of illicit spirit' made at Oldham.

> A woman named Sarah Ann Hedges was followed into a public-house, and in a basket it was discovered that she had three large bladders containing fifteen quarts of whiskey, which, on being tested, was found to be twenty per cent over proof. She gave no information as to what she intended to do with the liquor, but she significantly remarked that if the police had been two minutes later the whiskey would have been out of her possession. She appeared before the magistrates on Monday, and was fined £25.

The following account headed up 'Men and Women Who Smuggle: Chat With Custom House Officer' does not define locations but as it was in the *Lancashire Evening Post* (of 25 September 1895), then the assumption is that these were 'local' stories. It starts with a quote from the officer, who is not named. 'Smuggling is not carried on as largely as it once was, sir, not on as great a scale, I mean. But there's still a lot of it done.' He was asked if any cargoes were 'run' and replied,

> No, not here, at any rate. Further down the coast, fishermen may do a bit of that sort of thing occasionally, perhaps. But here it's all done on a small scale by the people crossing on the passenger boats. The old romantic days, when cargoes worth £6,000 were run, are all gone by. That was when I was a little shaver in short clothes. Nowadays it's mostly the hundreds of cigars stowed round the false side of a hat box, or the pint of *eau-de-cologne* put in a water cushion which the invalid lady carries off the boat in her hand, or the dozen yards of fine lace which another woman binds round her under her corsets. I've been at work now some ten years, and it would surprise you, sir, to know the dodges people are up to so as to escape paying a few shillings duty.'

The journalist interviewing the officer suggested that, 'Perhaps it's the excitement of smuggling that has something to do with it.' The reply was:

> I believe you've hit it, otherwise I'm thinking people wouldn't run the risks they do just for a few shillings, and all the bother, too. The ingenuity exercised is something extraordinary, I can assure you, and one would imagine that it might be employed to some better account. Of course, with some 100,000 tourists going over in the

> season for holidays, there is a good deal of amateur smuggling done, but it's those who go over and back again pretty frequently who're the worst offenders.

The officer had more stories to tell.

> Then there was that baby who wasn't a baby after all. Three or four years ago, a nice-looking lady, with equally nice-looking nurse, carrying a baby muffled up, as babies mostly are when quite young, came down to go aboard one morning, and did so a good many times afterwards. The nurse was a pretty young girl, and used always to speak pleasantly enough.
>
> He asked her if she had enjoyed her trip across, and she said, 'Rather. The missus doted on the water, and the doctor had said it was good for the baby.' The baby was a nice-looking little thing, what one could see of it, but it was always asleep and covered up. It seemed pretty heavy for its apparent size, I noticed, but for a time I didn't lay much store by that. One day, however … we had obtained some information which led to the nurse being taken into the female searchers' room. The baby proved to be an india-rubber one containing about a gallon of the best brandy. The face was a composition one, and so well done that even if we'd caught a casual glimpse of it, I dare say we mightn't have noticed anything wrong.

He was laughing as he continued.

> Then there was an oldish lady who used to come down and over two or three times a week when the weather was anything like good. She always carried a good-sized bible, closed together with a broad elastic band. Whenever I saw her reading it, which was not often, she

> was doing so quite near the beginning, somewhere about Genesis or Exodus. For a long time I thought that she was attached to some mission, or was a bible-woman or tract distributor, or something of that sort. But at last suspicion was aroused, and when next she came across I stepped up politely to her. She was going away having no luggage, and I said I should be much obliged if she'd allow me to look in her bible. At first she tried to put me off, saying she was in a great hurry, and that she was sure so good a man I looked to be had a bible of his own at home. And if I hadn't she'd bring me one down the next morning. In the end, however, she did give up the bible she was carrying, and we found that except for a few leaves at the beginning and at the end it was solid block, made of papier-mache, hollowed right out in the centre, where we found some £10 or £12 worth of lace. She had made some thirty trips, I should say, before she was caught, so she must have done well by her bible.

He had a final story about female smugglers.

> There were three girls who worked a clever system of lace smuggling some few years ago – or quite a long time before the dodge was found out. They were … respectable girls. They generally made a trip or two a week. For a long time this went on … at last the regularity of their trips, and the fact that though they weren't over-good sailors they always went once week anyway aroused some doubts. One day one of us asked a couple of them to step into the searching room. Nothing incriminating was discovered, except that the female searcher who attended to them said that they had the loveliest lace on their under-things ever she did see. We apologised for having given them the trouble, and they very politely said

> it didn't matter a bit. After a week or two had passed, we sent over someone with them one day, and when they got to the other side they were searched. There wasn't a scrap of lace trimming on either their petticoats or other underwear. They were watched to a certain house, where they remained all day, returning the next morning. When they landed they were searched again. As suspected, they were smothered in yards and yards of the costliest lace, five six rows on each of their petticoats, and the other garments in the same style. Of course the game was up.

The above accounts clearly show the changes that were happening when it came to smuggling, with men and – especially – women involved in smuggling by passengers on comfortable boats rather than in wet and windy open vessels. Somehow, the latter option has been romanticised over the years, but could hardly have been so.

Chapter Nine

Lincolnshire, Norfolk, and Suffolk

ALTHOUGH LINCOLNSHIRE, SUFFOLK and Norfolk have a huge coastline just a short hop over the North Sea to Europe, the involvement of women in their smuggling activities seems to have been pretty much ignored – or perhaps erased. Bearing in mind that these counties were close to the Dutch coast and the Dutch gin and tobacco markets, Richard Platt, in his definitive guide to British smuggling (*Smugglers' Britain*), suggests that 'perhaps the sparseness of the population accounts for this: the tight-knit communities would be reluctant to spill the local secrets to a stranger even a century or more later.' While on the one hand smuggling offered an 'easy' income for poverty-stricken villagers, it also seems that, conversely, smuggling in these counties was usually less than expected, given the widely scattered small communities, so that even fewer women were active than elsewhere – in fact, in Suffolk, it seems that the main hub of smuggling was actually inland in the nineteenth century, having been hit by being one of the first counties to establish a Coast Blockade, in 1817.

Lincolnshire

As regards Lincolnshire, the nineteenth century saw a change of emphasis from smuggling Dutch gin to smuggling tobacco which was manhandled from the coast to Lincoln to turn it into cigars or snuff, the transport thanks often to the villagers (male and female) of Louth and Horncastle.[1] Generally, however, local newspapers help to reveal glimpses of what was really going on.

For example, the *Lincolnshire Standard and Boston Guardian* of 3 October 1931 recounts the following story from the mid-nineteenth century. Their Mablethorpe representative visited a Mrs Haw, a widow aged 69 who lived in 'the old thatched cottage near the church'. The representative states that Mrs Haw had lived the whole of her life in Mablethorpe, being brought up by her grandfather, the late Mr Twidale. 'When I was a girl,' said Mrs Haw, 'the present *Book-in-Hand Hotel* was thatched and whitewashed, and you went down steps to it.' She recalled that 'the other side of the High Street was an open drain. The sea, on one occasion came over the pullover as far as the *Book-in-Hand*, causing much damage.' Asked if she knew any smuggling that went on at that time, she said that 'everyone knew Fanny Richardson', who lived in an old cottage at the foot of the steps now leading to the amusement park. It was believed that Fanny acted as a sort of decoy for smugglers. She entertained the officials at her cottage, while the stuff was being landed elsewhere. 'Plenty of wrecks, too, in those days,' said Mrs Haw, 'and we saved furniture, corn, and all sorts of things.' Note the idea of goods being saved rather than stolen.

Similarly, in the *Louth Standard* of 16 May 1936, there is an account of 'an old lady named Fanny Richardson, who always claimed that she was a smuggler's daughter'. This account says that she lived in an old thatched cottage 'adjoining Mr G. Sadler's house'. It seems that 'during the latter part of the last century the old lady lived alone, and she smoked a short clay pipe which was immediately thrust into the oven if any visitors arrived. Fanny never smoked in public.' It was said that in this cottage, or in the garden, 'many a load of gin and the like has been dumped prior to being removed to Alford, probably under a load of potatoes.'

In Douglas Wynn's entertaining book *Lincolnshire Villains*, he gives an account of two instances of women being involved in local smuggling activities. We have both found the 'stories' difficult to date, but the early nineteenth century seems the most likely. One features Mary West, young daughter of a known smuggler in Mablethorpe. His vessel was chased one night by a revenue cutter, with shots fired, injuring one smuggler, although the vessel escaped. The injured man was taken to the Wests' home and put to bed, but nobody told Mary. She was therefore woken in the night by groans and cries and peeped into the spare room, seeing a strange man in the bed. The doctor arrived next morning receiving a keg of brandy for his trouble, and the smuggler was soon ready to leave. The same account appears in David Robinson's book, referencing the cottage as being in a lonely position 'in the sand-hills at Mablethorpe' and adding that Mary sat on top of a cartload of potatoes just days later when her father led the horse to an inn at Alford, eight miles inland, where the 'cart was promptly backed into the coach-house and the door locked'. Mary was obviously aware of the 'kegs of brandy' under the potatoes, and the secret vault under the coach-house. There is a record of her marrying in 1836 which helps to date this event as being at the beginning of the nineteenth century.

Wynn's second story is regarding 'young Kitty' at Crook Bank, north of Mablethorpe, although this may well have been embellished with time. It seems that Kitty and her mother were disturbed by a call of, 'Come out, you smugglers!' one evening, accompanied by a sword 'pushed through the window'. Kitty bravely stepped outside and recognised the local customs man, 'Mr Gallakin', asking him why he was making so much noise. He explained that he had been following some lads from the Tom and Jerry (then an 'ale shop') because he had overheard them talking about 'getting stuff off the beach'. The lads had come in the direction of Kitty's cottage but she denied any knowledge, suggesting they take a look on the beach. Gallakin seemed to welcome the idea of accompanying Kitty through the dunes to the beach, which gave her brother, father, and the other smugglers time to unload the 'contraband in the sand cave at the back of the cottage'.

This same cottage is described in *The Book of the Lincolnshire Seaside* as being called The Curlew, a 'mile north of Oliver's Gap', being a 'brick cottage in the dunes, ideally situated for smuggling, with a clear view to the sea in one direction, and out over the Marsh in the other'. In the April/May 2018 issue of *Tidings*, Mablethorpe's magazine, Oliver's Gap is described as a 'pullover' between Mablethorpe and Theddlethorpe, one of several gaps through the dunes used by smugglers to drive their carts into the sea 'to where waiting ships would unload gin, silk & tobacco shipped across from Holland. They'd then return home, sometimes burying their stash in the sand hills.'

In this magazine is also a story dating back 150 years (i.e. to *c*.1860). One lady in her later years confessed how when she was a teenage girl she accompanied her father on numerous trips to Alford with a load of potatoes, just like Mary West. Underneath was the gin, the silk, and the tobacco. They would drive along the same roads used today, seeing the same dunes and cottages. Once in Alford they would enter the courtyard of the Windmill Hotel (now listed on the National Heritage List for England) and leave the cart. Late at night, apparently in room 105, 'transactions would take place and the illicit goods would be sold on'. Alford was quite a smuggling hotspot, illegally exporting wool and importing tea and alcohol.

The following account from the *Lincolnshire Chronicle* of 25 March 1870 is rather different, in that the nationality of the female smuggler is not revealed (though presumably German), nor exactly where she was heading or why, other than the reference to a 'Jew' in Grimsby.

> On the arrival of the *Eugenie* from Hamburg, on Friday morning, a passenger named Susannah Heinrich was observed to quit the vessel without giving up her ticket. One of the Dock police followed her and demanded her ticket. She pretended it was in her box on board, but took him to a Jew's house in Garibaldi-street, Grimsby, who paid her fare. Here she dropped a tin which had been concealed under her clothes, and which contained a gallon of spirits. He took her back, and she was examined at the Custom House, and three more bottles

of spirits, a lot of cigars and Cavendish tobacco were found on her person. She was taken before the borough magistrates on Saturday, and was fined £1 17s 5d and 7s 6d costs, which was paid.

Norfolk

Norfolk's miles of coastline, peppered with isolated beaches and secret streams, made this watery landscape a smuggler's dream with coastal areas like Wells-next-the-Sea providing a labyrinth of escape routes for small boat smugglers when the revenue cutter was in the vicinity. It was also a nightmare for the revenue men, with less reports of smuggling activity than most other coastal areas, which could just mean that they were on the take. Because smugglers didn't work alone. Fishermen, farmers, clergy, gentry, magistrates, and excise men were complicit, willing recipients of the gin, brandy-wine and rum they helped move inland.[2] Women and children played their part, lighting warning fires in case of an ambush, for many locals benefited from tax-free goods. In Norfolk, where commons and heathlands were used to move contraband inland, smuggling diminished in the nineteenth century when these areas were enclosed, leaving smugglers with only the open roads and the likelihood of capture.

However, several sources refer to the many women involved in the 100-plus crowd who went to the aid of smugglers landing eighty tubs of gin and brandy on the secluded beach at Snettisham in February 1822. Although local excise men had actually got their hands on the cargo, the waiting crowd, armed with 'bludgeon and fowling pieces', helped firstly to retrieve the goods and then escape in their boat, while the crowd had more than twenty horses and carts waiting to disperse the contraband inland. This features in Mackie's *Norfolk Annals* with specific reference to 'some women' helping smugglers.

Kenneth Hipper writes in *Smugglers All* of a woman recalling a childhood stay on a Norfolk farm a few miles from the coast in the 1820s who heard 'rumbling carts' and whispering men during the night which she was told was 'normal' farming work – until the preventive men arrived to search the farm, having followed tracks from the clifftop. They did not find the hiding place of the contraband, which was in a special store under sawdust in a sawpit. The child may have been innocent but not so the rest of the family on the farm.

Hipper also writes of a February 1837 incident when *Ruby Castle* was wrecked off Salthouse, North Norfolk in a gale. The wreck left the beach strewn with tea, oranges, nuts, toys, and, more significantly, spirits and wine, which meant that local men and women helped themselves, using any kind of container (e.g. their hats and shoes) to contain the liquids. Not just men but women were removed from the beach 'dead drunk' including some coastguard men who had been charged with guarding the wreck.

It was not unusual for whole village communities to be involved in the smuggling trade in Norfolk, as elsewhere. Hipper relates the story told to him by John Gray regarding Beckhithe (just west of Norwich) in the mid-nineteenth century when three generations of families, both sexes, would watch out for boats arriving on the beach even though this was several miles away, and then help to run any arriving cargo. Most houses in the village took in barrels, and it seems that everyone involved made a profit, a very welcome addition to their limited incomes.

Old Norfolk Inns by E. A. Cullyer in 1888 tells a story of an unnamed doctor's housekeeper and Old Martha, the cook at The Feathers in Holt, a few miles from Cromer. The housekeeper had received, on behalf of the doctor, an anonymous hamper full of spirits, cigars, and tobacco which he suspected was a way of one of the local poorer families, known to be smugglers, settling their bill. However, the doctor knew he would be in trouble if what was obviously contraband was found at his home so he asked the landlord of The Feathers to take it in – but that would present the landlord with the same problem. Undecided, he had a chat with The Feathers cook, Martha, described in the book as 'dapper' with a 'neat print dress' and 'high mob cap'. Not unexpectedly, the excise officers duly arrived at the doctor's house the next day apologising for the need for a search, and were shown around by the housekeeper but left empty-handed. They then decided to search The Feathers, although it had been searched just a week earlier. This worried the landlord, who was concerned that the mysterious hamper might have turned up in his pub but nothing was found – they left the kitchen until last, to Martha's annoyance, for they were upsetting her stores and her routine. She asked them if they thought she was a pirate while filling the oven with freshly made pies, becoming more and more angry as they approached her domain, the oven, and threatened them with a red-hot poker forcing them to retreat. The landlord persuaded her not to follow them, apologising to the men for her behaviour, and calming them down with lunch in the bar. When the landlord returned to Martha, she was no longer angry but chuckling, because the contraband was at the back of the oven, which she had not lit – for obvious reasons. She had told the doctor she would look after it and the landlord did not question her as to how she was going to dispose of it – but dispose of it she did, no doubt with the help of her friend, the unnamed housekeeper. The Feathers still features in Holt.

A few miles away exists a similar story involving another cook, Nannie Brett, at the Cherry Tree Inn at Plumstead a couple of years earlier, inns of course being on the custom men's radar as obvious choices to hide smuggled alcohol. Excise officers arrived without warning, and without being spotted in advance because of the Cherry Tree's lonely position, south of Holt and standing back from the road, three miles from the coast. The landlord had no opportunity to hide the spirits on his property, but Nannie persuaded the men to dine before searching and the smell of roast duck seems to have persuaded them. She managed to prolong the meal with ale and wine, while several young men removed every smuggled barrel away from prying eyes. By the time the search was started, all evidence had disappeared, and they had nothing to show for their visit apart from full stomachs.

Later in the nineteenth century, a man named John Buck hid a tub of smuggled gin at his friend Billy's house in East Tuddenham because he and his wife were ill in bed with smallpox and unlikely to be troubled by the excise men. Buck had chosen wisely, so he thought, because when the preventive officers arrived at his home and dug up his garden and the ponds nearby, finding nothing, he went happily to retrieve his gin from Billy and his wife only to find that they had drunk the whole tubful! This was one smuggler's wife who reaped the benefits without her husband having to do any smuggling.

In 1908 the Vicar of Gorleston, writing as Athol Forbes in *The Romance of Smuggling*, mentions an unnamed girl, the fiancée of the then vicar 100 years earlier, who ran four miles to where she knew local smugglers were landing contraband asking them to assist the wounded from a badly damaged naval warship that had limped into 'a Norfolk bay' – which they did. This really just establishes how aware local women were of what was going on, but also that, like most smugglers, they were not all law-breakers!

Nineteenth-century landowner and pioneering photographer, William Bolding, turned a blind eye to the comings and goings of local smugglers in return for a hefty share of the contraband, in common with many of his peers. He was living in Weybourne in North Norfolk, a location where large boats could get very close to the beaches because of its steep drop into the sea; this was at a time when landing parties came up with a way of communicating with each other in the dead of night. They buried themselves up to the neck in pebbles on the beach when customs men were around, but gave a whistled signal when the coast was clear so they could rise up from their shingle hollows like the returning dead and empty their boats. It is said that one smuggler (reputedly John Smythe) was late back to the beach after visiting his lover, the daughter of the local inn's landlord, and his companions left him, believing him caught. He waded into the sea to escape the revenue officers and drowned, still whistling in the hope of rescue, and is apparently still heard on nights in the village when the moon is full! The name of the inn, and the landlord's daughter, are not known. In many ways it must have been a shock to her, but it is a fact that few smugglers deliberately avoided learning to swim, believing that drowning was a better way to die than many bloodier options.

Incidentally, Norwich Quaker and philanthropist Elizabeth Fry was one woman not on the side of the smuggler, male or female. She in fact was responsible for providing comprehensive libraries for 500 coastguard stations and forty-eight cruisers around the UK.

It is interesting to see how nineteenth-century women on the coast could turn even something closely associated with smuggling into a home. The 1718 Hovering Act made it illegal for vessels smaller than fifty tonnes to wait within six miles of the shore, and brandy imported in ships under fifteen tonnes was also liable to seizure. Vessels involved in these offences were impounded and destroyed, usually by being sawn up, and their ropes unravelled. The divided vessels were useless at sea, but often found uses over the next century as illustrated by Clara Peggotty's house, of *David Copperfield* fame, which seems to have been the remains of a smuggling boat in 1840s Great Yarmouth.

Suffolk

Unlike eighteenth-century smugglers who landed contraband openly on the Suffolk beaches, the tightening of the net in the early nineteenth century meant that their activities moved to the estuaries and creeks where activity was less easily observed.

Bessie Catchpole, born in 1852, features regularly in Suffolk tales. She took over her dead husband's boat in the early nineteenth century and used the Suffolk coast to smuggle brandy and tobacco. She made a reputation for herself in the trade, following in her husband's footsteps when he was smuggler-captain and making a living against the odds. She had taken control of her husband's yawl, *Sally*, after her husband was killed by excisemen in what *Jack's Strange Tales* describes as 'a frantic skirmish'. Bessie was seemingly welcomed by the crew, although one man did laugh at the idea of a woman in charge, and was reputedly knocked overboard by Bessie as a result. She dressed as a man, complete with cutlass and smelly pipe. However, she did not smuggle on the Sabbath or resort to brute force, preferring to use wiles and trickery. One such manoeuvre was to have two sets of sails, white and tan, so that when watchers were looking for white, she would be heading for home 'decked out in tan' and, of course, vice versa.[3]

On one particular crossing from Dunkirk, Bessie ran into a small flotilla of Navy ships and revenue cutters, and steered towards the nearest cutter 'flying a yellow fever flag' which meant that they hoisted sail and fled to avoid being contaminated. On another occasion when the excisemen were approaching she waited for night and doused the lights, sunk her casks of smuggled brandy, and attached them to the seabed with grappling hooks. The next morning, able to play the innocent 'with aplomb', she is said to have welcomed the revenue men aboard to search freely. When asked why she had apparently evaded the search the night before, she claimed that she would have waited for them to come aboard if she had been aware of their presence, bearing in mind, however, that she regarded the 'King's men' as 'naughty characters' and she would have 'wished to protect herself'! The authors of *The Fabled Coast* claim that, although Bessie 'had to prove herself in a man's world there seems to have been no feeling that it was risky to sail with her just because she was female'. The book goes on to say that women were generally considered to be 'unchancy' (unlucky) at sea, especially in a 'smaller craft', but it seems to have been a different story for someone with the privileged status of captain and her own boat. She certainly seems to have been respected by her crew and by the law-abiding citizens of Ipswich and also Harwich in Essex, dividing her time between the two counties, mainly involved in the smuggling of tobacco and brandy. Certainly, her involvement in violent smuggling-related crime presented much less risk to the household livelihood than would be hazarded by her male counterparts.

A lesser-known female, with more elusive sources, was a Mrs Gildersleeves, described as 'a woman of fine physique, great courage and masculine bearing' in *Smugglers of the Suffolk Coast.* It seems she was the landlady of the White Horse at Leiston, near Aldeburgh, in the mid-nineteenth century and was apparently in demand for conveying small but valuable parcels of contraband under her 'voluminous garments' which were regularly, and obviously secretly, stored under the platform of the Friends' Meeting House at Leiston. This is reminiscent of the many hiding places in churches. Interestingly, in 1810 one of the customs officers who seized a consignment of geneva on the beach of the fishing village of nearby Sizewell was R. Gildersleeves – a relative on the other side of the law perhaps? There is a story in *Smugglers' Britain* of a 'certain lady' – presumably Mrs Gildersleeves – hiding a stock of brandy and silk beneath the floorboards of the Leiston Meeting House. Apparently, she kept the doors locked to prevent searches, and the locals realised that this indicated there was a hidden stash but it would hardly do to confess to this, given the purpose of the building and its Quaker congregation. This must have been late in the nineteenth century because the building was built in 1860, evidence that smuggling was ongoing.

Pub landladies seem to have been particularly empathetic to the smuggling fraternity. Mary Jane Key married Samuel Edwards some years before they took on the Duke of Marlborough pub in Weston, near Beccles (1851), funded by his smuggling lifestyle which had Mary's 'blessing and support'. This was according to Eliza Vaughan's 1934 book, *These for Remembrance*. Mary Jane's father was also a pub landlord, with his wife Martha, running the Queen's Head at Blyford in the Blythe Valley, which has quite a history in the smuggling world, known to have contraband concealed above its fireplace. Bootlegged liquor is said to have been hidden between the pews and the altar in Blyford church, taken there along a secret tunnel between the two. There is a story that when Mary Jane was a child she was heated and rubbed until red and put in her bed, surrounded by

Above left: *Rigging out a Smuggler*, Thomas Rowlandson, public domain (Wikimedia Commons CC0 1.0)

Above right: The Branwells' house, Chapel St., Penzance, Jowanipensans (Wikimedia Commons CC4)

Loading a Smuggler, Giles Grinagain, public domain (Wikimedia Commons)

Mortehoe Church Devon, nineteenth-century postcard

Above: The Free Traders Ogden's cigarette card, *c*.1900

Left: Dorchester Prison plaque, Simon Harryott (Wikimedia Commons CC 2.0)

Dancing Ledge Quarry near Langton Matravers, Charles Drake, public domain (Wikimedia Commons)

The Peter Boat, Leigh on Sea, Author

Shoeburyness coastguard station, early twentieth-century postcard

Above: View of Vereley Hill from Smugglers Rd., New Forest, Jim Champion (Wikimedia Commons CC 2.0)

Left: Jane Austen, James Andrews, public domain (Wikimedia Commons)

Blackgang Chine, Isle of Wight, Mypix (Wikimedia Commons CC4)

Will Watch and Sue, public domain (Wikimedia Commons)

Jenny Watts Cove, Ireland, early twentieth-century postcard

Hastings coastguard, Ecclesbourne, nineteenth-century postcard

Right: Rudyard Kipling, Elliott & Fry, public domain (Wikimedia Commons)

Below: SS *Great Eastern*, nineteenth-century postcard

Bottom: *Landing at Dover from the Steam Packet*, M. Sharp, public domain (Wikimedia Commons)

Above left: Fanny Burney, 1872, Edward Burney, public domain (Wikimedia Commons)

Above right: Smugglers' Cave near Cliftonville, early twentieth-century postcard

Left: Mother Redcap sculpture, Repton01x (Wikimedia Commons CC 3.0)

Above: Mother Redcap's arched gateway, ditto

Right: *Polly on the smuggling 'tack*, W. Heath, public domain

The Smugglers' Intrusion, Sir David Wilkie, public domain (Wikimedia Commons)

Bessie Catchpole and Crew, from *Compleat Smuggler*, 1938 (Bobbs-Merrill Co., US)

Above: The Custom House, London, Thomas H. Shepherd, public domain (Wikimedia Commons)

Left: 'Useful' Victorian crinoline, Edward Steele, Exeter (Victorian photographer)

Above: Cullercoats Beach, 1881, Winslow Homer, public domain (Wikimedia Commons)

Right: Dolly Peel, public domain (Wikimedia Commons)

Peggy Potts' house (permission from northeastlore.com)

Above left: *The Fair Smuggler*, *Strand* magazine, vol.1, 1891

Above right: Port Soderick Smugglers' Cave, Isle of Man, nineteenth-century postcard

Above: Smugglers' caves, Flamborough, early twentieth-century postcard

Right: Elizabeth Gaskell, public domain (Wikimedia Commons)

Smuggling Milliner, *Puck* magazine, May 1880

Suspect smuggler *Le Charivari* 4.7.1857, Martinet/Durnier/Destouches (Wikimedia Commons CC0 1.0)

smuggled bottles, which went undetected because customs officers did not want to catch scarlet fever! However, the dates don't seem to tally so historians and their researches have not been able to confirm more precise dating of these events.

The only other female identified specifically is Margaret Catchpole, no apparent relation to Bessie, who was transported to Australia at the beginning of the century (i.e. 1801) – not for smuggling, but for stealing her Suffolk employer's horse; although it certainly seems likely she had supported her notorious smuggler lover, William Laud. However, for the remainder of her life, she seems to have kept a clean sheet (unlike her husband) and is not recorded as being involved in smuggling, or any other crimes, in her new life. She was pardoned in 1814, and died in 1819, aged 57.

Chapter Ten

London

THE PORT OF London was Britain's (for some time the world's) largest port and its custom house in Lower Thames Street served as the headquarters of HM Customs. Alongside large numbers of local officers, the building accommodated officials and clerks responsible for national administration with the Board of Customs based there from the time of its establishment in the seventeenth century. However, the building was burned down in 1814, the third of a series of fires over two centuries, resulting in the destruction of many records relating to customs administration and smuggling. Author Trevor May has written of smuggling taking place in every coastal region in Great Britain with the 'Port of London being one of the worst affected areas'.

There were accounts of several seizures of tobacco which were 'landed within sight of the London Customs House in Lower Thames Street'.[1] But smuggling changed during the nineteenth century with less and less being smuggled over the English Channel in small fishing craft, and more being smuggled by passengers on packet steamers from ports like Rotterdam. The latter, for instance, introduced a regular return weekend service from 1830 for passengers alongside horses, freight, carriages, and mail, a regular mooring place being east of the Tower of London at St Katharine's Wharf in the days before Tower Bridge was built (1894). This was the *Batavier* line, which was updated and replaced in 1855.[2]

When looking at smuggling into the Port of London, a further complication is that some smugglers stood trial outside the county in which the offence was committed, e.g. they stood trial in London although the offence committed in Cornwall, Devon, and so on.

Newspaper reports of these trials did not always reveal where the smuggling actually took place. It seems that the Old Bailey was the preferred courthouse until at least 1814 rather than using juries in coastal counties who proved unreliable in returning convictions, as jurors were likely to be smugglers' relatives, collaborators, or customers.

On 21 November 1822, there was a report by the Thames Police in the *Public Ledger and Daily Advertiser*. This was in reference to Elizabeth Frazer, of Baker Street, Westminster, who was convicted 'in the penalty of £6 being two-thirds the value of a quantity of foreign wrought silk and Bandanna handkerchiefs, which she was attempting to smuggle from on board the *Vansittart East Indiaman*'. We are obviously looking at very different females involved in this kind of smuggling – these are not poverty-stricken women in coastal areas helping their menfolk to finance and feed their often-large families.

An account in the *Caernarvon & Denbigh Herald* of 30 April 1836 details the 'arrival of the Belfast steamer *France* off the London custom-house' when

> a smartly dressed young French woman named Maria Dufaur was questioned by John Kemp the revenue officer on board as to whether she had any smuggled goods about her. She declared she had none but the officer was ungallant enough to discredit her and she was handed over to the female searcher who discovered in the lining of her petticoat 739 ells of blond lace [one ell equating to approximately forty inches] valued at £78 and six muslin caps value £2 12s which were seized. She had been long suspected, and on being interrogated said she was in the employ of a lady of distinction at the west end, that she had made several smuggling trips … [being met on arrival] at the *King's Arms* in Thames Street.

She was fined £241 16s, triple the value of the goods.

A more commonplace case, of smuggling tobacco, was in the *Surrey and Middlesex Standard* of 14 October 1837.

> On Tuesday Mary Ann Smith, alias Mason, a very pretty young woman, was brought before Mr Ballantine, charged … with smuggling 7lb of foreign-manufactured tobacco, by which she had incurred a penalty of £100. The prisoner, on being called upon to plead, said 'Guilty'. Ellis, a Thames Police officer, said that on Saturday night be met the prisoner and her sister in Stepney Causeway. The prisoner's sister was in front, with an infant in her arms, and the prisoner was walking behind with what appeared to be another. Suspecting something wrong he stepped up to the prisoner, and said 'How is your baby, young woman?' at the same time touching what she was carrying in her arms. She immediately dropped her infant, exclaiming 'Oh dear, you have killed my baby.' Ellis picked up the 'baby,' which turned out to be a bundle of tobacco, made up so as to resemble a young infant. Mr Ballantine sentenced the prisoner to pay a fine of £100 to the Queen, and be imprisoned until it was paid.

As with many similar cases, there is no follow-up to be found regarding when and if the fine was paid.

A far more detailed account appeared in the *Weekly True Sun* of 30 September 1838. This was headed up: LADY SMUGGLERS: A NEW MODE OF 'CLEARING OUT' and was about a 'north of England woman, named Ann Read' who was charged with having

> pillaged the trunk of a French woman named Harriette Manning. The details of this case pretty clearly expose the extensive system of smuggling carried on by women between France and England. The complainant had, according to Childs, a constable, been several months

> ago apprehended upon a charge of smuggling, and sentenced to a fine of £100, or imprisonment for twelve months. She was, however, after repeated applications to the Board of Customs, discharged from prison after six months' confinement, and payment of £25 penalty. She had been taken into custody at Blackwall, on board the *Grand Turk*, and the contraband goods were found upon her person. Her trunk was taken in the steamer to the Custom house, and after she became an inmate of the prison she requested her friend, the prisoner, to clear it out of the stores; the prisoner, however, took advantage of the complainant's situation, and applied to her own purposes the articles contained in the trunk.
>
> Childs confirmed that he knew the complainant and prisoner 'Very well … They are most notorious smugglers', at which the prisoner intercepted with 'I get my living in as honest a way as anybody can, and by hard labour' and she denied any involvement in smuggling. However, Childs said that, 'When I went to the prisoner's house I found three gallons of smuggled spirits in the bed, covered up with the bed-clothes', to which the prisoner responded that 'Suppose you did, you didn't find me with it, did you?'

The Lord Mayor, also acting as prosecutor, pointed out that the prisoner seemed 'perfectly to understand what evidence is necessary to produce conviction' and she agreed that she was 'a good deal backwards and forwards between this and the Continent, and my husband being unable to work, I am obliged to maintain the family.' A custom house officer, named Jordan, said that she

> belonged to a gang of the most active and successful smugglers in the metropolis. They had articles fitted to various parts of their persons, by which they were

> enabled to convey contraband goods in inconceivably large quantities. They were in the habit of landing at Greenwich or its neighbourhood, because they were afraid to meet with the female searchers of London, and the officers who knew their practices durst not attempt to search them.

Jordan pointed out that the smugglers were

> all in excellent circumstances, my Lord. They have plenty of money, and live most comfortably. These two and their husbands are constantly at the business, and when anything disagreeable occurs, they go off to a Frenchman in the town who is in the wholesale contraband trade. The complainant said it was peculiarly hard upon her that while she was suffering in prison her friend should dispose of the goods in her trunk.

The prisoner said that she had supplied the complainant with money amounting to more than the value of the property in the trunk. The Lord Mayor commented that 'You have taken the trouble to clear it out effectually' but the prisoner pointed out that 'she has had the value. However, if your Lordship thinks the property ought to be restored to her, why I'll see what I can do on my next trip,' which produced a laugh in court. The Lord Mayor then claimed he could not detain her 'for the evidence is not sufficient, but I tell you that you are bound in honour to restore the property of which you possessed yourself in so ugly a manner.' The prisoner confirmed that 'she shall be all right when I have luck'. The Lord Mayor commented on her 'perfect command of the English language' and asked if she understood French, to which she said that 'To do business properly people must understand it', provoking another laugh. Jordan agreed she was 'perfectly well acquainted with it, my lord. They are both as well-known traders as are to be found.' The Lord Mayor closed proceedings with, 'Well, I trust they will be properly watched. This exposure must surely check them; but they seem, particularly the prisoner, to disregard the exertions of the revenue officers.' And they were not alone.

There are a couple of stories on the Bow Street Police Museum website regarding incidents a few years later. One refers to an article in the *Examiner* in December 1843 entitled 'Novel Bustle'. The article described how a 'slightly-formed young woman' by the name of Eliza Jones was charged by a customs officer with smuggling cigars into London. Jones travelled via steamer into Horsleydown (Bermondsey, South London) and claimed she had no articles liable to duty. However, the 'inordinately large' size of her bustle made the customs officer suspicious. The officer reportedly felt her bustle and 'found it was not composed of the usual material' rather, it contained 3.5lb of cheroots. Jones was fined fifty shillings.[3]

In 1857, the same source quotes the case of Lottie Dartdemere and her 'tobacco petticoat' that year. Dartdemere was described as a 'little Dutch woman' by the *Daily Telegraph*, who arrived at St Katharine's Wharf on a steamer from Antwerp. Similar to the story of Eliza Jones above, the 'extraordinary bulk' of her dress attracted the attention of customs officers. Despite her insistence that she was not carrying any goods liable to duty, Dartdemere was strip-searched by an 'unrelenting Englishwoman'. The search revealed 'a huge petticoat which encircled her person, and which was lined throughout with compressed tobacco'. Dartdemere insisted that she was simply trying to mirror the fashionable crinoline petticoats worn in England, but substituted tobacco because it was cheap in Holland. Her excuse was not believed, and she was taken into custody and prosecuted. At her trial, a custom house officer produced the petticoat. It was described as a 'large petticoat, made of canvas, with straps attached, to make it fast to the shoulders of the wearer ... filled with tobacco'. Dartdemere pleaded guilty. She was sentenced to pay a fine of £100 to the Queen. However, being unable to pay, she was imprisoned for six months and was permitted to take her eight-month-old baby with her.

The *Batavier* turns up again in the 17 September 1847 issue of the *Shipping and Mercantile Gazette*. This sported a brief account regarding 'an elderly-looking woman, named Elizabeth Askill, the stewardess of the Dutch steam-ship *Batavier*' who was charged 'before Mr Ballantine on Thursday, with smuggling 5lb of foreign manufactured tobacco and cigars. The case having been proved, Mr Ballantine said "You will pay a fine of £4 for this, and if you do not, you will go to prison for one month."' The penalty was immediately paid.

There is another reference to 'an elderly woman' in *Bell's New Weekly Messenger* of 14 April 1850, though no doubt 'elderly' then was very different to elderly now. This woman was

> Bridget Ellis charged with having smuggled upwards of three quarts of brandy. She had been observed on board a French steamer, apparently in a very interesting condition, and received from many on board those attentions which are considered so requisite to be observed towards a lady whose family is on the increase. The female searcher, however, thought that the bulk was removable without other attendance … [and pulled] a large bladder filled with brandy from the front of her person. The defendant, whose countenance and manner indicated that she paid devotion to the bottle, said she was not aware that the article was in her possession, and that it must have been placed about her person by some ill-disposed person who wished to derive amusement from the exposure. The Lord Mayor said he had no doubt … that the lady intended the bladder of brandy for her own private use and enjoyment, and fined her 20s.

There was quite a sympathetic case revealed in the *Oxford Chronicle and Reading Gazette* of 3 March 1855, headed 'INNOCENT FEMALE SMUGGLERS'. Three Belgian women were charged at the Thames Police Court with having smuggled tobacco over from Ostend.

> The female searcher found under the gown of each woman a large petticoat, ingeniously made for the purpose of smuggling, containing upwards of 40lb weight of tobacco. The petticoats were divided into compartments or packets, each pocket containing tobacco, and were partially supported by means of stays attached to each petticoat, and partly by straps fastened round their loins. The total quantity of tobacco in the three petticoats weighed 127lb. The prisoners were each charged with smuggling 40lb and all pleaded not guilty.

Mr Claridge, of the Queen's warehouse, said that the tobacco was of foreign manufacture liable to a prohibitory duty. One of the accused, Vanderplaas – a 'rather engaging young woman' – said she was accosted in a street in Ostend by a man who said he would pay her passage to London and back, and give her five francs, if she would carry the petticoat containing the tobacco, and showed her the way to wear it, and told her if she was asked any questions whether she had any tobacco on her person, to say no, and nothing else.

> Mr Yardley, who seemed to have a favourable impression of the young woman, questioned her, with a view of eliciting answers favourable to obtaining a mitigation of the punishment he was bound to indict upon her. She said the man who employed her to carry the tobacco was an utter stranger to her. He promised to meet her in London when the boat arrived … She had been three years in Ostend, and lived for some time as servant to Mr Bogler, an English gentleman, in King Street, Ostend, who ran away in the winter because all his money was gone … Her mother lived at Bruges. The man who gave her the

> tobacco to carry met her in Chapel Street, Ostend. She should know him again.

Mr Yardley indicated his surprise that 'for the wretched sum of five francs, or 4s 2d English money, you have incurred this ruinous penalty'. Vanderplaas then pleaded guilty and was fined £100, and in default of payment six months' imprisonment.

The next defendant, Mohler, 'who appeared older than she was stated to be', said that she came from 'Frankfort-on-the-Maine', and had two children in Germany.

> She was led into the commission of smuggling unconsciously. She had been out of a situation for days, and wished to proceed to London, where she had friends. A man met her in Ostend and took her to a public house, and gave her the petticoat, and said he would pay her passage to London and meet her when the boat arrived in England.

Mr Yardley asked if all the weight of the tobacco rested on the 'old woman's shoulders' and was told the weight would be partly on her shoulders and partly on her hips. It weighed, with the tobacco, about 45lb and she wore a large bustle petticoat as well. Mr Yardley asked her, through an interpreter, if she should know the party who gave her the tobacco. She responded that if she knew him, 'he should not escape with his life' and she would kill him! Mr Yardley said that she would be better off telling 'all she knows to the Custom house people. I fine her £100, or six months' imprisonment.'

The third victim, Moulton, sobbing loudly,

> was next arraigned, and the same evidence was repeated. The third petticoat like the others contained 41lb of tobacco. 'The young woman, who cannot speak a word of English, said she came from Altona [in Hamburg], and

> went to Ostend to meet her lover. She did not want to be stealing or murdering people. A man met her in the streets of Ostend, and said she could carry the petticoat containing the tobacco to London without incurring any risk. She was one day in Ostend only.'

Mr Beverley, from the customs solicitor's office, said the defendant was at least seven months pregnant. Mr Yardley confirmed that she would be taken care of. 'The weight of that tobacco was enough to make her ill in the situation she is in. It is not improbable she wore that tobacco petticoat all the voyage.' Mr Beverley emphasised that the system was 'dreadful' and that he would 'represent the whole matter to the Board'. Mr Yardley summarised by saying that

> If what these women say is true, great cruelty and rascality has been practised towards them, and I hope the matter will be fully investigated. I also fine this poor creature £100, and, in default of payment, six months' imprisonment. The jailor, Roche, will see that every attention is paid her before she is sent away in the van.

Cases at the Thames Police Court were reproduced in newspapers nationally, as in the *Durham Chronicle* of 13 August 1858. This account was regarding 'Ellen Carey, [a] neatly-dressed young woman' who had been charged on custom house information with smuggling 22.5lb of cigars, incurring a penalty of £100.

> She pleaded guilty … and the magistrate at once sentenced her to pay a fine of £l00 to the Queen, and in default of payment to be imprisoned for six months. Gardner, a tide-surveyor of customs, introduced to the notice of the magistrates three large petticoats, lined with cigars, and said the prisoner was passenger on the General Steam Navigation Company's ship, the *Moselle*,

> and on her arrival at St Katharine's Wharf, was about to step on shore, when her immense rotundity of dress excited his suspicions, and be asked her if she had anything about her liable to duty. She declared she had not, and explained that her blown appearance arose from crinoline, which she and every lady in the land considered as very becoming, whatever the gentlemen might say on the subject. He hinted to her that her crinoline petticoat was of extra dimensions, and handed her over to a female searcher, who stripped her in a private cabin, took the three petticoats lined with cigars from her person, and brought her out again with her size diminished to reasonable proportions, as she now appeared.'

Mr Yardley (again) said to Gardner that, 'You will have no faith in crinoline again,' the reply being, 'Never, sir. I shall always suspect every woman who wears crinoline.'

Similarly, on 7 June 1862, the *Stroud Journal* detailed the case of

> Louisa Touter, a married woman, aged thirty eight, brought before Mr Elliott, at the Thames Police Court, charged with smuggling 9lb of foreign manufactured tobacco. Mr Robert Grey, an examining officer of Customs, said that he came up the Thames with the General Steam Navigation Company's ship *Belgium* from Gravesend. The prisoner was among the passengers, and she embarked at Ostend. He observed that she looked very bulky, and asked her if she had anything about her liable to duty, to which she answered in the negative, and said that the ample dimensions of her crinoline caused her to look bulky, and that she was obliged to be in the fashion, absurd as it was. He told her that story was not believed, and that her crinoline must be overhauled for smuggled goods, on which she retired into a side cabin, came out

> with her crinoline reduced in size, and handed him 4lb of foreign manufactured tobacco, which she declared was all she had. He seized the tobacco, and placed her under arrest. On the ship arriving at her moorings, he conveyed the prisoner to the Arbour Square Police Station, adjoining the court, and caused her to be searched by a female, who still further reduced the dimensions of her crinoline by taking from among its ample folds 5lb more of tobacco, making in all 9lb. The value and duty amounted to £4 5s 6d. The prisoner said that what the officer had stated was quite true, and that she was not aware that she was doing wrong in bringing the tobacco to England.'

Mr Elliott asked why she had concealed it in her dress, at which point the prisoner's son stated that

> he was at Bruges with his mother three days ago, and his aunt and uncle remarked how cheap tobacco was at Bruges, and how dear it was in England. His uncle then went and bought some in the town, and gave it to his mother as a present to his father, and it was really intended for him to smoke, and not for sale. His mother had nothing to put the tobacco in but her dress.

Mr Elliott said the prisoner had been guilty of a violation of the revenue laws, and she must have known she was doing wrong when she concealed the tobacco in her dress and denied the possession of it to the officer. He convicted her of smuggling, and she must pay the single value and duty and £2 besides, in all £6 5s 6d, or be imprisoned for one month. The fine was immediately paid.

The *Batavier* also featured in the *Aldershot Military Gazette* of 23 November 1861, under the heading of 'The Use of Crinoline'. Back in the Thames Police Court, 'a well-dressed woman, named Elizabeth Barbara Lorinz, aged 36, a native of Holland, was brought on remand, charged with smuggling'. It appears that Inspector Major, of the Thames Police, and Dyer, constable, were on duty at the Dublin Wharf, Lower Smithfield, and

> saw the prisoner disembark from the *Batavier*, a Rotterdam steamer. There was something very peculiar in her gait, which induced the officers to watch her. Dyer put himself in her way. Something hard struck against his right knee as she passed him. The inspector and constable followed the prisoner as far as Burr Street, the back of the St Katharine's Dock, where the inspector spoke to her and intimated that she had goods about her liable to duty. She indignantly denied the assertion. She was then taken into custody. On the way to the Thames Police Station at Wapping, she offered Inspector Major a present to let her go, which he refused. On her arrival at the station she delivered to the officers a few sticks of Cavendish tobacco, and said she had no more. She was delivered into the care of Mrs Charlotte Nixon, a female searcher, to whom she declared that she was in the family way, and had no smuggled goods about her. Mrs Nixon, however, insisted on examining her dress, and discovered 5lb of cigars, 9lb of Cavendish tobacco, some tea, and a bottle of Holland's gin, concealed beneath her clothes and about her capacious crinoline. The evidence having been interpreted to the prisoner, she pleaded Guilty.

There was more smuggling from Holland reported in the *London City Press* on 16 April 1870. This time it was 'Christiana Williams, aged 32, residing at 20 Panton Street Haymarket' who was charged with smuggling.

> The prisoner, a native of Holland, was a passenger on Tuesday morning by the steamer from Rotterdam and on

> being asked if she had anything liable to duty she said she had not. It was discovered, however, that she was wearing a bustle in which was concealed 3lb of tobacco and cigars. She had besides in her pocket three bottles of spirits, containing in all 32 gills. Mr Mogg, an examining officer of Customs, said that women were frequently engaged in smuggling in this way, and he fancied that he had seen the prisoner several times before. Her husband was waiting her arrival and on hearing that his wife was charged he went home to get money to pay the fine, which he anticipated would be inflicted. The Lord Mayor said that the practice of smuggling by women like the prisoner must be stopped. He fined her £4 being treble the value and duty of the tobacco and spirits with the alternative of twenty-one days' imprisonment.

The fine was paid.

A London newspaper, the *Southwark and Bermondsey Recorder*, of 31 May 1879 reported a local case.

> At Southwark Police Court in Monday Alice Heron, 33, described as a married woman, who refused to give her address, was charged with having in her possession and conveying 28lb weight of foreign manufactured tobacco, and having concealed upon the premises at 16 New Street, Bermondsey, a further quantity of 69lb of tobacco liable to duty, with intent to defraud her Majesty's Revenue. Mr Beverley prosecuted on behalf of the Commissioners of Customs. The woman was carrying the bundle along Maltby Street, and was followed by Detective Sergeant Howard to the above address where she was arrested. After further evidence, Mr Slade had no alternative but to fine her £100, or to be imprisoned until such sum be paid.

Not only female passengers but the female staff on late nineteenth-century ships were involved. The *Taunton Courier and Western Advertiser* of 28 December 1881 relates the account of

> a woman named Wells, the stewardess on board the German ship *Strauss,* lying in the river ... charged at Southwark with smuggling. As the officer of the Customs suspected her, he threatened to have her searched, whereupon she produced a smuggling petticoat, a garment furnished with large pockets all round, and these contained, in flat packets, ten and a half pounds of foreign tobacco. The defendant was found to be in possession of five other smuggling petticoats. She was fined £15 7s 6d or one month's imprisonment.

Some smugglers were well known in London and appeared in court regularly. In the *South London Press* of 15 April 1882, 'Alice Harvey (35), described on the charge-sheet as a mantle-maker, but well known to the police as a notorious smuggler, was brought before Mr Bridge charged with having in her possession 11lb of foreign manufactured tobacco, with intent to defraud her Majesty's Revenue.' Called as a witness, Alice Smith, an

> intelligent girl, living with her grandmother in Queen Street, Horselydown [Bermondsey] said that the prisoner lived with her father, and Thursday morning she sent her with a large parcel to the parcel delivery station at an oil-shop close by, to be forwarded to Three Colt Street, Limehouse. On the same afternoon she sent her with another, and told her to ask the shopkeeper to weigh it. While he was doing so, she saw it was directed to Mr D. Hays, 34 Little Colt Street, Limehouse. The shopkeeper told her it weighed 11lb and she left it. George Reed, an inspector of police and officer

> of Customs said he proceeded to Three Colt Street, Limehouse, on Thursday evening, when he saw the cart of the delivery company stop at 34, and saw the parcel produced addressed to Mr Hays. He told the car-man who he was and took possession of the parcel, and finding it contained 11lb of smuggled tobacco, he conveyed it to the Queen's Warehouse. Mr Bridge asked how he knew the tobacco to be smuggled. The witness replied that it was never imported in that state. It was in pound compressed packages ready for the smugglers, who were employed on board the Hamburg and Bremen steamers. Mr Bridge asked if he knew anything of the prisoner and the witness replied that she had been a notorious smuggler for years, and had been recently fined three times at this court for that offence … The prisoner, who declined to say anything, was accordingly remanded.

Tobacco was obviously the most popular product being smuggled by women at this time. In the *Sheffield Daily Telegraph* of 21 December 1894 was yet another such account, this time at Westminster Police Court. The woman involved was

> Annie Voss, 51, a German subject from Hamburg charged with smuggling cigars. The prisoner, *en route* from Port of Spain, Trinidad, to join her husband, arrived on Wednesday by the Continental train at Victoria Station, and said that she had nothing excisable to declare. The Inland Revenue officers noticed that the depth of the interior of her trunk did not accord with its outside appearance, and, investigating the matter further, discovered that there was a false bottom of four inches lined with 5.5lb of cigars. Mr Foreman, the Examining Officer of Customs, said prisoner was liable to treble the duty and value amounting to £12 7s 6d, and additional

> fine of £l. Assuming that the prisoner had declared the cigars the duty would have been taken and returned on satisfactory proof of export. But in such a flagrant case as this accused could expect no consideration. She was ordered to pay penalties amounting to £13 7s 6d or in default two months imprisonment.

While many such stories indicate that the fine was paid, not all clarify this particular ending to proceedings, although the following does provide a finale.

This was when the following year, back at the Thames Police Court, Mrs Catherine Peters of 24 Suffield Road, Walworth was named in the *Tamworth Herald* (28 September 1895), having been

> charged with attempting to smuggle 2lb of cigars, 1lb of tobacco, and a quantity of foreign spirits, the single value and duty of which amounted to £1 18s 8d, with intent to defraud her Majesty's Customs. The defendant pleaded guilty, and the examining officer of Customs stated that she was a passenger by the steamship *Holland* from Rotterdam. The defendant denied having anything liable for duty but on being searched the tobacco, cigars and spirits were found artfully concealed in packets attached to an under-dress. Mrs Peters now said she was very sorry. She bought the things in order to make presents to relatives. Mr Dickinson ordered her to pay the single value and duty. The money was paid.

Smuggling was therefore by no means confined to coastal towns, and was increasing among women passengers travelling to the UK from Europe in direct proportion to their declining involvement in the landings on the beaches.

Chapter Eleven

Northumberland and Tyne and Wear

THIS PART OF the United Kingdom does not feature prominently (and is less well documented) when it comes to smuggling, but, bearing in mind its distance from Europe across the North Sea compared to the coasts in the South of England, it is not surprising. One comparison is the 200 miles from Poole to Calais compared to the 485 miles from Sunderland to Antwerp. Enough to deter all but the hardiest smuggler, until a regular service of steamers between the two coastlines changed the face of smuggling altogether.

However, in *Smugglers' Britain*, Richard Platt refers to an author in 1909 writing of childhood memories (i.e. from the nineteenth century) of a woman in Boulmer keeping an eye out for the 'salt man' and announcing his arrival to the other villagers, because smuggled salt was retailed by local women carrying it around on their backs. If caught by an excise man they would slash a knife to spill the cargo, which carried a heavy duty at the time. Boulmer and other coastal areas north of Newcastle were influenced by the proximity of Scotland and the cross-border smuggling of whisky, but there was a thriving trade in gin from Holland as well as salt in the early part of the nineteenth century, the latter valued for curing pork and fish.

Research shows that one of the most interesting smugglers was Peggy Potts, born in 1789, who, for many years, was one of the principal public characters of the town of Sunderland. It seems Peggy was known as a 'daughter of the soil', for she had lived in the town all her life. Her maiden name was Havelock, her father a sailor and then a fisherman, and her second cousin the celebrated General Havelock, the hero of Lucknow distinguished in the 1857 Indian Mutiny. Peggy's husband, who predeceased her by several years, was 'likewise a fisherman, and latterly a pilot, and he had the reputation of being a somewhat lazy fellow, who was glad to supplement his gains by those of his more energetic wife. However this may have been, Peggy managed to make a good fend for herself.' Her apparent eccentricity not only furthered her own ends in making a livelihood, but made her a universal favourite wherever she went. She was seemingly wonderfully ready-witted; and 'her command of the Sunderland vernacular, which she never dreamt of spoiling by any sort of refinement, was so perfect as to give a zest to every word she uttered'. Those who knew Peggy in her youth testified that she was a

> very handsome, well-favoured, buxom lass; and she retained to the last the traces of having been so. She was of middle stature, and rather stout. Her dress latterly, when attending to her usual vocation, was a blue gown, a flannel petticoat of the same colour, an old fashioned black silk bonnet that set off her comely face to advantage, a silk handkerchief round her neck, and a snow white apron. She was always as clean as a pin.[1]

For many years, Peggy made a living by selling fish and other produce, and for some time she had a small shop in the market, where she sold cheese. Her custom was to buy a quantity of stale cheese, at a very cheap rate, although often of the finest and richest quality. This cheese she sold at 4d per pound when it was selling at 10d in the shops, and she would let her friends have mates' rates at 2d per pound. One day a friend of the teller of the tale[2] went to her stall, when she addressed him thus: 'Noo, then, hoo are ye the morin!' The reply being, 'I am very bad i' my stomach.' She instantly rejoined, 'Eat a bit rotten cheese, hunny. Aa had a bit mesel this mornin', an' aa'm nicely noo. Thor's nowt like a bit o' rotten cheese for mendin' the stomach'! However, in the

> old palmy days of contraband trade, Peggy is said to have turned over hundreds of pounds in the smuggling line. She

> had her regular customers whom she supplied with goods that had never paid toll to the Imperial Revenue; and no one could more deftly than Peggy outwit the custom-house officers, however keen on the scent. Also, when contraband stuff was not forthcoming, Peggy would go to old Solomon Chapman's and get a temporary supply (along with a permit), and go round and dispose of it as smuggled.

There was one incident when she was tramping into the country with a small keg of whisky to serve a friend, when

> she was met by an officer, who guessing what it was she carried, made her turn back, meaning to take her before his superiors. She went along quietly for a good way, when she begged the officer to walk forward a bit. He did so. No sooner was his back turned than she emptied the keg, re-filled it with water, and walked on quickly with it after the officer, on reaching whom she transferred it to his custody, telling him she was tired of carrying it. On arriving at the custom-house, the keg was found to contain nothing but the pure element. The laugh was turned against the officer, and Peggy came off chuckling.

It seems that Peggy's

> favourite seat on a fine summer's night was on the steps of the Rendezvous, next door to her home. Here she knitted stockings and gossiped with her neighbours. This was formerly the quarters of the Press Gang, and the captives used to be conveyed secretly away through passages and stairs in the rear up to the High Street.

(This was presumably an inn, but has proved untraceable.) Peggy died in October 1875 in a house in Aikenhead Square on the Low

Quay, aged 86, so says her obituary in the local paper, although in fact she was believed to have died in the workhouse.

A second prominent smuggler was born just a few years before Peggy, in 1782. Dorothy (Dolly) Peel, née Appleby, was born on the riverside in Shadwell Street when South Shields had been the most important salt-making town in Great Britain, with shipbuilding, fishing, and glass-making also prominent. She grew up to be the person you needed if you wanted to smuggle booze, cigarettes, or even budgies. Like many others she was able to smuggle contraband under her fish-basket by day, and specialised in tobacco, cigars, brandy, perfume, and lace, supplementing her meagre income. 'She wasn't a big fan of the pressgang, enforcing young men to join the military, and would regularly hide local sailors … until the coast was clear.'[3]

She married Cuthbert Peel in 1803, but he was pressed into naval service in 1808 on the HMS *Amelia* warship during the Napoleonic Wars. Dolly 'was known to be a strong muscular woman and utterly fearless, which is why she probably managed to get away with smuggling for so long'. Nearby Marsden Bay was a well-known secluded centre of smuggling along this stretch of the coast where she was presumably party to the nefarious activities that took place. One story is of a man running through the streets of the town to escape the press gangs that were chasing him when he bumped into Dolly.

> Ever the quick thinker, Dolly lifted up her voluminous petticoats and long skirt and told the man to hide under them. Fearful for his freedom the man duly obliged and dived underneath. As the press gangs came shooting round the corner they too bumped into an innocent-looking Dolly who sent them off in completely the wrong direction in search for the man. Once they were out of sight the man underneath the petticoats emerged back into the daylight and was sent on his way in the opposite direction to the press gang.[4]

With yet another war looming, this time with the United States, a press gang in March 1812 (known locally as the Hunter's Gang) was again in 'hot pursuit of Cuthbert Peel who had returned home to Shadwell Street from service in 1811'. Single-handed, Dolly managed to keep the press gang at bay whilst her husband escaped out of the window. He didn't get very far as he was captured, along with their son Ralph, both pressed into service on the HMS *Lyra* which was waiting at nearby Peggy's Hole in North Shields. A huge crowd had congregated at Peggy's Hole and understandably the situation was a bit tense. Tempers flared and a huge fight kicked off. At one point it was said that a pistol was fired with the bullet passing through the lapel of an officer's coat. Whilst all this commotion was going on, Dolly was hiding on board the HMS *Lyra*, having sneaked on board the ship to be with her husband and son. She remained hidden for three days until discovered. The captain and crew wanted to dump her off the ship on the west coast of Africa; however, she ended up working in the sick bay as a nurse to sick and wounded sailors. She did such a good job that she was allowed to stay on board with her family, often being used as a 'powder monkey' in addition to nursing duties, which meant that she supplied gunpowder to the cannons during battle. She may even have worked as a nurse in the ship's cockpit where crude surgery was performed on injured sailors.

In late 1815, following the Battle of Waterloo, the Peels were allowed to return home where 'Dolly received a pardon for her initial attempts to interfere with naval practice. The Peels were also made exempt from any future press-ganging.' Regardless, Dolly didn't take too kindly to what had happened to her and her family. So she became a ringleader in 'organizing groups which prevented the Navy's ships from docking in South Shields and was also known to lure vessels on to the rocks in the River Tyne where she could board them and … give their contents to the poor of the town'. This won her many admirers and for the rest of her life she championed the down-and-outs of South Shields and continued to hide men from the press gangs as well as handling contraband.

She was also an entertainer, using her wit and humour to become a

> famed poet and story teller at Market Place in South Shields [still in evidence] where she would make up rhymes and stories about subjects such as the loss of the barge *Dove of Sunderland* which ran aground on the Herd Sand in November 1836 carrying tallow which would have been a godsend for the local people during that cold winter.

It's also possible that Dolly herself may have lured the doomed ship on to the sands, although this is not proven. 'She would regularly imitate the quack doctors by waving a box of pills and repeating their sales patter' and was

> popular with the town's first M.P. Robert Ingham for whom she composed a poem congratulating him for his election victory in 1832. Quite why a Member of Parliament would associate himself with a dubious, albeit popular character such as Dolly is not known. Perhaps she supplied with him cheap contraband?[5]

By 1841, she was living at Ropery Stairs near Shadwell Street, and later relocated to Lookham Stairs nearby. Cuthbert Peel died in 1856, Dolly joining him the following year after a severe attack of bronchitis. She was 75, a great age for the time, perhaps confirming how tough she was.[6] The *Falkirk Herald* of 29 October referred to her as 'noted virago, fish-woman, smuggler, and poetess, with whom has perished a rich fund of reminiscences of the French war, the pressgang, etcetera'. Fishwives were often associated with smuggling in coastal areas like Cullercoats.

Stories about Dolly linger on to this day in a variety of ways. In 1923, South Shields playwright Eva Elwes wrote *Dolly Peel*, a play based on her life, setting it in 1832 at the time of the election of Robert Ingham. The play was first performed in 1913 and revived a few times but was lost until a hand-written copy was discovered in South Shields in 2004. The play was performed in South Shields' Customs House Theatre in 2005. There is a statue of Dolly, representing the resilience of local women, commissioned by Reg Peel of South Tyneside Metropolitan Borough Council, who is her great-great-great-grandson. It was unveiled in 1987, in River Drive looking out over the River Tyne. There is also a Dolly Peel public house in Commercial Road, South Shields, with various tributes to her amongst its furnishings and decor.

There are a few further accounts of female involvement in local smuggling in the 1860s. One, headed 'ABUSES OF CRINOLINE', was in the *Newcastle Daily Chronicle* of 18 May 1861.

> At the Hartlepool police court, on Monday, Elizabeth Colvert, stewardess of the new steamer *Osprey*, which arrived from Hamburg on Sunday night, was charged with smuggling 5lb 4oz of tobacco, and three gills of spirits. Edwards, a tide waiter, who saw her come ashore from the steamer, and expected she was conveying smuggled goods, questioned her, and not obtaining a satisfactory reply, took her to the office, where the female searcher took her in charge, when the prisoner pulled out from under her crinoline – to which it was stitched – a quantity of tobacco. She denied having any more, but careful search resulted in the discovery of a further quantity concealed in her bustle. Prisoner then produced a bottle of spirits which had been tied by the neck to the under part of her crinoline, and gave it to the searcher. The Bench fined her £3 12s 7d and 12s 6d costs.

Another is from the *Cardiff Times* dated 21 September 1866, about a woman arriving at Sunderland Dock. This is headed 'FEMALE SMUGGLER', continuing with:

> On Saturday a somewhat unusual case of smuggling came before the Sunderland magistrates, when a woman

> with a child in her arms, and who called herself Mary Clarke, was charged with smuggling on the previous night. Mr McKenzie, a Customs officer at the dock, saw the woman lurking about, and her suspicious conduct induced him to watch her. She went towards a French vessel in the dock, and soon afterwards returned, and was making away by the south end, when he stopped her, and in a basket she was carrying found two gallons of French brandy, in two bladders, out of which some had already leaked. The woman alleged that the captain of a French vessel met her in the street, and promised her something if she would go to the dock and carry a bundle for him. She did so, and waited for some time, until the captain brought her the bladders, and he had just left her when the Customs officer arrived. Mr McKenzie said he believed that the woman had been made a fool of, but he could not bring the captain, as the liquor was found on the woman. The bench remanded the prisoner, and ordered the Captain to be produced on Monday next.

While almost identical accounts appear in another fifteen newspapers nationwide, not one has a follow-up as to whether the captain was 'produced' or what happened to Mary, who does sound as if she was duped… but may also have been a very good liar!

Of course, there were obviously many others involved in smuggling in the area, but few have achieved legendary status, probably because so many, and their stories, have been airbrushed from history.

Chapter Twelve

Scotland

AS EARLY AS 1806, it seems that the fisherwomen of Arbroath had developed the smuggling habit, according to Jack Strange's book.[1] He also refers to fisher wives in Scotland helping to physically carry men to and from their boats, helping with the launch, 'baiting the lines', and, of course, selling the catch, mainly but not only whisky. To a Scot, smuggling had a dual meaning as there was also illegal whisky distilling. It certainly had financial benefits because in 1803 the duty in Scotland on a gallon of whisky was three shillings, compared to the English eight shillings. The difference was what fuelled the smuggling of the drink over the border, often in earthenware jugs called grey hens, hidden among the other contents in innocent-looking carts.

Women and children were involved in helping smugglers and illicit still operators to avoid excise men, giving signals when they would witness the arrival of an excise man into their neighbourhood. They also would help waylay the officer by talking to them or offering them something to eat.[2] In Argyll, particularly, the illicit distillers were generally small tenants. Transactions show that large numbers of women were engaged in making illicit whisky on their own account. Farmers seem to have delegated the task to maidservants and other 'inferior persons', who acted as covers in order that more substantial individuals would escape detection. Illicit distilling may have been regarded as part of general domestic duties, or as a source of pin money, especially for widows or single women, providing a ready source of income.[3]

Both producing whisky and smuggling it for money or for salt was an essential part of the local economy, and entire families were engaged in it, but there were dangers as in the following example in 1817. On 27 March, a small boat carrying whisky 'produced at a distilling place called Black Cave on the Struie burn' (on the Isle of Arran) was spotted by the gaugers (excise men). The gaugers gave chase, forcing the smugglers to retreat to the shore. In desperation, they threw stones at the gaugers to keep them away. But the gaugers fired their guns in return, killing Isabell Nicol, and a father and son, William and Donald McKinnon. These deaths had a considerable impact on the local community and as late as the 1950s a memorial service was held where they were killed. Their graves can still be seen in Kilmory graveyard. Meanwhile, at his trial for murder at Edinburgh's high court, despite opening fire on a group of unarmed islanders, John Jeffrey, who led the excise party, was found not guilty.[4] This account also appears in the *Caledonian Mercury* with Isabell (or Isobel, spellings vary) 'at the head of a crowd of at least 200' with 'not one third of the number being men'. A witness at the High Court of Justiciary, which investigated the charge of murder against the revenue officers, described Isobel as a 'rash clever woman' who 'had no idea of the danger she ran'. The language tellingly adopted contemporary prejudices which regarded 'violent criminality amongst women as irrational or aberrant'.

Despite this cautionary tale, however, it is clear that women participated in smuggling-related crime because, more often than not, the gamble paid off.

> Although there has not been enough archival work completed to estimate the overall quantities of goods involved ... reports suggest that local men and women 'recovered' a not insignificant proportion of the contraband that Revenue officers managed to intercept. Women were not bystanders or mere accomplices; they organised, motivated, and led a sustained pattern of social upheaval and rejection of authority.[5]

There are several stories of the involvement of smugglers' wives in *The Compleat Smuggler* but it is not clear if these are eighteenth- or nineteenth-century tales, so they are not included.

Prior to 1823, when smuggling was more lucrative, a substantial number of cottagers and labourers in Kintyre were said to support large families on the profits of the business. Interestingly, early marriages were frequent as a wife was regarded as an indispensable part of the enterprise. Much of the work was assigned to women who were 'fit for' or 'employed in' nothing else. Certainly, women dominated home brewing, although some men were also involved, whereas alehouses were usually run by men. Some women may have brewed largely for home consumption and sold their produce only once or twice a year when they had a surplus. For others, it provided their main income, to the extent that they would buy in malt if their holding did not produce enough, selling the ale from home or on market stalls. There is evidence that richer peasants sometimes invested substantially in brewing, with husbandmen being recorded using the profits from the sale of their agricultural produce to purchase the vats and cauldrons which their wives needed to set up brewing on a larger scale, but it was also a common source of income for poorer households. The Illicit Distillation (Scotland) Act of 1832 strengthened the hands of the excise men, giving them the power to confiscate or destroy stills, spirits, carts, or barrels, wiping out much of this source of income for the Scots.[6]

Early in the nineteenth century, the women of Scotland were often less violent, and more peripheral, than in reports decades later. For instance, during the Regency period, wives of smugglers sent presents such as poultry, butter, veal, and, predictably, whisky, to the wives of excise men. In return for these gifts, they were informed when the patrol were out searching for smugglers. Presumably they did not tell their husbands about their involvement![7]

Author Hugh McMillan felt that often the women were 'smugglers' molls … rather than smugglers themselves' but that they also 'certainly played the leading part in the food riots that took place in some Solway ports' in the early 1800s. These centred on ships exporting food at a time of shortages and high price, with the organisation, planning and execution of these raids – often extremely and unusually violent – being carried out 'exclusively by women'. He mentions one example in 1801, when Marie Milligan, Agnes Glover, and Marion Ireland forcibly boarded a ship in Kirkudbright laden with potatoes, taking them 'without authority' and 'distributing them at a price they deemed just'. Not content with that, they sought out the farmer who was exporting the potatoes, dragged him to the harbour 'and threw him in'! So, smuggling was not all about whisky…

One woman, mentioned by McMillan and also by Richard Platt on his excellent website, was apparently an 'attractive local Amazon'. This was Maggie McConnell, described variously as a 'very comely woman aged about 40' and as having 'brawny arms' with a 'judo-like grip … and a matronly bulk sufficient to hold down an officer's wriggling form'. This was further reinforced by Helen Susan Swift,[8] who quotes her description as strong enough 'to hold up a two year old stirk' – a stirk being a young cow or bull! Swift also adds some additional information regarding Maggie's origins, for example that she was a farmer's daughter from Dailly in Ayrshire known to help run cargoes for the local 'free traders' (smugglers). Here is a relevant and entertaining extract from *Smuggling Days and Smuggling Ways* of 1890:

> A few miles from Lochnaw is the little Harbour of Dallybay. Here … some smugglers had landed a cargo of their usual wares, such as brandy, wines, and tobacco, and these were carried up the hill of South Cairn, waiting till a band of volunteers arrived with a string of pack-horses to transport them inwards for distribution. The Custom House officer in charge of the district received information of their doings, and hurrying to the spot with the only coastguardsman disengaged, he promptly effected a seizure of the whole of the goods. The smugglers

> skulked off, and the one coastguardsman was sent back to Stranraer. The officer … sauntered sentry-fashion round and round his prizes which were all heaped before him in rich profusion, his sword and a brace of formidable pistols by his side. Presently Maggie McConnell approached the great man, bade him good morning, to which he affably accepted Maggie's proffered hand. He had unwittingly sealed his own fate. His arm was thrust upwards, and at the same instant he was encircled by the siren's arms, and with a heavy fall was thrown helplessly upon his back. Maggie then sat coolly down upon her victim, and having placed her apron over his eyes, she held him firmly down as if bound in a vice. In vain he struggled; he coaxed and threatened her by turns; he shouted for help in the king's name, and for a moment his hopes ran high; footsteps approached; he roared louder and louder, but no friendly voice replied. At last, but only when it suited her pleasure, Maggie released him from her grasp. But oh, the vanity of human hopes! When he looked up not one of the articles lay in its old place, as he had himself seen them just before upon the ground. By and by his companion reappeared, but only to find the head officer *tete-a-tete* with this Galloway matron who, bidding them adieu, disappeared without further loss of time, wishing them both a pleasant ride into Stranraer.

(Note: The coastguard was formed in 1822 and this account seems to have been a couple of decades before that; a common mistake. No sources give a firmer date for the story.)

Another non-violent, but very different, kind of assistance was given to smugglers by Bessie Millie, regarded as one of the last witches from Stromness in Orkney. She earned a living by selling 'fair winds' to sailors who had called into Stromness for supplies, but she is also reputed to have cursed a revenue cutter that appeared to suppress the smuggling trade, making it clear what side she was on. The curse certainly worried the revenue men, who wanted their captain to burn her house down unless she withdrew the curse! She seems to have achieved a level of fame for her activities, with Sir Walter Scott visiting her in 1814 when she was well over 90, and using her story in his novel *The Pirate*. He described her in his journal as being like a 'dried up mummy' with a corpse-like complexion and light blue eyes.

Smugglers' wives in the coastal village of Ballantrae were heavily involved in smuggling activity, especially the Coulter family. On 29 October 1807, Thomas Coulter's wife Sarah, Robert Coulter's wife Janet, and Alexander Coulter's wife Grizel actually managed to seize hold of the local customs officer, Robert Williamson, and dragged him into Robert Coulter's home where he was held, though how long for is unclear. Presumably long enough for husbands, or contraband, to disappear. One account suggests that it was Janet who was responsible for actually wounding Williamson with 'the Board of Customs' accepting responsibility 'for his medical bills'. Interestingly, Janet had also attacked Williamson in another report in 1799 along with other members of the Coulter family. The Coulters were well known locally at the time – in August 1804, William Coulter brought salt on *The Nancy* which he landed at Larne, a mile north of Ballantrae, where it was hidden in the house of widow Grizel Main; the salt was eventually seized by Ballantrae customs officers.

On Wednesday, 31 May 1809, both James Coulter and Thomas Coulter's wife, Sarah, were charged 40s per pound for landing salt in bulk from Ireland. (Interestingly, two of the seafaring male Coulters were delivered to the Navy in December 1807, because they had been found on board a smuggling boat with contraband salt. They both deserted!) The family turn up again in October 1814 when they helped to unload from a small boat quite a haul of alcohol: thirty-seven casks containing 570 gallons of gin, and three casks containing thirty gallons of brandy, worth over £25,000 in today's money. Their customers included Mrs Agnes Ross, wife of a Ballantrae innkeeper, plus Mrs Mary Ferguson Kennedy and Mrs Mary McWhirter.[9]

Then in January 1816 there is an account of another Ballantrae family – the Peacocks.[10] This time two customs officers seized six bags of salt that had been smuggled to the south of the town by Robert Peacock and his wife, neither of whom could prove that the legal import duty had been paid. They were apparently fined more than the equivalent of a massive £140,000 each (!) for helping to unload and land the salt from a boat and carrying it to their barnyard where it was hidden from view. The salt had been offered to John Harrison's wife at 'Big Park' and to Thomas Milroy's wife at Shallochwreck, a farm with a large acreage. The Ballantrae website comments that it is 'not impossible that there would be women among the smuggler's crews' but sadly offers no evidence. Until the twenty-first century there was an annual Smugglers' Festival in the village but its future seems uncertain.

Also in 1816, Largs – a seaside town on the Firth of Clyde – opened a revenue office with coast-waiter (custom-house officer) Robert Brown in charge, his role being to superintend the landing and shipping of goods. Some of the seizures made in the town between 1812 and 1834 are listed in *Clyde Coast Smuggling*. They include a smuggled cask of 'nine gallons of whisky' found at the home of Janet McVairn, listed as a vintner, and 'two and a half gallons of aqua vitae' (a strong alcoholic spirit, probably brandy) seized in the house of Janet Paterson, innkeeper.

Research has revealed some quite violent accounts of women involved in smuggling later in the nineteenth century in Scotland. There is a detailed thesis written by Christine Lodge when at the University of Glasgow studying for her Philosophy doctorate. She writes in some detail about women outwitting the excise man (or gauger, because men had to gauge the amount and value of spirits) and of their involvement in the production and distribution of illicit whisky. There are references to records of a number of Kintyre smugglers, including women, purchasing malt for this purpose, and of how they tried to destroy evidence of such transactions, like 'the MacNeill woman' who bent down to tie her shoe but in bending down deliberately smashed the jar of whisky she had been carrying. Another woman, from Knockhanty, Campbeltown, who 'appealed to the exciseman to allow her a final swig of her smuggled whisky before surrendering it' but promptly spat it into his face when her wish was granted, and then managed to elude him.

Charles Harper wrote about this subject in 1909, with one particular incident in Glenlivet in the 1820s when the excisemen

> considered that the best time for a raid would be Monday morning, after the debauch of the Sunday afternoon and night in which the Roman Catholics [local smugglers were mainly Catholic] were wont to indulge, and marching out of Elgin town on the Sunday, arrived at Glenlivet at daybreak … but they presently discovered that their arrival had not only been observed but foreseen … several hundred men, women, and children were assembled on the hill-sides at Glenlivet to bid active defiance to them. The excisemen keenly desired to bring the affair to a decisive issue, but the thirty seamen who accompanied them had a due amount of discretion, and refused to match their pistols and cutlasses against the muskets that the smugglers ostentatiously displayed.

The distilling of illicit whisky was a serious pastime, highly organised and heavily invested in. Illegal production required a degree of commitment that sanctioned violence, and even murder. Tales abound of women outwitting the excise men throughout Scotland, with financial, literary, and judicial records bearing out women's involvement in illicit distilling, for themselves or as part of a group. Ian MacDonald was among the first to publish stories of whisky smuggling, and a number of tales that have subsequently appeared are taken from his work. Women most frequently appear in these tales smuggling whisky to the point of sale. He refers to the women outwitting the gaugers in a variety of ways with 'a woman from Abriachan escaping with her whisky by squirting the spirit into an officer's face'. There is also a story of 'an old woman brought before Sheriff Duncan Campbell who presided for about thirty years prior to 1822'. The sheriff was seemingly a bit uneasy, but suggested that, 'No doubt my good woman it is not often you have been guilty of this fault.' Her reply was, 'Na, Na, Shirra … I hae'na made a drop since yon wee keg I sent yoursel'!'

It is perhaps not surprising that legal records have yet to be uncovered to confirm stories such as these. It may be, of course, that the very lack of evidence is confirmation in itself. However, legal documents do attest to women distributing the illicit spirit. Women's attire allowed the concealment of a variety of appropriate vessels: stone jars, bottles, small casks, and skins. The usual practice was to secrete the chosen vessel beneath their long skirts, cloaks, shawls and hatboxes. Evidence given to a parliamentary inquiry in 1823 described how women carried the whisky. For example, at Inverness, women apparently favoured the use of band-boxes (lightweight and commonplace Victorian boxes), with female whisky smugglers in Scotland in the 1820s operating near port towns and in broad daylight, under the eyes of the authorities. They were bold enough in these locations and at this time of day to wear two-gallon 'belly canteens' made of sheet iron around their waist, which, when covered with the cloth of the dress, looked like pregnancy bumps. Women also concealed bottles in unplucked dead geese; note that this was mainly whisky being smuggled *out* of Scotland rather than into it.

A Mrs Watson of Auchterhouse, Tayside, was regarded as one of the finest makers of illicit whisky. Distillation of whisky had been a family activity for several generations and Mrs Watson had been active in the process since childhood. Following the death of her husband when she was in her early 30s, Mrs Watson continued her practices for more than three decades in the nineteenth century. Another Auchterhouse woman, Jeannie Gray, had a still concealed beneath her kitchen and the whisky was hidden in the woodpile. While the excise officers watched the woodpile in anticipation of retrieving the spirit, the women of the community were distributing the whisky concealed in the false bottoms of the milk pails they carried and in bladder-skins beneath their skirts.

There was also Mary McRae, a widow who operated an illicit still on Kishorn Island, Ross-shire, and a Knapdale woman, known as 'Sarah of the Bog', who concealed her smuggling activities by practising necromancy. The people of the district were very superstitious and to encourage her favour they provided peat, potatoes, and meal. Legend has it that she cultivated the image of being a witch, keeping the excisemen of Oban away from her door. It seems 'this was still being talked about in Oban decades after Sarah's death, showing her enduring legacy in the town'.[11] Growing old, and having acquired a taste for whisky, Sarah took too large a dose from her keg one night and apparently stumbled into the fire. She was found with her head 'black as a cinder, and thus, in 1853, the last known witch was burned'.

On the same website, there is also reference to the Isle of Arran as being 'an illicit distilling hotspot' with court records showing how deeply ingrained the practice was within family dynamics. One mother informed the authorities it was 'her fault her son had been caught with bottles of whisky, as she would send them to the mainland with bottles to fund their stays there'. In the same region, 'Arranach woman Mary McKinnion was caught with a small barrel of whisky hidden under her skirts.' Despite the risks, some women 'embraced their involvement, evidenced by Mary's reflection on her imprisonment at Rathasay: "[I have] never enjoyed a holiday so much!"'

Certainly, women were part of the violence surrounding the smuggling fraternity. The use of stones as missiles thrown by crowds largely composed of women emerges as a common response in many parts of the Highlands against attempts at law enforcement. There were several detailed accounts, in newspapers such as the *Inverness Courier*, of mobs mustering against the excise men, dominated by women and girls. In March 1816, for instance, John Proudfoot, a revenue officer, was surrounded and pelted with stones, the first stone thrown by Margaret McLennan according to the *Inverness Journal and Northern Advertiser* of 27 September. They unyoked his horse from his cart when he was attempting to remove smuggled malt from a 'farm in Redcastle Ride'. Prevented from making the seizure, he instead ripped open the sacks and scattered the malt, provoking the women to follow him to another farm and pelt him with stones. He threatened the mob of women with his stick, striking McLennan, resulting in a 'cry of murder'. The women who had followed him tied him with ropes, dragged him though a dirty pool, and continued pelting him with stones, resulting in his needing medical attention for several days when he was finally rescued by two of the farm men and managed to make his way back to Inverness. The trial that followed resulted in McLennan being sentenced to twelve months' imprisonment in Dingwall jail.

In the *Shetland Times* on 26 May 1888, headed 'Smuggling in Shetland', is an anonymous account of someone looking back on his life fifty or sixty years earlier.

> Well I remember how my dear mother managed to have under her thumb a good few gallons of Hollands gin, or Schiedam, a large quantity of the finest tea (black and green), and a considerable quantity of book tobacco, and, honest woman as she was, she did not think it a sin to act the part she did, neither was it at any time thought wrong to cheat the Excise or Government … The best gin was generally in the case or square bottle, which we got for one shilling; there was an inferior kind stored in bladders at tenpence. The *modus operandi* of the bladder trick was to fill the bladders about three quarters full, and then have them, hung in pairs, equally balanced around the person. They were under the inner clothes, and were kept close to the body so that the sound of clinking or jolting (or swinkling as it was called by the natives),

was unheard … The trade done depended greatly on the locality, and the dangers to be encountered. If the coast guard officers were about, trade was dull, but if the coast was free from those sharks, a roaring trade was carried on. My mother's spirit store was the peat stack at the head of our well-kept garden. The garden was surrounded by a good stone wall … and was under lock and key. When our peats were carted home, the mistress of the house … superintended the building of the peat stack. The reason why, we dared not ask, but, we thought mother could do nothing wrong, and we were allowed to watch in silent admiration. We saw that in places a space was left and marked an enclosed, small tuft of grass or a small piece of peat. In course of time, when we became older we … saw that the grass was a bed for bottle. I knew of more than one place of concealment. The bottom of one press could slide aside, and underneath was a large chest or locker for tobacco. In another press some of the shelves could be taken out … leaving two presses of equal dimensions. Upstairs, in the best room, there was more than one concealment, between the lath and plaster of the roof of the room below, and the floor of the upper one. By a simple contrivance, some of the skirting was forced out by a spring; turning a screw you then raised some of the wood off the floor, and found a nice little locker for the tea … generally well secured and cosily wrapped up to preserve the fine flavour and aroma so much loved by my mother, who prided herself on her matchless skill in preparing a cup. The water had to be brought from a particular well, the kettle boiled on a clear fire … the tea aired at the fire and put into the hot pot, and infused to a moment, the great secret of which was the sinking of the leaves. Our house was never searched, my mother

> had never been suspected, having at all times managed her own affairs in such a way that no one, not even my father, knew how. I have seen a very large cod fish safely delivered of a very large bladder of gin. The cod was caught by a Dutchman, carefully disembowelled by the gills, and a large bladder of gin put into the empty space. All looked so very natural, that no suspicion was directed towards the poor innocent cod. At times a carpenter's tool basket was used as a commodious tobacco pouch, while the skipper's tall hat was often a convenient tea caddy.

The Kentish Gazette of 1 April 1873 carried another anonymous story entitled 'A Highland Smuggler'. This correspondent wrote about 'Elizabeth, better known all over Deeside as Lizzie Davidson' as 'the last of a daring band who, during the first quarter of the present century, carried on the traffic in smuggled whisky between the illicit distillers in the Highlands and the Sassenach consumers in the low country'. She had recently died at Kidcluny (?),

> on the estate of Durris, at the age of 76. She was the youngest and last survivor of a family of smugglers, and was born at Inver, near Balmoral, where her brothers, men of great fame in the district for agility and prowess, for many years lived in a state of chronic warfare with the officers of the Excise … The sisters frequently joined the brothers in their smuggling excursions, and, like most of their class, the whole family were nearly ruined when they found it necessary to adopt a more settled mode of life. The last Duke of Gordon kindly conferred a house and a small croft on the two sisters, where they carried on a small shop and inn till about fifty years ago, when, on the death of the elder, Elizabeth gave up business.

An account entitled 'SMUGGLING by A WOMAN AT LEITH' in the *Dundee Courier* of 27 August 1878 referred to a 'Justice of Peace Court held at Leith yesterday' when

> Ann Jones, stewardess aboard the screw-steamer *Berlin*, of Leith, was charged by the Customs authorities with having had 23lb of tobacco concealed about her on Monday last. She pleaded guilty, and was fined £100, with £2 17s of expenses, or in default, to be imprisoned until released according to law. It is expected that the fine will be mitigated if the Board of Customs are petitioned.

This feature in the *Alloa Circular* on 23 June 1880 gives an idea of how different male and female smuggling (not just in Scotland) was:

> The smuggling devices made use of by women have elicited admiration for their ingenuity. Not only do they wear false teeth, great cavities in which are filled with valuable diamonds, but they bring over diamonds set in the hollows of their natural teeth. The skilful inspector must be able to recognise the difference between a boil or contusion and a sore made by the insertion of a valuable gem beneath the skin. Mustard plasters have been torn off and hundreds of dollars' worth of laces revealed folded in a pamphlet shaped sack of oiled skin.

Ouch.

The *Dundee Courier* of 27 January 1886 gave a brief account of 'Two Women Convicted of Smuggling at the Falkirk Justice of Peace Court'. Mr James A. Henderson, JP, was presiding when

> Margaret Black or Nelson, and Isabella Black, of the firm of Nelson & Black, general merchants, Grangemouth, were brought up on charge of smuggling 55lb of foreign

> manufactured tobacco and 1.25lb of cigars. Both prisoners pleaded not guilty, and evidence was provided, at the close of which the charge was held proved, and they were fined £15 each, with £1 each costs, the option being one month's incarceration.

As proprietors of a general merchants, this supply was presumably not for personal use, and it is unlikely to have been their first offence unless they were very unlucky.

In the *Dundee Evening Telegraph* of 22 April 1895, it was confirmed that 'Many women were quite as active and daring in the traffic as the men, and … attempts to arrest certain strong limbed and fleet members of a smuggling gang' were remembered.

> On one occasion a raid was made upon a notorious bothy near Rattray, where its frequenters were wanted for more offences than the working of the sma'still [small still]. The men escaped: but two young women were seized. The mother of the gang, however, mounted a big mare, put her to the gallop, and soon led the gaugers in pursuit amongst a series of intricate morasses, through which she steered her steed, but in which those in pursuit found themselves in a perfect trap. Women used to sell whisky openly in the streets of Perth and Dundee but now used the villages adjoining, where they had no difficulty in securing runners, and very frequently women offered their services for that purpose. In many cases the women bought it from the smugglers and took the risk of running upon themselves. At one time the coopers turned out kegs adapted in size for women carrying on their backs, in creels, or in sacks. If they chanced to see the gaugers while carrying the kegs they used to sit down the roadside and endeavour to cover the kegs with their skirts. The gaugers soon discovered this dodge, and never hesitated

> to deprive them of their treasure by methods far from agreeable. Milk pails with false bottoms were often used. The uninitiated saw the strapping country lass with her pail and milk openly displayed, never suspecting that under the milk there was a good supply of whisky. The tinkers exercised all manner of ingenuity many a time in making flagons for running purposes. However, bladder-skins from different animals were by far the favourite articles … for smuggling by the female runners of Angus from the Strathmore [Valley] and Sidlaw Hills … An immense amount of whisky was run in this way, and there are many still alive who were engaged in the bladder-skin trick. On one occasion a notorious old hand was seized by an officer, who proceeded to search her in very rough-and-ready style. In a twinkling, she produced a loaded bladder-skin from beneath her dress, brought it with a bang over his face, and drenched and blinded him with the rank and fiery contents.

The Banffshire Advertiser of 18 June 1896 harks back to 'The Old Smuggling Days', reporting an event in about 1820 when a quantity of gin, brandy, and tobacco was landed at Portlong on the Moray coast.

> It was hid in the drain that still carries the water across the road. There was a considerable number of casks in all. Information was given, and the King's men came from Sandend [a small fishing village] and seized the whole. The bystanders were so obliging as to help to carry the casks to the boats. In spite of the vigilance of the officers, however, one of the casks found its way to the Crannoch Hill instead of to Sandend. On such occasions fierce conflicts sometimes occurred between the preventive men and the crowd.

Here the writer mentions other similar incidents involving local women:

> The Cullen gauger once discovered fourteen half-ankers and one anker of gin hid near where the United Presbyterian Church now stands. He sent off east and west for assistance, but a crowd, especially of women from nearby Seatown, was soon on the scene. One woman tried several times to snatch off a half-anker cask, but the gauger's staff came smartly down on her head. At last, she succeeded, and got into the crowd … A well-understood system of signals warned the inhabitants of the parish of Deskford of the approach of the gaugers. Betty Dougal, from the height opposite Squaredoch [a house in Deskford] hoisted a sheet on the end of her stack of peat, and soon the news was telegraphed from point to point till it spread all over the parish …
>
> An ingenious device once saved the farmer of Mid Skeith from the consequences of a seizure. Betty Dougal's sheet was hoisted, when he had an exceptionally large quantity of malt on hand. He filled a number of sacks with it, and carted them off to the field, and, as it was seed time, he had the sacks placed at regular intervals all over the field. The gaugers soon arrived, saw the sacks very orderly placed, and passed them without suspicion.

On another occasion, two Glenlivet wives were

> nearing Cullen with a horse and cart. Meeting Robert Leighton, they asked him what they should do if they met the gauger. 'Fill your lap wi' stones,' said Robert, 'and stone him.' Soon after they met Randal Macdonald, and faithfully carried out Robert's injunctions. Randal was forced to retreat, and before he could return to the scene,

young stout fellows had the smuggled whisky carried off to a safe spot, and all he found when he returned to the place was the empty cart.

So, women in Scotland, perhaps more so than elsewhere in the UK, commonly used violence when deemed necessary – until the increased border patrols by excise officers eventually made smuggling too risky for both sexes.

There is a lengthy poem on the website of the National Library of Scotland called *The Female Smuggler*, dated 1850 but unauthored, about 'young Jane' of which the following is an extract:

With her pistols loaded she went on board,
By her side hung a glittering sword,
In her belt two daggers – well arm'd for war,
Was the female smuggler, who never fear'd a scar.
Not far they sail'd from the land,
When a strange sail put them all to a stand;
Those are sea robbers, this maid did cry,
The female smuggler will conquer or die.

Exactly! Although this same poem indicates the cheapest and easiest form of disposal and control of the nineteenth-century female offender was to marry her off to a respectable citizen…

If you pardon that maid – said the gentleman,
To make her my bride is my plan:
Then I'd be happy for evermore,
With my Female Smuggler,
said the bold Commodore

Chapter Thirteen

Wales and the Isle of Man

IN WALES, AS elsewhere, the need merely to survive propelled whole families, including wives, mothers, sisters, daughters, and even grandmothers into the realms of what some historians would describe as 'social crime', i.e. activities such as wrecking, smuggling, and poaching which were effectively legitimised by popular opinion as being a necessity. For women living adjacent to the

> treacherous sands and shallow waters of Cefn Sidan, to the east of Carmarthen Bay, wrecking, for instance, was a way of life. There, as in other coastal locations, they, along with family and friends, braved storms and heavy seas in order to pillage wrecks, the contents of which they saw as being theirs by right. At such times, the fever-pitch excitement and danger led to discoveries of alcohol being immediately and avidly consumed.[1]

Newspapers reported hundreds of men and women being reduced to drunkenness when the Norwegian brig, *Bergetta*, lost her cargo of wines and spirits on Cefn Sidan Sands in 1817. It seems that besides openly defiant and aggressive direct action, women behaved

> more covertly in silent protest against unpopular taxes and tariffs by using stealth and furtive, deceitful ruses to trick authority figures. Bailiffs, excise and revenue officers and police constables who represented higher authority took the brunt of women's deceit. When hiding smuggled contraband of gin and tobacco from searching

> revenue officers, women in Newport, Pembrokeshire, used the traditional female trick of feigning imminent childbirth or at least advanced pregnancy in the hope that male authority figures would beat a retreat from such a traditionally female-orientated concern … one girl at Solva [on the Pembrokeshire coast] was caught red-handed illicitly brewing her own smuggled malt for her wedding day.[2]

There were certainly some enterprising women in Wales.

According to Platt's *Smugglers' Britain*, the gently curving beach at Rhossili was a natural landing spot. Smuggling continued here long after it was stamped out elsewhere by the 'stationing there of a preventive boat and a force of eight stout Sea Fencibles'. (A part-time organisation recruited from fishermen and boatmen, under the command of naval officers, formed for local defence and mobilised when needed.) However, by 1805, the various preventives had realised what was going on at Rhossili, and had 'become a little more watchful'. There were various clashes on the sands, some violent, with women 'assisting the men by throwing stones, sometimes injuring Customs officers' and usually featuring a prominent smuggler called William Stote. One story concerns two customs officers who asked Mrs Stote for

> stabling for their horses. She realized that they had probably come to search for a cargo of run spirits that were concealed nearby, so she delayed them with a drink. When they commented that the spirits were too strong, she topped up their glasses from the kettle on the stove. This, however, also contained spirits, and the customs men soon fell asleep. At this point Mrs Stote was able to raise the alarm, and the hidden contraband was dispersed.

The Stote family lived in a cottage at Middleton, but perhaps William Stote would not have been so 'successful' without his wife.

Another member of the Stote family appears in the same period: Isaac Stote was arrested after a similar affray, and his wife, Mary, was issued with a subpoena to give evidence at his trial but she returned it to the customs officer with 'a suitably impudent message'.[3]

On 12 April 1804, Lieutenant Sawyer of the Sea Fencibles, with a customs officer and his sons, pounced upon the farms of Great and Little Highway on the Gower Peninsula, renowned for smuggling activities. These farms, and the Beaufort Inn at Pwll Du nearby, were effectively staging posts for gangs of smugglers. The officers found a huge pile of casks in the farmyard of Little Highway which the officers would have to remove, but needed help to do this, so another fourteen Sea Fencibles were called upon. Local wagons were brought, thanks to threats, into service to remove the casks. But it seems everyone in Gower was aware of what was happening and a large crowd of men and women surrounded the casks, and the officers, using 'violent means' to retrieve what they could before it was hauled onto the wagons, drinking as much as they were removing. 'Nor was it only men who indulged to excess but the women in the crowd were equally as eager to obtain it', and some of these women, having 'secured a seven gallon cask of raw spirits immediately took it to a neighbouring field where they indulged in a drunken debauch'! These remote Gower farms were among hundreds involved in smuggling, and that one night of plunder resulted in the remaining goods being seized totalling '1500 gallons of brandy, 1000 gallons of gin, 330 gallons of brandy, and 15 gallons each of port and sherry'.[4]

In 1805, two officers travelled to the small beach-side village of Marcross in the Vale of Glamorgan, intent on serving a summons on the 'wife of Thomas John for smuggling'. They met up with John outside Marcross walking beside a horse upon which his wife was seated. 'Evidently her garments were covering more than a woman's dress is entitled to do.' The officers were suspicious and ordered her to dismount, revealing three small kegs of brandy in a bag beneath her 'robes'. Mrs John was lucky because the revenue officers were compassionate enough to take into account her eight children, which meant she escaped punishment.[5]

Another wife features in a smuggling story of treachery and loyalty dating from 1825. This was at Swanlake, an area only accessible from the Pembrokeshire coastal path or by boat, where a local man confided in his wife that 'a local smuggler' referred to only as 'Mr J' had temporarily stowed barrels in their cellar. The following day the wife went downstairs, counted the barrels, and set off to inform the local customs officials, hoping for a reward of some £200. En route through Manorbier, she told a friend of her plan, who in turn told 'Mr J' himself. 'The smuggler rallied his troops, the Swanlake house was cleared within an hour or so, with the contraband being transported to Sunny Hill [inland] and elsewhere. The reactions of the customs officers at their discovery – or lack of it – were not recorded.'[6]

Later in the century there were reports of smuggling by female passengers on regular pleasure steamers. In 1879, at Penarth, a case of two women smugglers was reported in the *South Wales Daily News* (8 Feb). Described as 'two washerwomen' they were convicted of smuggling tobacco and cigars from the steamer *America.* 'The master made enquiries regarding the fine inflicted on the women and very good naturedly proceeded at once to the gaol, paid the money and obtained their release.' On Feb 15, *The Pontypridd District Herald* names them as Mrs Mary Ann Nelson and Mrs Emma Jones, 'charged at Cardiff before Mr Corbett' having 'concealed the cigars in their petticoats, but some of them dropped and the circumstances were observed by a customs officer'. The fines were detailed as £1 14s 3d single value and duty for Nelson, and £1 11s 7d for Jones.

Isle of Man

According to Platt's *Smugglers' Britain*, much of the untaxed brandy 'quaffed on Anglesey' came into Britain via the Isle of Man. Due to its convenient offshore location, the Isle of Man became an important centre for illegal contraband throughout much of the fifteenth and sixteenth centuries. The government at Westminster attempted to legislate against such trade with the Smuggling Act of 1765 – known locally as the Mischief Act – which had quite an impact in the eighteenth and nineteenth centuries. Also, the final sale of the Island by the Duke of Athol to England in 1825 virtually ended the trade, its reputation as a smuggling hotspot ending, much to the outcry of the Manx people. But the smugglers just shifted their operations elsewhere with Guernsey and Flushing in Holland being other preferred ports. A popular song at the time declared:

> The babes unborn will rue the day
> That the Isle of Man was sold away;
> For there's ne'er an old wife that loves her dram
> But who'll lament for the sale of Man.

There are, nevertheless, a number of smuggling stories in the *Cumberland Pacquet* well after this date, so the men had certainly not given up on their trade. One specific reference to women, however, is on 2 December 1828 in connection with a niche product, the early nineteenth-century version of the smartphone, given the portable information it contained: the almanac. The feature is frustratingly brief:

> Several hundred almanacks, without stamps, have lately found their way into this port from the Isle of Man, for the purpose of being circulated in England, to the injury of the Revenue and the fair dealer, and in defiance of the existing laws on this subject. They are, we understand, publicly carried about, chiefly by female hawkers, and retailed at one shilling each.

Possibly even more relevant, on 5 October 1847, a feature appeared in the *Kentish Gazette* under the heading of 'A Smuggler'. As this also refers to smuggling out of the Isle of Man rather than into it, the reference throughout to 'a Boltonian' and 'his good lady' on a 'pleasure excursion' to the Isle of Man seems to be a reference to the Bolton in Massachusetts rather than Lancashire! But the reference to his 'good lady' and her involvement make the story worth telling. So, the unnamed Boltonian was

> drawn to the dexterity employed by custom house officers in preventing outward-bound passengers taking from the Isle brandy, etc., at too cheap a rate, he determined on trying his hand with some of these gentlemen, and to see whether he or they were most expert. Accordingly, on the day of his departure from the Island, he proceeded to the pier with a trunk containing a quantity of clothing but something more, to wit, a stone bottle filled to the brim. Just as the steamer was expected to start, the Bolton gentleman was at a short distance carrying the trunk, his spouse being little in the advance. When about to step on the packet he was accosted by one of the closely-watching individuals, who desired him to step back with his trunk into the searching-house. 'After feeling in the trunk for some time' apparently with no concern for the pristine nature of some of the clothes a cold substance was found, which proved to be the very bottle. The taster was called upon to perform his part of the business, but how great his disappointment when, instead of real cognac presenting itself to his tongue, the saline flavour of the bottle's contents assured him that nothing more or less was in the vessel than a quantity of liquid, such as abounded in the Irish Sea! … off the cunning boy set to the boat full of glee, at having, after all, outdone the officer. This he had managed by causing a quantity of the real stuff to be placed in the pockets of his wife, which, in consequence of the officer's attention being distracted by the trunk, escaped detection.

On the manxliterature.com website there is a relevant, though to some extent fictionalised, account of a Kitty Caveen, in love with a young revenue officer (John Tate), although her father, Jimmy, 'kept himself in touch with both revenue men and smugglers. The latter he termed respectable traders.' When Old Caveen and his daughter were returning home one night they overtook Tate 'sauntering along the road leading to the beach. "Good evening, Mr Caveen," said Tate, respectfully raising his cap to Kitty.' Tate admitted that his men were 'stationed along the cliffs' and he intended to watch the 'old cave' (at the shore end of the glen at Port Soderick, a few miles from Douglas) that he suspected was being used by 'a band of smugglers'. Kitty followed him to where he had discovered a new cave, branching off the old one where he 'perceived what he thought to be a glow-worm. On closer examination it proved to be a light coming from a small hole in the ground … "Putting my ear to the hole, I could hear voices murmuring below in a foreign language, which I believe to be French. I will soon find out, for I intend to spy on them in the cave."' He gave Kitty his watch and pistol with instructions that if he was not back in half an hour, she should fire one barrel to signal his men that he needed assistance. Kitty reluctantly agreed and Tate easily reached the entrance of the inner cave because the guard was 'dead drunk'. He discovered

> small kegs of French brandy and other contraband goods … stacked along the sides … but had not gone far before he heard footsteps and voices coming in his direction. Looking round for some suitable place to hide in, he found nothing but bare rocky sides. There was nothing to do but return to the outer cave and hide among the smuggled goods.
>
> He was just emerging through one of the narrow places on his way back, when he was suddenly seized and gagged, but not without a struggle.

The other smugglers arrived on the scene and Tate, who understood French, 'heard with horror that he was to he tied to a stake and burnt, in revenge for having captured some members of their gang the year before. They carried him to the outer cave, bound him to a barrel filled with stones, and began to heap gorse and barrel staves round him', but he then heard the faint echo of a gunshot, stopping the smugglers in their preparations. While some smugglers began to run, the French captain declared he was going to avenge the death of his brother (at the hands of the revenue) by burning Tate to death.

> So saying, he applied the torch to the gorse; but at that moment a report rang out from the other side of the cave, and the smuggler's captain fell face forward on the fire he had kindled. Two of his gang dragged him out, just as Kitty bounded in. Picking up a knife, which one of the smugglers had dropped, she cut at the cords that bound her lover, who was soon dragged out of danger. Tate's men now came rushing in, and chased the smugglers to the water's edge, discharging their pistols at them. Too late, however, for the smugglers were well out to sea in their small boats to a schooner which was seen bearing in towards them. The only reply they got to their pistol volley was a hard mocking laugh.[7]

So this was a story of a woman caught between her father's known activity and her law-abiding husband. She may not have been a smuggler, but she was involved in a very different way. (The couple were apparently married soon after, moving to England because of Tate's promotion – but fact and fiction are blurred.) The existence of these particular smugglers' caves, however, are confirmed by many websites.

Other than this fascinating story, the archives for the Isle of Man drew a blank when searching for women smugglers in the period covered by this book. This did not mean it did not happen, just that it went unrecorded. It should also be remembered that in 1814 official records regarding smuggling in this area stored at the Thames-side custom house were destroyed in a fire.

Finally, there is one woman, an unnamed smuggler's wife, who is the subject of what is now a traditional, undated, folk song. The idea is that it is sung to the baby ostensibly as a lullaby, but in fact it warned her husband of the presence of excise men as he was landing his boat and contraband. She knew that, as a fisherman, he was an obvious suspect so she sang in Manx Gaelic, knowing that the English excise men would not understand, but her husband would have enough warning to drop his cargo overboard to retrieve later. The lyrics were written by J. Kelly from a small village on the east coast of the Island called Baldrine, identified in chiollaghbooks.com as John James Kelly, born in 1860. This is the translation:

> See the Excise men are coming
> Sleep my little hero
> They'll be seeking wine and whisky
> Sleep my little hero
> Daddy's late and we must warn him
> Sleep my little hero
> This run he'll have naught illegal
> Sleep my little hero
> Oh the Englishmen may board us
> Sleep my little hero
> Nothing wrong will they discover
> Sleep my little hero
> Let them search in boat or dwelling
> Sleep my little hero

Chapter Fourteen

Yorkshire

YORKSHIRE'S COASTLINE WAS ideal for smuggling, with miles of deserted beaches where contraband could be landed, and caves for storage. The Bridlington Collector (employed by HM Customs) is quoted in 1851 as saying that 'no part of the coast of England affords greater facilities for smuggling than the coast of this district'. The principal smuggling ports were Staithes, Whitby, and Robin Hood's Bay, the latter regarded in the nineteenth century as the stand-out smuggling village in the area, with women and children helping to move goods inland or to Whitby.[1] Flamborough Head, near Bridlington, is dotted with caves associated with smuggling.

As the smugglers grew old, their tongues loosened, the evidence was long gone and they loved to tell the stories. One such case was an 'Aunt Peggy' who Meadley writes of in his 1890 book *Memorials of Scarborough*. She told how, in 1810, she had ridden on her husband's horse on a pillion seat. When they found themselves followed by the customs officers she dropped from the horse with a couple of half ankers of spirits. She had a few bruises, unsurprisingly given that a half anker was around five gallons, but managed to remain hidden. Eventually the preventives caught up with her husband who was of course now carrying no contraband. Meadley also writes of an old lady who had run 'numerous kegs of gin to places of safety in the town' and described her memories as being of the 'good old days of smuggling'! She pointed out that many valuable cargoes of contraband spirits were landed between Scarborough Castle and Robin Hood's Bay and ended up, with the help of local women, in many locations around Scarborough.

Scarborough is also the scene of a violent scuffle in 1822 between the preventive men and the smugglers, when William Mead was persuaded to name the ringleader. He named a well-known local smuggler, James Law, and a mob descended on Mead's house, enraged at his being an informer, with Mead ending up shooting Law in the ensuing attack. When tried the following year in York, the location chosen to avoid being mobbed by Scarborough men and women, a number of local witnesses were nevertheless called upon, including one brave girl who gave evidence that Law had threatened Mead, so that he only ended up with a manslaughter charge.

Whitby also features in stories showing that women were adept at aiding the smuggling effort with skilful subterfuge when it came to distributing the contraband. Large ships hovered off the coast and local cobles (the open, traditional boats), fishing boats or luggers (with sails) ran the goods ashore where the housewives of the town waited in loose fitting clothes. When the women returned, 'their buttons were bursting with contraband'.[2]

Nineteenth-century author Elizabeth Gaskell, a Whitby resident in 1859 when she was doing some research, remarked how the whole town supported free trade – even two local Quaker brothers who 'bought smuggled goods'. Mrs Gaskell commented on 'The clever way in which certain [Whitby] women managed to bring in prohibited goods; how in fact when a woman did give her mind to smuggling, she was more full of resources, and tricks, and impudence, and energy than any man.' Her 1863 novel, *Sylvia's Lover*, set in the fictional town of Monkshaven, a seaside whaling town modelled on Whitby, has one particularly revealing sentence: 'Everybody in Monkshaven smuggled who could, and everyone wore smuggled goods who could.' Another famous nineteenth-century author, R. D. Blackmore (*Lorna Doone*, etc.), wrote *Mary Anerley, A Yorkshire Tale*, a romance about Mary and her smuggler lover.

There were so many women involved in smuggling in Whitby that they employed a female 'searcher' by 1800 to aid the Customs Board collectors. One particular suspect, Eliza Howard, appeared to be running 'a rather nice profitable business in smuggled goods from her house' according to *Smuggling in Yorkshire*. Customs searchers found tea, chocolate, geneva, lace, and cambrics in enough quantity to confirm her status as a supplier of smuggled goods. Smith also writes of Beth Howlett, who was 'stopped alongside the quayside with tea, coffee and tobacco' in her basket, believed to have come from the *John and George*, a Newcastle collier 'that had left the port on the evening tide'. A third female, Mary O'Brian, a 'market woman' also had her home searched, with smuggled tea and geneva found, which she was believed to sell on market days, having been active in the smuggling trade 'for some time past'. Her trade in tea had been on the decline for more than a decade since the duty on tea had been slashed from over 100 per cent to just over 12 per cent. It had been what drove the smuggling trade where many Yorkshire women were concerned, with the punitive levels of taxation on that most popular of Yorkshire (and British) drinks, meaning that at one point it had cost up to thirty-five shillings a pound – whereas in Holland it was only seven pence! Smugglers seized the opportunity to buy it for next to nothing and sell for sixty times what they paid, and the trade operated from 1700 until about 1850.

Jane Bell, the landlady of the Mulgrave Castle Inn, high on the cliffs near Whitby (until coastal erosion saw its demise in 1887) was another supposedly deeply involved in the smuggling trade, thanks to the number of luggers that landed their contraband at nearby Upgang beach. She was one of many such landladies around the UK.

The port of Hull was another smuggling hotspot. For example, in July 1837, Margaret Quillash was charged with smuggling six and a quarter gallons of foreign brandy. This was concealed below a false bottom under a bed in a steam packet cabin. The false bottom certainly suggests pre-meditation and planning and perhaps frequent activity – by the steam packet employees if not by this particular individual. Such smuggling was a far cry from the traditional and romanticised image of smuggling, and there was 'little apparent glamour'.[3]

In the *York Herald* on 22 September 1860, the headline features 'Extensive Smuggling'. One reference is to a 'Josiah Sherwood, steward, and Mrs Lines, stewardess' both of whom were working on the screw steamer the SS *Normanby*. They were brought before the county magistrates, on remand, for smuggling 104lb of foreign-manufactured tobacco, and were fined £100 each, or six months' imprisonment. This shows how everyone, regardless of gender and status, appearance and profession, seemed to be tempted by the rewards of smuggling.

Hull features again in the *Yorkshire Gazette* of 21 August 1886. There is an account of a 'tailoress' called Catherine Anderson, who was fined there for smuggling tobacco in 'five pockets of her dress'. She had the ideal profession for this kind of concealment, and her fine was £6 5s 7d plus costs for smuggling 13.5lb of 'foreign manufactured tobacco'. She was obviously not expecting this outcome, for she apparently fainted on hearing the penalty. This case is reported in more detail in the *Driffield Times* on the very same day, headed 'Clever Smuggling by a Woman in Hull', giving the details of the hearing at the Hull Police Court a few days before, in front of 'Mr E. C. Twiss, the stipendiary magistrate'. She is described as 'a woman about thirty years of age, and of delicate appearance' charged with smuggling 13.5lb of tobacco 'from on board the SS *Hansa*, lying in the Humber Dock'. The customs officer on duty at the time is named as 'W. Fletcher' who stated that he was on duty 'watching the ship' when the prisoner came on shore 'with some black bread'. During the time he was examining the bread he asked her several questions as to whether she had any uncustomed goods in her possession. After some hesitation she replied, 'I will speak the truth. I have two pounds of tobacco.' He then requested her to go to the Customs' Watch Office, where she was searched by a female searcher, and 13lb of tobacco was found, the single value and duty of which was £4 5s 9d. The female searcher stated that 'the petticoat in which the tobacco was concealed appeared to be specially designed for the purpose of smuggling. There were four or five pockets in different parts of it.' Mr Twiss imposed a fine of £6 5s 7d and costs resulting in the prisoner 'on leaving the dock' falling 'in a fit'.

It was not just local women who were involved in smuggling. There was an account regarding a Mary Neilson from Scandinavia, tried at Hull Police Court in 1887. The *Hull Daily Mail* of 5 September described her as a 'Danish woman' charged with smuggling 25lb of 'other manufactured tobacco'. The stipendiary magistrate was, once again, Mr Twiss. Evidence was given by Customs Officer Lynch, who was on the Alexandra Dock 'on the arrival of the SS *Orlando* from Gothenburg', and saw the prisoner go on board. Shortly after she came ashore, and in reply to the officer's questions, she denied that she had in her possession anything liable to duty. He took her to the watch-house, and there she produced 25lb of tobacco. At first she said that she had got the tobacco from 'a carpenter', and afterwards from 'an emigrant'. A Mr Denovan (sic) acted as interpreter, and she was remanded, bail being allowed. A slightly different account of the same trial appeared in the *Yorkshire Post and Leeds Intelligence* of 9 September referring to Mary Neilson as 'a married woman, a Swede' and also details her fine which was £6 17s 6d, the single value and duty, plus costs, which she apparently paid.

On the same day, a Polly Hansen was charged with smuggling 11lb of 'other manufactured tobacco', single value and duty, £3 0s 6d. A different customs officer, Mr Connor, saw the prisoner leave the *Orlando* the night before, and on being questioned she admitted that she had 11lb of tobacco concealed under her dress. The place of concealment was described as 'very ingenious' being the 'bottom of the prisoner's dress' which was produced in court, revealing 'eleven pockets, each made to hold a 1lb package'. A busy Mr Twiss felt that 'having regard to the appearance of the dress he was inclined to think this was not the first time Hansen had been guilty of such conduct' and therefore fined her £4 10s 9d and costs, or in default thirty days' imprisonment.

Another court case detailed in the *Beverley Independent* on 26 January 1895 was described as 'Smuggling by a Woman in Hull'.

The woman was Emma King, 'a young married woman' who had been summoned at the Hull Police Court 'for harbouring on her premises, 12 Salthouse Lane, smuggled tobacco'. The Examining Officer T. C. Forth prosecuted and 'said the defendant carried on business as a general dealer at the above address'. The Commissioner of Customs was suing for treble value and duty, which amounted to £4 4s. Giving evidence, Mr Forth said that on the tenth of January he and other officers 'visited defendant's premises under a writ of assistance'. He asked the defendant to produce her stock of tobacco, and she produced 5oz tobacco 'steamed from compressed cake'. He searched the warehouse at the back of the premises and found '2lb 7oz of steamed tobacco, and 1lb 9oz of Cavendish'. The single value and duty was twenty-eight shillings. Mr Forth then said he asked Mrs King to account for the tobacco, and she said she 'bought 2lb of compressed tobacco from a neighbour the night before, and also bought the Cavendish from the same man'. This man, giving evidence, had drawn her attention to the fact that the tobacco was still warm, and had been told, 'Yes. I only steamed it this morning.' It seems there had been several complaints respecting the defendant's shop, which had been 'under observation for the last two years'. The defendant had nothing to say in response and was fined £2 2s and costs.

Tales of how the local community around Saltburn-by-the-Sea outfoxed the customs officers soon became part of local folklore and indeed feature on the BBC's website. One tale has an old woman hiding a keg of spirits underneath her voluminous skirts whilst customs officers performed a spot raid of her house. Wood's book identifies the woman as the miller's wife with a hiding place for gin near the millwheel, not far from the Ship Inn, but preventing the search by turning on the water from the 'great wheel', nearly drowning the officer. Its owner around the beginning of the nineteenth century was John Andrew – 'King of the Smugglers' – the recognised leader of Saltburn's smuggling operation for over forty years, with local justices and landed gentry profiting from his activities. He used a network of underground tunnels, which are believed to survive to this day. (Andrew was captured and imprisoned by the authorities in 1827 and died in prison seven years later).[4]

According to the BBC, a Reverend Grant wrote a sympathetic account of the area's smuggling antics, with the ladies of nearby Marske, some two miles from Saltburn, delighting in hoodwinking the officers: 'They sanded the streets at night with leaves of tea, leading the officers to believe that the contraband had gone in a certain direction and when the latter were busily engaged following the supposed track, the men of Marske were equally busy in transferring the tea to a totally opposite direction.' Even infants were not above pitching in, though unwittingly in some cases. One enterprising mother, who found herself victim of a surprise search, wrapped a jar of spirit in her baby's clothes, and walked past the guards with it cradled in her arms. This would have been very early in the century following the huge reduction of the tea tax.

It is a shame that so few records exist of the smuggling on this part of the north-east coast. It was an activity which was carried on in secret and supported often by customs officers in private. The memories of the smugglers are passed down in many cases by word of mouth. Villagers were insular and wary of customs men from the outside, so they kept their mouths shut and took the smugglers' backhanders. It was a very serious matter to be accused of smuggling and very dangerous to accuse someone of smuggling. As for the women, they were as usual protected from publicity by their menfolk, and by a general unwillingness to admit their involvement, however peripheral.

Chapter Fifteen

The USA and Canada

IN THE NINETEENTH century, smuggling into the USA and its environs was very different to the kind of smuggling that went on in the UK, especially where women were concerned. On the one hand, women were smuggling luxury goods from Europe rather than smuggling to feed their poverty-stricken families. On the other hand, the Union blockade during the American Civil War (1861–1865) hindered the passing of crucial supplies to the Confederates in the South so that women and girls, some very young, were used as blockade runners, with the Confederates using creative ways of smuggling supplies over the blockade. Even dolls were used to smuggle drugs and anaesthetics through the Confederate lines. A simple doll made of papier-mâché was used by the niece of Confederate Major General James Patton Anderson for this purpose. Initially, the South had been winning the war against the North but then the North cut the South's access to all kinds of supplies, 'including anaesthetics which were vital for the work of the Confederate medical corps, but had become limited and scarce although the need was increasing'.[1]

Dolls were probably shipped from Europe, already packed with drugs, in the hope that Union troops would not inspect toys when looking for contraband. Two dolls, called Nina and Lucy Ann, discovered to have hollowed-out heads, and kept in the Confederacy Museum, were X-rayed in the twentieth century at the Virginia Commonwealth University Radiology Department. Their conclusions

> were that the probability of the dolls being used for smuggling was very high because of evidence such as Nina's head being secured by clips instead of it being

> sewed to the body giving easy access, plus Lucy Ann's head had a gash on the back, again suggesting the necessity for easy access to items inside. It therefore seems highly likely that these dolls were used to smuggle some kind of contraband during the Civil War. Morphine and quinine were the most likely medicines being smuggled, due to the prevalence of malaria among the Confederate troops.

However, according to the Women History blog, Civil War women smugglers carried a lot more than drugs across enemy lines, i.e. weapons, ammunition and food.[2] Flowing skirts could conceal all sorts of supplies, and were often attached to the hooped frame. One Union official called them 'fashionable women spies'. One named individual, Belle Boyd, was described as a Jill-of-all-trades for the Confederacy because she did indeed carry information between generals such as Stonewall Jackson, 'becoming a courier in all but name by 1861'. Jackson went as far as crediting her with assuring some of his victories and with boosting Southern morale. After working briefly as a nurse, Belle Boyd then became engaged in blockade-running and smuggling, making good use of her skilled horsemanship and geographical knowledge. She led a network of Southern women 'creeping around Union camps late at night', when they would gather thousands of unattended swords and pistols, ending up with a whole arsenal of weapons in the steel coils of their hooped skirts. She, like the dolls, also smuggled quantities of the best treatment for malaria to where it was needed, i.e. quinine.[3]

While Belle was successful, Emma Kline, aged just 20, was less so in 1864 because she was arrested for smuggling in Vicksburg, Mississippi. She too had been part of a group of women smuggling much needed supplies *out* of Vicksburg (held by Unionists) to an area east of the Big Black River, held by the Confederacy. A photograph was published in the newspapers as a warning to other women involved with smuggling. The supposition on The Wild Geese website is that it is unlikely that Emma Kline was ever tried for her crime, but she 'probably spent some time in the Warren County jail'.[4]

After the Civil War, the products being smuggled changed from lifesaving to the practical or frivolous. It was 'fashionable smuggling' that was the most popular attraction for female smugglers. It involved European, especially French, gowns and goods such as ribbons, lace, and accessories. The influence, in particular, of Paris fashions affected business practices of dressmakers and milliners, 'who studied and copied patterns but needed to purchase fabric and trims from France to keep their clients happy'. This meant they had to travel overseas to bring back textiles, trims, and, when possible, full gowns to use as samples. Women reported to be involved were 'highly likely to be the dressmakers and milliners themselves'.

These elite providers of fashion to American women saw smuggling as a necessary risk to decrease costs (by avoiding import laws), and it also allowed them access to European fashion which increased their commercial profile as well as their profits. According to Hind Abdul Jabbar, who has written extensively about fashion smuggling, bribery between smugglers, inspectors, and members of the crews involved was 'well known' with travellers leaving money on top of illicit items in their luggage to encourage the inspector 'to look the other way'.[5] Often the loose garments became the base for other garments to be stitched onto, with pockets sewn to carry extra fabrics, and this became common practice. The US Custom House began hiring female inspectors to assist with seizures, the first arriving in 1861, changing their title to 'inspectress' in 1867.

Other items than fashion did feature, as in an account in the *Kentish Chronicle* of 16 September 1865, which told of a lady who tried to smuggle a clock across the Canada border. She had given the Canadian clock-seller particular directions to fix the alarm apparatus so that it would not strike but he actually set the alarm to make it strike at the moment he knew the lady would arrive at the custom house!

> The lady fastened the timepiece securely to her hoops and started on her homeward journey. Arriving at the

> Custom-house the officer found nothing contraband among her effects, and was passing to the next traveller when a loud wh-r-r-r was heard under the lady's skirts. The strange noise was kept up for the full space of a minute; but to the lady it seemed an hour, and she became tremulous and excited … the Custom-house officer, not daring to lay hands on the woman save in the way of kindness, obtained an iron rod, with which he felt around the crinoline for the concealed clock, and succeeded in bringing it down.

Nothing to Wear is a poem by W. B. Butler published in *Harper's Bazaar* in 1872, about Flora McFlimsy returning to the US from a shopping trip to Paris, and includes the lines:

> Her relations at home all marvelled no doubt
> Miss Flora had grown so enormously stout
> For an actual belle and a possible bride
> But the miracle ceased when she turned inside out
> And the truth came to light, and the dry goods beside
> Which, in spite of Collector and Custom-house sentry
> Had entered the port without any entry

An insight into how custom house officials in Detroit were coping is shown in an account headed 'Crossing the Border' in the *Norwich Mercury* of 30 November 1872.

> At least every tenth woman who crosses the Detroit river carries smuggled goods. Though officials at the Ferry dock are as vigilant as officers can be, what chances have they against monster hoop skirts and gigantic bustles? They cannot stop to peep under shawls, examine pockets, look into baby carts, hold a crowd on the boat, and so they must continue their work with the knowledge that

> goods are being smuggled, and that only one grand and sudden haul of their nets can trap the guilty and frighten the innocent so that they shall never dare to pursue the business.

On 21 October,

> the officers commenced about two o'clock walking fifteen or twenty women upstairs in the Customs' room, and handing them over to a woman to be searched. Every boat load which landed for about three hours was treated in the same manner – that is all the female portion. During the afternoon about 150 women were confronted by Uncle Sam, and the old man had a good deal of fun, and made some wonderful discoveries. For instance, a modest little woman, who was in a great hurry to go home to her sick child, pulled out a few pins and ten yards of English flannel fell to the floor. A tall woman who with tears in her eyes asserted that she would sooner chop her head off than think of smuggling, unfastened a pound of tea from her skeleton, and asserted that it must have been placed there by some designing person. Another indignantly denied the right of search, but after remaining a prisoner for an hour or two told the searcher to 'take it and go to grass' throwing a package of ribands [sic] and lace to the floor. A lot of calico was found on another, some velvet on another and at least ten per cent of the whole number were found to be engaged in smuggling. The officials were satisfied with confiscating the goods.

This account seems to have originated in the *Detroit Free Press*.

While women were now recognised as playing a strong role in smuggling in the USA, they had no political voice or way to affect changes in tariff reform. In one article published in 1873 entitled

'Smuggling as a Fine Art', the author comments on the motivations behind female smugglers and correlates her indifference towards cheating Uncle Sam with the lack of representation that women had in government, as they were neither allowed the right to vote nor to be part of the law-making process. It suggests that women had no choice but to devote their full attention to fashion since they were not useful in a political sense. The author's belief was that dress and deception are tied together![6]

Because professional dressmakers were so good at creating elaborate gowns for their rich clientele, they were also able to find original hiding places. Having spent years perfecting their skills, they could create the dress 'confections' admired by their upper-class clientele. Their tricks of the trade fascinated and bewildered the customs inspectors and are detailed in several nineteenth-century American journals. One example was published in *Frank Leslie's Popular Monthly*, July 1878, which refers to 'the swell milliner' as being 'adept in the art of packing, and can force a room full of silk into a Saratoga trunk. As fold after fold comes forth from its limited receptacle, both wonder and admiration are excited, that so very much can go into very little.'

The subject became quite popular in the American media. Issues of the *New York Times* from 1879 suggested that the newer trend of a fitted skirt was a 'direct result' of excessive smuggling, with the tight fit adopted to avoid the 'trouble and vexation' of undergoing a thorough examination at the hands of the searchers. *Harper's Magazine* (in an issue of 1884), referred to the illegal activities of travellers, mainly dressmakers and milliners, pointing out that the customs inspectors were faced with searching and interrogating those arousing suspicion 'without causing them offence. Inspectors learned to rely on visual clues, particularly dress, to help them. If their garments seemed to be worn incorrectly or fitted badly, this would ring a bell with the inspectors as this meant they could have been purchased for someone else, not the wearer.' One – named – dressmaker (Delia Gladstone), who had seven dresses in her trunk, came under suspicion until she tried them all on, confirming that they fitted her! She still had to pay the appropriate duty, but no more than that.

In 1880, Cynthia Westover was hired specifically to uncover female smugglers, as part of her civil service position in a customs house.[7] The New York Customs House was one institution propagating its positive image by creating new jobs for women at a time when they were in short supply: by 1888 there were twenty women hired as inspectresses for the New York Customs House, half of them unmarried.

Their job was made even more difficult by instances of male officers, crews, and stewards of transatlantic steamers who forced unwilling women passengers to 'don several valuable dresses' (according to the *Suffolk and Essex Free Press*, 11 June 1890) and conceal other dutiable articles! When the *City of Chester* docked in New York a few days earlier, custom house detectives found in one officer's locker several dresses, cloaks, and billiard cloth, valued at about £60. They had procured a tip-off from one of the women who had been scared by her involvement in a similar incident. The goods were seized, and the officer was arrested on the day the *City of Chester* started on her return to Liverpool. The custom house authorities said they had proof of his smuggling activities since he entered the service of the company eight years ago. His practice was to have women come aboard the night before the steamer sailed and take them to the stateroom, where each donned several valuable dresses. In fact, a correspondent in the *Kilrush Herald and Kilkee Gazette* of 21 June 1890 points out how men were cashing in on the popularity of fashion smuggling, claiming that the New York Customs House detectives had discovered

> an organisation of smugglers, bound by oath, among the officers, crews, and stewards of Transatlantic steamers. It has been suspected for a long time that large quantities of fine London made clothing have been smuggled regularly into New York, but no trace of the methods had

> been obtained till a few weeks ago when a considerable quantity was found concealed on board the Inman Line steamer *City of New York* ... Other dutiable articles were concealed about the apparel of the women, who, as soon as they were clear from the espionage of the Customs officials on the dock, went to certain places, where the smuggled goods were disposed of to the homes for whom they were intended [with some] carried out of the ship in bags concealed among the soiled linen of the vessel destined for the laundry.

The agent of the Inman Company published the following: 'We beg to state that it is the invariable rule of this company summarily to discharge any officer or employee found engaged in smuggling', but the women were obviously regarded as innocent.

There were also a number of accounts of fashion smuggling in the British press in the nineteenth century. One distinctive story featured in the *Dundee Weekly News* of 30 May 1891. An unnamed American widow, whose husband had died abroad, had his body returned to the US and planned an 'elaborate mourning dress, all of the materials being purchased abroad'. She was, it seems, already an 'accomplished smuggler' along with 'many of the society women of Gotham [in New Jersey]' and she had no intention of paying the duty involved. She was particularly fond of one costly bolt of silk which she felt would adorn her as 'the most stunning widow in New York'. She therefore placed this bolt in the coffin, under her husband's embalmed body. Once through customs, she buried her husband, had the silk made up into a dress and 'strutted' her way around Fifth Avenue and Broadway. The story continues with an account of her two broken engagements, blamed on the 'candidates' being told how she had used her husband's cadaver!

Another, less grisly, account appeared in *The Otley News and West Riding Advertiser* (4 January 1889). This was about Mrs Rose Ludvigh, a fashionable New York dressmaker, and her travelling companion

Bessie Montour, who brought in 10,000 dollars' worth of 'imported Charles Worth dresses' without paying duties. Rose posed as Bessie's maid, claiming that Bessie was an actress who needed the garments for performance. One investigator, however, found that some of these dresses were being sold on to high-society New York women, and the remaining garments were confiscated from their homes.

On 15 February 1890, there was an opinionated article (uncredited) on the subject of smuggling in *The Leeds Times*, headed up 'Fashionable Women get their diamonds into America by all sorts of dodges' and starting with the words 'Men and women in the higher walks of life are now the representatives of the sea rovers of a century or two ago. Women are chronic smugglers. Men are stupid in their smuggling operations and are more likely to be detected.' There is then a specific example: 'There is a lady with a wealth of blonde hair, great blue innocent eyes, and a face in which no one could discover traces of deceit. Around her waist is a Worth's corset studded with diamonds.' (Charles Worth was obviously the in-vogue designer of the time.) More generally is a reference to women who do not 'hesitate to … stow away diamonds rolled in wadding'. One woman who falls into this latter group is named as Elizabeth Howe, 'a handsome Boston lady' who had arrived

> by a French steamer. She was elegantly attired, but to the female inspectors seemed rather stout and ill-proportioned for her youthful face. They took her in charge and made a full investigation. Beneath her silk dress and seal sacque [unfitted garment with large crinoline] she wore four full suits of London make intended for her brother … nothing further was heard of the case

which suggests that she may not have been prosecuted. The article finishes with one Mary Arnold, 'a Philadelphia lady', who was 'highly indignant when taken into custody. A search resulted in the discovery of twenty-six watches firmly fixed here and there on her corset in which holes had been cut for the purpose', although again there are no details of the outcome.

The Dundee Courier of 3 August 1888 ran a fascinating article headed: 'WOMEN AS SMUGGLERS'. It quotes a *Chicago Tribune* feature about a veteran of its custom house who 'has searched more trunks in more parts of the world than any of Uncle Sam's officials', a man who had served on innumerable revenue cutters. He is quoted as saying that

> the principal smugglers of today are women. The daring of other times is unnecessary now. A Saratoga trunk properly prepared is worth more than all the dirks and cutlasses that a smuggler ever wore at his belt. I remember when I last came back from Europe, a fine young woman, exceedingly plump, whom everybody admired. The young fellows on board were infatuated, especially those who liked a stout, well-rounded girl. All the way over, she wore the same dress – blue cloth, tailor made. It fitted her, if possible, just a little bit too well … I can imagine a belle rigging herself in this when on parade at Newport, but for the deck of a Cunarder it is a trifle too chic. At quarantine, after the health officer came aboard, a boat pulled out from Fort Hamilton and wanted to take my charmer off. I touched her on the shoulder: 'You can't leave this vessel,' said I 'until we reach the Battery.' 'Who are you?' she demanded, turning pale. 'I'm a Custom-house officer,' said I, 'and as soon as we land I shall have you searched.' She hadn't the heart to say much. Still pale, she sat down, licking her lips and looking round to see that nobody had heard us. 'Officer,' she said at length, 'how much will make it square?' 'Well,' said I, with a sly glance at her shapely figure, 'I don't know how much it took to make it round but I guess there is about 5000 dollars' worth of lace and jewellery in the

> lining of that dress of yours.' And so it was. When the women-searchers had undressed her she looked like a scarecrow – old, haggard, a regular skeleton. The haul just doubled my estimate.

The custom house officer continued to reminisce about his experiences, talking about strange hiding places, like fruit,

> perhaps the handiest covering. Who would look for cigars in a pumpkin or for snuff in a turnip? Yet pumpkins and turnips, carefully lined with wool, have brought any amount of tobacco into this country … Jewellery generally travels in boot-heels. The boots are specially made in Paris. I remember unscrewing one of those heels in New York. A shower of brilliants fell all around me. There was a fortune in that little shoe … At Liverpool they told me how, on a vessel coming from Stettin, in the Baltic, they found cigars in casks of camomile flowers … cigars in cases of glue … tobacco in potato sacks … tea lying on furze bushes waiting to be shipped … tobacco stowed away in loaves of German bread, to say nothing of a boat drifting in the harbour with fifty barrels of snuff in it … And the ladies are born smugglers. They think it no harm to defraud Uncle Sam. They are rabid free-traders. They will hide jewellery in their hair, wrap laces round their bodies, pack their husband's cigars among their petticoats. The commonest device of the feminine smuggler is the false-bottomed trunk. In a box filled apparently with cheap ginghams and calicoes may lie the finest dress … No matter how honest the woman, she loves to fill her trunks with new dresses for her friends.

There are other accounts of women who were not just smuggling fashions. *The Otley News* (above) has further; one of a 'stout, elderly female' who was searched on arriving in the US because her young companion had been found to be hiding lace and uncut diamonds – and, more unexpectedly, revealing a number of very expensive violins beneath her skirts! Another was hiding gold English watches in her underwear, 'requested' by several friends, and yet another hid precious stones in her elaborate head-dress. Enterprising indeed. *The American Register* of 13 November 1887 has an account of two ladies who smuggled cigars for male members of their family, but had to stand all the way home from Paris to New York to avoid crushing them!

Another article, in the *Leicester Daily Post* of 13 October 1891, details 'How Women Smuggle' from another point of view, that of the inspectresses in the employ of the New York Customs House. These women had

> to work all hours and in all weathers whenever ships come in, and are well paid. One day last summer I made the acquaintance of one of these female detectives, and she enlightened me on various points connected with the smuggling trade. She was a tall, well set-up, well dressed, comely young woman of somewhat weather-beaten complexion. 'Now tell me,' said I, 'have you any means of recognising or suspecting a woman smuggler, apart from her bulky appearance?' 'Certainly … she has a peculiar way of biting her lips and trying to look innocent that is unmistakable. Yes, you bet, I have some queer experiences sometimes. Look at that scar on my wrist. It's a little memento of a black-eyed French woman, who tripped off the steamer wearing a rather marked crinoline. I searched her, and found a lot of valuable French china concealed under her skirt, and as she volunteered to cut the strings by which the articles were attached, I lent her my scissors, and no sooner had she got hold of them than she gave me a gash across the wrist. She's in prison now.'

The interviewee continued:

> Very little false hair has been worn until lately, but since the pyramid coil and the Cadogan coiffure [chignon] became popular, switches are in demand, and the hair smugglers are on the alert. The choicest supplies come from the convents of Germany, and command very high prices … we inspectresses do a great deal of feeling whenever a costume has a thicker appearance than the regulation umbrella skirt. When the *Augusta Victoria* came in on her last August trip a very business-like young woman came over the gang plank. She was assisted to the retiring room, and relieved of a little silicia [tiered and draped] skirt with a well-stayed belt fringed with switches of the most beautiful human hair imaginable. There were tresses of gold, blonde, bronze brown, jet, and cow's-tail-red – that most fashionable of all shades – all clean and fine as silk, without a trace of dye or bleach, and worth at least twenty dollars a switch. The skirt weighed forty pounds, which accounted for the deliberate pace of the unhappy adventuress …
>
> I remember having my suspicion once aroused by the restlessness of a slightly-built, girlish looking woman. She had a very thin neck, slender feet, arms as thick as a pair of spermaceti candles, and the figure of a Juno. On being searched the goddess-like figure came off, hips and all. But it was very precious. It consisted of superb Florentine mosaics, Etruscan jewels, pearls, and fine old cameos, smothered in rose, point, and Portuguese lace. The padding alone was worth a lot of money … One fine afternoon a steamer came in, bringing, among other passengers, a man and wife suspected of trying to smuggle a quantity of pearls and unset stones. I searched the woman's person in an improvised custom office on

> the pier. Every consideration was shown to the fair tourist, who submitted graciously, and appeared so innocent that I was about to release her. The woman was effusively grateful, and fell to thanking me. She called me 'a perfect lady,' said she had 'been treated perfectly lovely' etc. Her compliments were so profuse that I resumed operations … In the side gore of the tourist's under-waist was found a long, narrow bag, made of the same material as the garment, which was literally stitched with whole pearls. The gems were pierced for necklaces, strung on fine linen threads, and the threads were basted together as closely as the lovely stones would permit.

This account does not give the outcomes of these finds.

In Volume 49, No. 3 of the *Tredyffrin* (Pennysylvania) *Easttown History Quarterly* there is a story from an 1892 *New York Times* report of attempted smuggling by two sisters from Devon. It seems that customs officers in New York examined

> four trunks which were owned by sisters Miss E.R.B. Simmons and Miss M.E. Simmons, which were searched after the landing of the steamship S.S. *City of Paris*. The trunks were found to contain Paris-made ballroom dresses which had not been declared. The customs officers also found other contraband goods, including rings valued at about $2,500.00, in the trunks.

This seizure was apparently the result of a 'tip received by the customs officers from Europe'. The *New York Times* article stated that the trunks were

> found to contain new costumes, and the Misses Simmons were asked to show the bills from the dressmakers. In producing these papers one of them also dropped another

> receipt from Maret Frères of Paris for a fifteen-hundred-franc ruby ring, set with diamonds. Miss Simmons wore a ruby ring, but H.C. Clark, an appraiser, decided that it was a comparatively cheap affair, and an inspectress found the other ring, with a pearl ring as well, in a little pocket in her dress.

Smuggling into Canada could be from much nearer home. *The Toronto Daily Mail* of 20 May 1893 details the smuggling of a 'coloured wrap with three capes' by a young Canadian woman, purchased in Port Huron in the States and smuggled into Sarnia in Canada. A Canadian officer had accosted her on arrival securing an immediate confession, resulting in a fine, although the news item expresses the concerns of Port Huron residents who had felt a real drop off in trade as a result of the duty anyone from Canada – and elsewhere – were 'liable to pay with regard to goods such as boots and shoes'.

In the *Lincolnshire Chronicle* of 27 June 1899 is a tale of a 'Lady Smuggler Trapped' with 'one of the largest seizures of dutiable articles ever recorded' by customs officials from the American liner *St Paul* which had docked at New York. The property, which comprised a

> valuable assortment of diamonds, jewellery, laces, etc, valued at $50,000, was brought ashore by one of the passengers, Mrs Phyllis Dodge, a handsome and fashionably-dressed woman residing at 80th Street. Mrs Dodge went abroad a month ago, and detectives in the service of the Treasury Department shadowed her to Paris, and cabled information of her extensive purchases, and probable attempt to smuggle. When Mrs Dodge arrived at New York she made a sworn declaration of the contents of her baggage, but as she failed to mention the dutiable property, it was immediately seized. Forty thousand dollars' worth of diamonds and jewellery alone was found in a small handbag she carried. Mrs Dodge

> vainly protested that she had worn the jewellery, and that it was not dutiable. The seizure created great sensation. Mrs Dodge was not arrested, but was allowed to drive home with her maid.

Whether she was fined, or prosecuted, is not recorded.

It certainly appears that female smugglers into the US and Canada in the nineteenth century did not resort to violence in the main and did not put themselves at risk of injury or worse. They were also generally more well-heeled, even genteel, more interested in fashion than tobacco and alcohol, and not always working for or in cahoots with men, often acting independently. So, very different smuggling stories with regard to women in the USA, but an insight into how smuggling played its part on both sides of the Atlantic.

Chapter Sixteen

Europe

INTER-COUNTRY SMUGGLING WAS widespread in Europe, usually done overland, obviously, without the need for using some kind of watercraft. Some sources mention Spanish female smugglers in the early 1900s travelling on steam trains between San Roque and Ronda peddling their contraband wares.

Spain had imposed tariffs on foreign-manufactured goods to protect Spain's own fledgling industrial enterprises including a heavy tax on tobacco, one of the government's principal sources of revenue. Therefore, inevitably, Gibraltar became a centre of intensive smuggling activity because of its cheaper tobacco and goods. The depressed state of their economy caused smuggling to become a mainstay of their trade. The mid-nineteenth-century Irish traveller Martin Haverty described Gibraltar as 'the grand smuggling depot for Spain'.[1] In a letter to Prime Minister Lord Palmerston, General Sir Robert Gardiner described the daily scene:

> From the first early opening of the gates there is to be seen a stream of Spanish men, women and children, horses and a few caleches, [light carriages] passing into the town where they remain … until about noon. The … carriages and beasts, which come light and springy into the place, quit it scarcely able to drag or bear their burdens. The Spanish authorities bear part in this traffic, by receiving a bribe from every individual passing the Lines … Some of these people take hardware goods, as well as cotton and tobacco, into Spain.[2]

The problem was eventually reduced by imposing duties on imported goods.

It seems that Gibraltar was one of the top smuggling hotspots in the nineteenth century, with this comment in the 1879 Gibraltar directory: 'the traveller will see' close to the road groups of men and women 'packing themselves and each other with cotton and silk goods, tea … tobacco, and other contraband'. These had to escape search 'by the carabineros' (revenue officers) or 'it would not be worthwhile to run the risk'. Women smugglers were known locally as matuteras.[3]

In the *London Morning Post* of 13 September 1890 is a letter headed 'Smuggling in Gibraltar' where a 'retired soldier' points out that a previous article

> hardly conveys the idea of the very open manner in which smuggling tobacco into Spain was practised a short time ago, and is, I believe, still carried on. When I was there I could see almost any day men and women carrying parcels of it through the British lines on to the neutral ground. There they would sit down and proceed to stow away in all parts of their person the tobacco in small packets, tying them round their legs, filling the bodies of their dresses, etc, with them. This was done openly, though the road was patrolled by the Spanish Guardia Civilia; they would then face the Custom House officials with impunity. On the steamer which runs from Gibraltar to Algeciras I have seen the same thing, and out of curiosity watched to see how the smugglers would fare on landing. The official would go through the farce of running his hands' over their clothes, and though naturally he must have felt the packets concealed there would let them pass on.

The Cotton Factory Times of 30 October 1896 confirmed that as

> Gibraltar … is a free port … a good deal of smuggling goes on across the Spanish lines. A common plan is for a

> Spaniard to take a lot of mongrel dogs with him into the town, tie tobacco round their bodies and send them off home at full gallop to take their chance of escaping the sentinels' rifles. It was suspected that a good deal of lace was being carried across duty free. There was a lady in the habit of driving about with an invalid husband in the carriage, who seemed to 'devote the utmost attention to her wifely duties. Her conduct was admired until some suspicion falling on this exemplary person, the carriage was stopped and searched. The sufferer proved to be a dummy made up entirely of bundles of lace.

These are a few lines from a nineteenth-century Spanish fandango, translated from Spanish:

> I'm the smuggler
> I get so rough
> I'm going with my spouse
> to Gibraltar Square.

One Spanish woman worthy of inclusion is Eliza Welsh, born 1806, who lived with a Captain Graham in her youth, and convinced his crew on HMS *Devonshire* to turn to piracy, apparently a successful ploy. This is quite a step up from mere smuggling in that she joined in Graham's more violent piratical activities. He and his officers were eventually captured and hanged in London, and Eliza was imprisoned in Tasmania, with other seamen, where she spent twenty years, after which she married another naval captain, hence her surname of Welsh.[4]

France was also a prime centre for smuggled goods. Charles G. Harper quotes from an 1816 copy of *The Times* in his book *The Smugglers* regarding the smuggling of 'cotton stockings and thread lace into Dieppe using large stone bottles with the bottoms knocked off, filled with merchandise, false bottom used, mouth left open so that any challenge could be met with the response that the bottles were going to be refilled at the spirit merchant'. He also wrote of lace smuggling which

> exercised great fascination for the ladies, who – women being generally lacking in the moral sense [!], or possessing it only in the partial and perverted manner in which it is owned by infants – very rarely could resist the temptation to secrete some on their way home from foreign parts. The story is told how a lady who had a smuggled lace veil of great value in her possession, grew very nervous of being able to carry it through, and imparted her anxiety to a gentleman at the hotel dinner. He offered to take charge of it, as, being a bachelor, no one was in the least likely to suspect him of secreting such an article. But, in the very act of accepting his offer, she chanced to observe a saturnine smile spreading over the countenance of the waiter at her elbow. She instantly suspected a spy, and secretly altered her plans, causing the veil to be sewn up in the back of her husband's waistcoat.

Presumably this was successful.

'A Smuggling Adventure' is how the *Newry Examiner and Louth Advertiser* of 27 March 1852 head their account:

> A gentleman, holding a high official position in the courts of law in Paris … went, in company with his wife, on a tour pleasure in Belgium. After having travelled through this interesting country, they were returning home by the railway, the husband with his mind quite at rest, like man blessed with an untroubled conscience, while the lady felt that uncomfortable sensation which arises from the recollection of some imprudence, of a dread of some approaching danger. When they were near the frontier,

the lady could no longer restrain her uneasiness. Inclining herself towards her husband, she whispered to him 'I have lace in my portmanteau – take and conceal it, that it may not be seized … it is beautiful Malines lace, and has cost a great deal.' Her husband told her it was impossible and he could not do it. 'On the contrary, it is very easy' was the reply. 'The lace would fit the inside of your hat.' 'But do you recollect,' rejoined the gentleman, 'the position I occupy.' 'But recollect,' said the wife, 'that there is not an instant to be lost, and this lace has cost me 1,500 francs.' During the conversation, the train rapidly approached the dreaded station. Imagine the consternation of the worthy magistrate, who had been always in the habit of considering things with calm and slow deliberation … overcome and perplexed by his difficulties, and losing all presence of mind, he allowed his wife to put the lace into his hat, and, having placed it on his head, he forced it down almost to his ears, and resigned himself to his fate. At the station … the gentleman concealed his uneasiness as best he could, and handed over his passport with an air of assumed indifference. When his position as judge became known, the officials of the custom-house immediately hastened to tender their respects and declared they considered it unnecessary to examine the luggage … of one who occupied such a high and important situation in the State. Never had the magistrate more sincerely valued the respect attached to his position…

While a severe examination was passing on the property of the other passengers, the head of the custom-house and the commander of the local gendarmerie … came to offer him their respects. … To their profound salutation, the judge responded immediately raising his hat with the utmost politeness … but, alas, this polite obeisance [was so rapid and involuntary that he forgot

> the contents of his hat]. He had scarcely raised it from his head, when a cloud of lace rushed out, covering him from head to foot, as with a large marriage veil. What language can describe the confusion of the detected smuggler, the despair of his wife, the amusement of the spectators, or the astonishment of the custom-house officers, at this scene? The offence was too public to be overlooked. With many expressions of regret on the part of the authorities, the magistrate was detained … After a short delay, he was allowed to resume his journey to Paris, and can easily believe that the adventure formed subject for much gossip and amusement in that gay capital.

This indicates that he – and his wife? – escaped prosecution.

On the subject of lace, french-lace.com details how only England could produce perfect 'bobbinet tulle with a hexagonal mesh' at the time. This was apparently very desirable in France, but could only be obtained as contraband! In the UK workers were breaking the looms they deemed responsible for their unemployment as part of the Luddite Revolts, but some looms were smuggled into France to produce bobbinet tulle and lace – 'an extremely valuable commodity – initially in the Nord-Pas-de-Calais region'.[5]

The heading of the *Morning Chronicle* of 8 April 1857 was 'Smuggling in Paris', regarding 'the seizure of 60,000 smuggled cigars and of a ton of smuggled tobacco, at Gravelle Saint-Maurice, near the wood of Vincennes, occupied by a Belgian, who had long been known as a smuggler, but who had always contrived not only to avoid arrest, but even to prevent his residence from being known'. When the seizure was taking place, the man arrived at the house in an omnibus, but

> seeing that something strange was going on in the house, he told the driver not to set him down at his own door as usual. His wife was, however, taken into custody. The cigars and tobacco seized were secreted in double floors,

in recesses in the walls, in a secret well in the garden … in fact, the house was fitted up with as many hiding places and trap-doors as a man can see in a Christmas pantomime. After the seizure, the officers of the indirect taxes made many searches after the Belgian, but could not discover anything of him. A few weeks back they learned that cigars similar to those which he was accustomed to smuggle had again made their appearance in Paris … the Belgian was in the habit of passing through the Barriere de L'Etoile almost every day, and they … resolved to follow him.

However, he was 'constantly on his guard' turning up and down different streets, but at last … they succeeded in ascertaining that he went to No. 26, Rue de Cormeilles, in the village Levallois, near the Barriere de L'Etoile. This house was occupied by a family deemed highly respectable, and supposed to be living on their property … A watch was set on the movements of the said family. The mother and her two daughters were accustomed to go every day to … Rue de Longchamps, at Chaillot, and as they wore tremendous crinolines, it was thought probable that they conveyed tobacco there. Yesterday a descent was effected on both houses. In that of the Rue de Cormeilles not a trace of tobacco or cigars was seen; but … secret passage leading to a garret was discovered, housing an enormous quantity of tobacco and cigars. In the house in Chaillot also a large quantity was found, as was a thin box, bearing the name of the Belgian, and containing a large sum of money, and all the man's account books and papers – the latter showing that be carried on his smuggling trade in a very methodical manner, and on a very large scale. A seizure was effected of all these objects in both places, and the three women of the family of the Rue de Cormeilles were arrested; but the Belgian was not taken. On examining the crinolines

> of the females, they were found to contain large pockets smelling strongly of tobacco, in which they, without doubt, conveyed the smuggling.

What happened to these women does not seem to have been covered in the British press, nor are they named.

The *Buxton Advertiser* of 6 April 1872 tells of

> All Paris … at present laughing over a clever smuggling device which the vigilant French octroi men [duty collectors] have just detected. The heavy duties on spirits have of course made the smuggling sisterhood (most of the smuggling now-a-days is by women) doubly eager to bring into Paris an extra quantity of the precious liquors, and this they have accomplished in a most ingenious manner, viz., by wearing zinc corsets provided with rotundities which can easily contain four or five gallons of brandy. For a time the trick succeeded admirably, but at length the officers began to be suspicious of the magnificently developed busts which contrasted oddly in some of the ladies with the inadequate necks and faces. A staff of female searchers was enrolled, and the cheat discovered.

The innovation of female smugglers was confirmed in the *Fife Herald* on 21 March 1872, referring to a 'new mode of smuggling'. This mentions the augmentation in the duty on alcohol which had led to a 'great increase of smuggling spirits into Paris, and has developed the ingenuity of the fraudsters. Hollow blocks of stone, carts with double bottoms, and bladders suspended beneath the petticoats are now quite out of date, and the women employed in the traffic have invented something new', i.e. the zinc corsets.

While the above account does not give the source of the spirits, the *Bicester Herald* of 15 November 1895 reaffirms how much tobacco was being smuggled from Belgium into France. A couple had been 'at length' arrested by the French Customs officers after 'suspicious detectives had for a considerable time travelled upon the train which runs between Paris and Antwerp'. Their vigilance was rewarded when a man and a woman, who had occupied a special compartment, threw several packages from the windows 'as they approached Creil'. They were at once arrested, while the receiver was also taken into custody. The latter had managed to get the tobacco

> into Paris in quarry stones which were scooped out in order to admit the packages. The arrested persons said that they had been carrying on their smuggling operations with considerable success for two years. They made £36 a trip, the tobacco, worth roughly three francs per kilogramme in Belgium, being sold in Paris for sixteen francs. The smugglers acted with the complicity of Belgian railway men.

The *South Wales Daily News* of 19 September 1890 seemed to be looking at the more humorous side of smuggling. It refers to

> those humble but useful officials in dark green uniforms who collect octrois, or municipal tolls and dues, at the different *entravers* to Paris ... Generally speaking, the toll-taker ... has keen eyes for bumpers, sacks, bags, and bundles. Nevertheless, he has frequently been taken in by artificially obese persons, principally of the fair sex, who conceal alcoholic supplies in their habiliments, and who, while passing the tail-gates, exert their blandishments on the officials who come to them if they have anything to declare. The toll-keeper, reassured by the answers and smiles of the fair sex, returns to the lodge, and the fiscal authorities of the city are defrauded to a considerable extent, the female smugglers having contrived to introduce numerous bottles of wine and

> spirits into the capital free of toil. A man who tried these tricks the other day at the Northern Railway station did not succeed so well as the women … The abnormally stout stranger was led to the police-station. There his coat and vest were unbuttoned, and it was discovered that he had secreted ten quarts of spirits in a pair of gutta percha [hooped] stays which he wore around his body… The stays trick is … an old dodge with the women smugglers of Paris, while tavern-keepers living in the city are often known to send trampish-looking boys and men, who are really their relatives or servants, outside the fortifications for spirits. The apparent tramps are provided with the usual gutta percha corsets or vests, which they line with bottles, and return … in the evening with impunity, their miserable looks and ragged garments precluding them from any close inspection on the part of the octroi officials.

There is one particularly notorious female smuggler from, unusually, Sweden. This was Johanna Hård, also known as Johanna Jungberg. She was widowed in 1817 and had some difficulty supporting herself, resulting in an arrest for smuggling after she sailed to Copenhagen and sold textiles against custom regulations. It seems she ran a speakeasy and lived off her smuggling when it was a 'common past-time as a consequence of the reintroduction of harsh trade importation laws in Sweden'. However, she was accused of piracy in 1823 following the attack and plundering of the Danish ship *Frau Mette*, when the crew were killed. Her co-accused testified that, while Hård had not been present during the attack, they had planned the act in her home, with her as the leading brain behind the plot. She was found not guilty thanks to lack of evidence, but three of her cohort were beheaded for piracy and murder, and one sentenced to 'forced labour'. She subsequently lived a much quieter life in Stockholm, and died in a charity hospital there in 1851 (translation of geni.com/people).

Germany also featured. For instance, in the *Ampthill and District News* of 1 April 1893, there is an account of 'a newly married couple, who had been taking a wedding trip to the Ardennes, the miniature Alps' and were returning to Germany. 'As they neared the frontier station … the young lady became curiously silent and depressed', finally revealing that she had 'some lovely pieces of fine Brussels lace' which she knew were liable for a 'large sum of money' in duty. She asked her husband to help her get through customs. He initially rebelled and objected but 'then, you see, he was only newly married, and had not yet learned to be stony-hearted. Therefore it was decided in the end that the airy fairy laces should be housed in his high hat till the station and the Custom-house were safely passed.' This has virtually the same outcome as that of the French magistrate who forgot about the lace in his hat, for 'the grateful husband, in a forgetful, fatal moment, bade the stationmaster a last farewell by lifting his hat in the orthodox fashion. In a second, a thin lovely veil of old Brussels lace fell over his face, and – and – well, you can easily imagine the rest.'

The same newspaper features 'another and more terrible discovery made some years ago … at Eydtkuhnen [now part of Russia]' where officers at the

> frontier station …were particularly prying and objectionable… It was midnight, and … two very grand Russian ladies were among the passengers on the Prussian/German side. Their boxes were of the size of lions' cages, and they affirmed with great dignity that they had absolutely nothing by the importation of which into Russia the state could turn an honest penny. But there was one officer who could not bring himself to let the trunks pass without satisfying his curiosity … One of the ladies waxing exceedingly wrath over what she said was an insult, the officer – perhaps naturally – grew the more determined to see exactly what the boxes contained. The heap of clothing, etc.,

> that was put upon the low endless table … was truly astounding. Deeper and deeper the hirelings burrowed, the elegant officers standing by, and the ladies and their maids chiding loudly from the other side of the table. And what do you think the men found deep down in the trunks? Yards and yards and pieces upon pieces of beautiful new Lyons silk. The change from haughty ire to utter annihilation on the faces of these two ladies was too painful for words.

Unfortunately, as is often the case, no outcome of the event is recorded.

The fascinating epoch-magazine.com website refers to the concealment of contraband beneath women's petticoats 'in Hamburg during the French occupation of 1809' when merchants

> employed local women to carry packets of coffee past Napoleon's officers. They were also frequently customers, turning a blind eye to the providence of cut-price goods. Illicit tea, alcohol, and tobacco graced the table of households across all sections of society including, it is rumoured, the table of at least one prime minister … Given that women were commonly involved in the management of the household budget, it is no surprise to find them implicated in the illegal economy.

Belgium had goods smuggled in as well as goods smuggled out. The website of the Bow Street Police Museum has an 1844 account, when a lady arrived by train from Prussia to Belgium with 'not less than one hundred and seventeen pairs of white stockings attached to her crinoline – all of which were confiscated … through the use of crinolines, fashionable skirts grew even wider in the 1850s than they were in the 1840s.'[6] There is also a fascinating story in the *Family Herald* magazine of 6 December 1845 which points out

> The enormous development lately given by ladies to their back hair was last week applied to smuggling purposes. A well-dressed woman was stopped when entering Belgium for concealing about 130 yards of Valenciennes lace in what is called the chignon. Since then any unusual dimension of that portion of the coiffure is strictly examined by the Custom-House officials.

Travellers to and from Italy by the St Gotthard Railway, which connects Switzerland with Italy, were given a warning in the 9 February 1884 issue of the *North British Advertiser & Ladies' Journal*.

> Smuggling, which has always been rife in the neighbourhood of the Italian lakes, is, moreover, becoming more active than ever, and the revenue officers are at their wits' end how to keep it under control. Besides the lakes and mountains they have now to watch the railway, which is calling into existence a new class of smugglers … Some of the stratagems adopted by the railway smugglers are both curious and original. Loaves of bread are gutted and filled with tobacco, game is treated in like fashion; the fragrant weed, coffee, jewellery, and sometimes lace, are hidden in hollow cabbages, pears, apples, and potatoes, in wheelbarrow handles and bedstead legs. Sheep are shorn, their bodies enveloped with the lace, and the fleece so artistically replaced almost to defy detection … the greatest adepts both by reason of their keener wit and their more voluminous garments, being women. The Custom-house officers do their best, but they sorrowfully admit that the women are really too many for them, and that they are often taken in.

Small items, such as salt, were popular with female smugglers in Europe. In Piedmont-Sardinia (Northern Italy) after the defeat of

Napoleon, a heavy tax on salt was imposed, increasing the incidence of salt smuggling which remained cheaper on the Swiss side of the border along with coffee, chocolate, and sugar, plus meat from the fertile French valleys. Sometimes there was a barter system, dependent on mutual trust, with items like butter and meat being left under a pre-arranged stone, to be exchanged for coffee and sugar, which would be picked up later. Although men often carried packs of up to forty kilos, it was the women who handled the bulk of many other items.[7]

Even books were being smuggled in the nineteenth century, especially across the border between Lithuania and East Prussia. Lithuania opposed Russia's occupation and in 1866 there was a total ban on the Lithuanian press in an attempt to 'eradicate their language and promote loyalty to Russia'.[8] Book carriers appeared with works being printed overseas and smuggled into Lithuania. There were reports of 'female smugglers dressed as beggars hiding books in sacks of cheese, eggs and bread and strapping tool belts to their waists and pretending to be craftsmen, disguising newspapers under clothes' (see *Forty Years of Darkness*). The risks were high and the borders not easy to cross with Russian security who burned any journals found. In 1897, Russia's Council of Ministers declared the ban a failure.

Although the following is obviously a Europe 'event' it is difficult to pin down which of France's various 'neighbouring kingdoms' is featured. The anecdote is from the *Sheffield Independent* of 10 November 1821 quoting 'A French Paper':

> A diligence [a large French stagecoach] was on the point of passing the French frontiers to enter the neighbouring kingdom, where several articles of French manufacture are not admitted; a beautiful female, who was a passenger, expressed her hopes that she should be enabled to smuggle a fine lace veil, which was concealed very secretly about her person. A taciturn gentleman, who was one of the passengers … said nothing, but on arrival … he, on some pretext, alighted … on entering the office, the lady received

> a hint to retire into another room, and divest herself of the lace veil which she had about her, with which request she, of course, found it necessary to comply. Resuming their seats in the diligence, the lady … broke out into a torrent of invective against the taciturn gentleman, whom she accused of having been the informer, and the other passengers joined her in heaping abuse upon him. On their reaching a considerable distance from the frontier, 'Madame,' said the gentleman, who had hitherto said nothing in return for the invectives poured profusely upon him, 'you are right; I am the guilty individual; but please tell me what was the value of the loss …?' 'It was worth nearly 100 Louis [one Louis = 20 francs], monster that you are!' said the lady in a great passion … 'Well, Madame, dry your tears, and if you will accept one of 1000 crowns [?], I am ready to offer it to you when we alight … Do not imagine, however, that my offer is the effect of remorse or conscience; I have introduced … contraband goods of the same kind, of the value of nearly 100,000 francs into this country. My denunciation against you turned aside all the suspicions … against me, and you see that only one of us has been caught, thanks to the trifling reparation which I owe you.' This explanation had immediate effect; the taciturn gentleman was then pronounced one of the honestest men in the world; and the fair traveller, quite delighted, cried out, in which she was joined by the other passengers.

(Comparing three different nineteenth-century French currencies is not an easy task, but the reader will get the general idea.)

So, European smugglers were a resourceful bunch. Their methodology – beams, quarry stones, corsets, vegetables, bedstead legs, hair – and their range of products being more than just tobacco, fabrics, and alcohol but including books, coffee, and looms. With women involved every step of the way.

Endnotes

Introduction

1. Jo Stanley (ed.), *Bold in Her Breeches* (HarperCollins, London, 1995)
2. https://core.ac.uk
3. Lieut. the Hon. Henry N. Shore, *Smuggling Days and Smuggling Ways* (Cassell, London, 1890)
4. Mary Waugh, *Smuggling in Kent & Sussex 1700–1840* (Countryside Books, Berkshire, 1985)
5. http://cornwallsmugglers.com
6. Jan Toms, *Isle of Wight Villains: Rogues, Rascals and Reprobates* (The History Press, Slough, 2012)
7. www.johnhmoore.co.uk
8. Chris McCooey, *Smuggling* (Amberley, Stroud, 2014)
9. https://customsmuseum.org
10. www.educationblog.oup.com
11. Richard Platt, *Smuggling in the British Isles* (Tempus, Stroud, 2007)

Chapter One: Cornwall

1. www.timetravel-britain.com
2. http://cornwallsmugglers.com
3. https://cornishbirdblog.com
4. Ibid.
5. Ibid.
6. http://cornwallsmugglers.com

7. Richard Platt, *Smugglers' Britain* (Cassell, London, 1991)
8. www.cornwalllive.com
9. Ibid.
10. http://cornwallsmugglers.com
11. www.burtonbradstock.org.uk/history
12. John Rattenbury, *Memoirs of a Smuggler* (J. Harvey, London, 1837)
13. http://mysticengland.freeservers.com
14. Bernard G. Wood, *Smugglers' Britain* (Cassell & Co. London, 1966)
15. www.cornwalllive.com
16. Mary Waugh, *Smuggling in Devon & Cornwall 1700–1850* (Countryside Books, Berkshire, 1991)
17. www.rameheritage.co.uk
18. Ibid.
19. www.plymouthherald.co.uk
20. Richard Platt, *Smugglers' Britain* (Cassell, London, 1991)
21. www.cornwallmuseumspartnership.org.uk
22. www.toys-toys-toys.co.uk/2013/07/looe-is-place-of-smugglers-tales
23. Richard Platt, *Smugglers' Britain* (Cassell, London, 1991)
24. http://cornwallsmugglers.com

Chapter Two: Devon

1. www.combemartinvillage.co.uk
2. Richard Platt, *Smuggling in the British Isles* (Tempus, Stroud, 2007)
3. www.salcombemuseum.org.uk
4. Mary Waugh, *Smuggling in Devon & Cornwall 1700–1850* (Countryside Books, Berkshire, 1991)
5. http://cornwallsmugglers.com
6. Ibid.
7. www.salcombehistorysociety.co.uk

8. Richard and Bridget Larn, *The Shipwreck Index of the British Isles* (Lloyds Register of Shipping, London, 1995)
9. www.woolacombemortehoevoice.co.uk
10. www.johnhmoore.co.uk/hele/smugglers
11. W. White, *White's Gazeteer and Directory of Devon 1878–1879* (W. White, Sheffield, 1879)

Chapter Three: Dorset and the Channel Islands

1. www.dorset-ancestors.com
2. Roger Guttridge, *Dorset Smugglers* (Dorset Publishing Co., Sherborne, 1984)
3. www.dorset-ancestors.com
4. Roger Guttridge, *Dorset Smugglers* (Dorset Publishing Co., Sherborne, 1984)
5. www.portlandmuseum.co.uk
6. www.dorset-ancestors.com
7. Geoffrey Morley, *Smuggling in Hampshire and Dorset 1700–1850* (Countryside Books, Berkshire, 1993)
8. www.bbc.co.uk/dorset
9. www.smuggling.co.uk
10. Carol Showell and Roger Guttridge, *Smugglers' Trails* (Red Post Books, Poole, 1997)
11. www.dorset-ancestors.com
12. David Phillipson, *Smuggling: A History 1700–1970* (David and Charles, Exeter, 1973)

Chapter Four: Essex

1. Graham Smith, *Smuggling in Essex* (Countryside Books, Berkshire, 2005)
2. Ibid.

3. Paul Wreyford, *Essex Villains, Rogues, Rascals and Reprobates* (The History Press, Slough, 2012)
4. Sheila Pitt-Stanley, *Legends of Leigh* (Leigh Society, Essex, 1989)

Chapter Five: Hampshire and the Isle of Wight

1. Jan Toms, *Isle of Wight Villains, Rogues, Rascals and Reprobates* (The History Press, Slough, 2012)
2. Keith Dyer, *Blackgang 1835* (G2 Rights Ltd., Kent, 2012)
3. www.customscowes.co.uk
4. Ibid.
5. www.shanklinhistory.net
6. Richard Hutchings, *Smugglers of the Isle of Wight* (Isle of Wight County Press, Newport, 1973)
7. Graham Smith, *Something to Declare* (George Harrap & Co., London, 1980)
8. Trevor May, *Smugglers and Smuggling* (Shire Books, Oxford, 2014)
9. Geoffrey Morley, *Smuggling in Hampshire & Dorset 1700–1850* (Countryside Books, Berkshire, 1993)
10. www.newforestexplorersguide.co.uk

Chapter Six: Ireland

1. Mary Waugh, *Smuggling in Devon and Cornwall 1700–1850* (Countryside Books, Berkshire, 1991)
2. www.waterford-news.ie
3. www.sunnybangor.com
4. www.headstuff.org
5. Adam, Robert James, *Papers on Sutherland Estate Management* (Boydell & Brewer, Suffolk, 1972)

Chapter Seven: Kent and Sussex

1. John English, *English's Reminiscences of Old Folkestone Smugglers and Smuggling Days* (John English, Folkestone, 1888)
2. Mary Waugh, *Smuggling in Kent and Sussex 1700–1840* (Countryside Books, Berkshire, 1985)
3. Geoffrey Morley, *Smuggling in Hampshire and Dorset 1700–1850* (Countryside Books, Berkshire, 1993)
4. Charles G. Harper, *The Smugglers* (Chapman & Hall Ltd., London, 1909)
5. www.margatelocalhistory.co.uk
6. R. Philp, *The Coastal Blockade: The Royal Navy's War on Smuggling in Kent and Sussex 1817–1831* (Compton Press, Horsham, 1999)
7. John English, *English's Reminiscences of Old Folkestone Smugglers and Smuggling Days* (John English, Folkestone, 1888)
8. https://lynnesfamilies.wordpress.com/aldington-smugglers
9. Mary Waugh, *Smuggling in Kent and Sussex 1700–1840* (Countryside Books, Berkshire, 1985)
10. www.bexhillmuseum.org.uk
11. http://btckstorage.blob.core.windows.net
12. Frederick Jones, *Sussex County Magazine*, Vol. 3, 1929
13. Information provided by Brian Phillips at The Keep in Brighton
14. www.osborne.house/tdprofile

Chapter Eight: Lancashire, Merseyside, and Cheshire

1. www.historyofwallasey.co.uk
2. www.wirralhistory.uk
3. Richard Ayton, *Voyage Round Great Britain* (Longman, Hurst, Rees, Orme, and Brown, London 1814)
4. https://h2g2.com
5. www.hslc.org.uk

6. www.wirralhistory.uk/redcap.html
7. www.wirralhistory.co.uk

Chapter Nine: Lincolnshire, Norfolk, and Suffolk

1. Richard Platt, *Smugglers' Britain* (Cassell, London, 1991)
2. www.benorfolk.co.uk
3. *The Sphere* magazine, 18 November 1936

Chapter Ten: London

1. Graham Smith, *Smuggling in Essex* (Countryside Books, Berkshire, 2005)
2. www.theshipslist.com
3. https://bowstreetpolicemuseum.org.uk

Chapter Eleven: Northumberland and Tyne and Wear

1. https://sunderlandglobalmedia.org
2. J. Morton on www.northeastlore.com
3. www.fabulousnorth.com
4. https://coastwalkblog.wordpress.com
5. www.fabulousnorth.com
6. www.southshieldslocalhistorygroup.co.uk

Chapter Twelve: Scotland

1. Jack Strange, *Jack's Strange Tales Collection* (Next Chapter, USA, re-published 2023)
2. https://ir.lib.uwo.ca
3. www.northumberlandnationalpark.org.uk
4. www.coast.scot/stories

5. www.epoch-magazine.com
6. J. R. D. Campbell, *Clyde Coast Smuggling* (St Maura Press, Largs, 1994)
7. https://regency-explorer.net/smuggling-moonshine
8. Helen Susan Swift, *Women of Scotland* (Next Chapter, USA, 2019)
9. www.ballantrae.org.uk
10. https://issuu.com/carolinesmithdesign/docs/ballantrae_smugglers
11. https://whiskyauctioneer.com

Chapter Thirteen: Wales and the Isle of Man

1. Wilma R. Thomas, *Women in the Rural Society of South-West Wales c.1780–1870* (University of Wales, Swansea, 2003)
2. Ibid.
3. www.wikitree.com
4. www.walesonline.co.uk
5. www.wikitree.com
6. Richard Platt, *Smugglers' Britain* (Cassell, London, 1991)
7. https://manxliterature.com

Chapter Fourteen: Yorkshire

1. www.godsowncounty.co.uk
2. Graham Smith, *Smuggling in Yorkshire 1700–1850* (Countryside Books, Berkshire, 1994)
3. Scarborough Maritime Heritage Centre
4. www.gazettelive.co.uk

Chapter Fifteen: The USA and Canada

1. https://stmuscholars.org/innocent-faced-doll-and-smuggling-drugs
2. www.womenhistoryblog.com
3. https://recollections.biz/blog/crimes-of-fashion-the-civil-war-hoop-skirt-smugglers

4. https://thewildgeese.irish
5. www.fashionstudiesjournal.org
6. Ibid.
7. https://investigatemidwest.org

Chapter Sixteen: Europe

1. William G. F. Jackson, *The Rock of the Gibraltarians* (Associated University Presses, Cranbury, New Jersey 1986)
2. George Hills, *Rock of Contention: A History of Gibraltar* (Robert Hale & Co. London, 1974)
3. https://gibraltar-intro.blogspot.com
4. Arne Zuidhoek, *Pirate Encyclopedia* (Brill, Holland, 2022)
5. https://lacemakersproject.com
6. https://bowstreetpolicemuseum.org.uk
7. www.cicerone.co.uk
8. www.atlasobscura.com

Bibliography

Adam, Robert James, *Papers on Sutherland Estate Management* (Boydell & Brewer, Suffolk, 1972)

Ayton, Richard, *Voyage Round Great Britain* (Longman, Hurst, Rees, Orme, and Brown, London, 1814)

Baring-Gould, Sabine, *A Book of the West: Devon and Cornwall* (Methuen, London, 1902)

Bidgood, Ruby Frances, *Two Villages: The Story of Mortehoe and Woolacombe* (Self-published, 1965)

Burrows, Bob, *Infamous Cheshire* (The History Press, Slough, 2006)

Campbell, J. R. D., *Clyde Coast Smuggling* (St Maura Press, Largs, 1994)

Chappell, Gavin, *Wirral Smugglers, Wreckers and Pirates* (Countryside Books, Berkshire, 2009)

Coxe, Antony D. Hippisley, *Smuggling in the West Country 1700–1850* (Tapp House, Cornwall, 1984)

Cullyer, E. A., *Old Norfolk Inns* (Jarrold & Sons, Norfolk, 1888)

Dyer, Keith, *Blackgang 1835* (G2 Rights Ltd., Kent, 2012)

Elias, Twm and Meirion, Dafydd, *Smugglers in Wales* (Gwasg Carreg Gwalch, Llanrwst, 2017)

English, John, *English's Reminiscences of Old Folkestone Smugglers and Smuggling Days* (John English, Folkestone, 1888)

Farjeon, Jefferson, *The Compleat Smuggler* (Bobbs-Merrill Co., Indianapolis, 1938)

Forbes, Athol, *The Romance of Smuggling* (C. Arthur Pearson, London, 1909)

Gordon, Dee, *Infamous Essex Women* (The History Press, Stroud, 2009)

Grant, Elizabeth, *Memoirs of a Highland Lady* (John Murray, London, 1898)

Guttridge, Roger, *Dorset Smugglers* (Dorset Publishing Co., Sherborne, 1984)

Guttridge, Roger, *Heritage in Dorset and the New Forest* (Ensign Publications, Salt Lake City, 1991)

Hardcastle, Felicite, *Aspects of a New Forest Village: Records of Burley* (Chameleon International, London, 1987)

Harper, Charles G., *The Smugglers* (Chapman & Hall Ltd., London, 1909)

Harvey, E. G., *Mullyon: Its History, Scenery and Antiquities* (W. Lake, Truro, 1875)

Hesketh, Robert, *Devon Smugglers* (Bossiney Books, Ilkley, 2007)

Hills, George, *Rock of Contention: A History of Gibraltar* (Robert Hale & Co. London, 1974)

Hipper, Kenneth, *Smugglers All* (Larks Press, Dereham, 2001)

Hodgson, George B., *The Borough of South Shields from Earliest Period to the Close of the Nineteenth Century* (Forgotten Books, London, 2018)

Holyoake, Gregory, *Deal Sad Smuggling Town* (SB Publications, Eastbourne, 2001)

Hutchings, Richard J., *Smugglers of the Isle of Wight* (Isle of Wight County Press, Newport, 1973)

Jackson, William G. F., *The Rock of the Gibraltarians* (Associated University Presses, Cranbury, New Jersey, 1986)

James, Derek, *The Smugglers' Coast* (Fast-Print Publishing, Peterborough, 2016)

Jarvis, Stan, *Smuggling in East Anglia 1700–1840* (Countryside Books, Berkshire, 1987)

Kingshill, Sophie, and Westwood, Jennifer, *The Fabled Coast* (Arrow Books, London, 2014)

Larn, Richard and Bridget, *The Shipwreck Index of the British Isles* (Lloyds Register of Shipping, London, 1995)

Lee, Mary and Catherine, *Goldhanger Woods* (originally apparently self-published, 1887)

Lely, Bridget, *Smuggling in Kent* (Jarrold, Norwich, 1990)

Lodge, Christine, *The Clearers and the Cleared: Women, Economy and the Land in the Scottish Highlands 1800–1900* (University of Glasgow, 1996)

Macilwee, Dr Michael, *The Liverpool Underworld: Crime in the City, 1750–1900* (Liverpool University Press, 2011)

Mackie, Charles, *Norfolk Annals* (Norfolk Chronicle, Norwich, 1901)

May, Trevor, *Smugglers and Smuggling* (Shire Books, Oxford, 2014)

Mays, James O'Donald (Ed.), *New Forest Book, An Illustrated Anthology* (New Forest Leaves, 1989)

McCooey, Chris, *Smuggling* (Amberley, Stroud, 2014)

McDonald, Ian, *Smuggling in the Highlands* (Eneas Mackay & Son, Stirling, 1914)

McMillan, Hugh, *McMillan's Galloway* (Luath Press, Edinburgh, 2016)

Meadley, C., *Memorials of Scarborough* (Simpkin, Marshall, Hamilton, Kent & Co. London, 1890)

Morley, Geoffrey, *Smuggling in Hampshire & Dorset 1700–1850* (Countryside Books, Berkshire, 1993)

Newcombe, Lisa, *Smuggling in Cornwall and Devon* (Jarrold, Norwich, 1989)

Pearce, Cathryn, *Cornish Wrecking 1700–1860* (Boydell Press, Suffolk, 2010)

Phillipson, David, *Smuggling: A History 1700–1970* (David and Charles, Exeter, 1973)

Philp, R., *The Coastal Blockade: The Royal Navy's War on Smuggling in Kent and Sussex 1817–1831* (Compton Press, Horsham, 1999)

Pitt-Stanley, Sheila, *Legends of Leigh* (Leigh Society, Essex, 1989)

Platt, Richard, *Smugglers' Britain* (Cassell, London, 1991)

Platt, Richard, *Smuggling in the British Isles* (Tempus, Stroud, 2007)

Rattenbury, John, *Memoirs of a Smuggler* (J. Harvey, London, 1837)

Robinson, David, *The Book of the Lincolnshire Seaside* (Barracuda Books, Buckingham, 1981)

Shore, Lieut. the Hon. Henry N., *Smuggling Days and Smuggling Ways* (Cassell, London, 1890)

Showell, Carol and Guttridge, Roger, *Smugglers' Trails* (Red Post Books, Poole, 1997)

Smith, Rev. G. C., *The Wreckers* (William Whittemore, London, 1819)

Smith, Graham, *Smuggling in Essex* (Countryside Books, Berkshire, 2005)

Smith, Graham, *Smuggling in the Bristol Channel 1700–1850* (Countryside Books, Berkshire, 1989)

Smith, Graham, *Smuggling in Yorkshire 1700–1850* (Countryside Books, Berkshire, 1994)

Smith, Graham, *Something to Declare* (George Harrap & Co., London, 1980)

Stanley, Jo (ed.), *Bold in Her Breeches* (HarperCollins, London, 1995)

Stonehouse, James, *The Streets of Liverpool* (Edward Howell, Liverpool, 1870)

Storey, Neil R., *Norfolk Villains, Rogues, Rascals and Reprobates* (The History Press, Slough, 2012)

Strachey, Lady (ed.), *The Autobiography of Elizabeth Grant 1797–1830* (John Murray, London, 1898)

Strange, Jack, *Jack's Strange Tales Collection* (Next Chapter, USA, re-published 2023)

Swift, Helen Susan, *Women of Scotland* (Next Chapter, USA, 2019)

Thomas, Wilma R., *Women in the Rural Society of South-West Wales c.1780–1870* (University of Wales, Swansea, 2003)

Thompson, Leonard P., *Smugglers of the Suffolk Coast* (The Boydell Press, Ipswich, 1968)

Tompkins, Herbert W., *Marsh Country Rambles* (Chatto & Windus, London, 1904)

Toms, Jan, *Isle of Wight Villains, Rogues, Rascals and Reprobates* (The History Press, Slough, 2012)

Vaišnora, Juozas, *The Forty Years of Darkness* (Franciscan Press, Brooklyn, 1975)

Vaughan, Eliza, *These for Remembrance* (Benham & Co., Colchester, 1934)

Vivian, John, *Tales of Cornish Smugglers* (Tormark Press, Redruth, 2012)

Vivian, John, *Tales of Cornish Wreckers* (Tormark Press, Truro, 1970)

Waugh, Mary, *Smuggling in Kent & Sussex 1700–1840* (Countryside Books, Berkshire, 1985)

Waugh, Mary, *Smuggling in Devon & Cornwall 1700–1850* (Countryside Books, Berkshire, 1991)

Wilkins, Frances, *The Smuggler of Kyle* (Wyre Forest Press, Ashbourne, 2007)

Williams, Gomer, *History of the Liverpool Privateers and Letters of Marque* (William Heinemann, London, 1897)

Wood, G. Bernard, *Smugglers' Britain* (Cassell & Co., London, 1966)

Wreyford, Paul, *Essex Villains, Rogues, Rascals and Reprobates* (The History Press, Slough, 2012)

Wynn, Douglas, *Lincolnshire Villains, Rogues, Rascals and Reprobates* (The History Press, Slough, 2012)

Zuidhoek, Arne, *Pirate Encyclopedia* (Brill, Holland, 2022)